Aging in Black America

Aging in Black America

EDITED BY

James S. Jackson
Linda M. Chatters
Robert Joseph Taylor

SAGE Publications
International Educational and Professional Publisher
Newbury Park   London   New Delhi

For information address:

SAGE Publications, Inc.
2455 Teller Road
Newbury Park, California 91320

SAGE Publications Ltd.
6 Bonhill Street
London EC2A 4PU
United Kingdom

SAGE Publications India Pvt. Ltd.
M-32 Market
Greater Kailash I
New Delhi 110 048 India

Printed in the United States of America

Library of Congress Cataloging-in-Publication Data

Main entry under title:

Aging in Black America / [edited by] James S. Jackson, Linda M.
  Chatters, Robert Joseph Taylor.
        p.   cm.
    Includes bibliographical references and index.
    ISBN 0-8039-3535-8 (cl).—ISBN 0-8039-3536-6 (pb)
      1. Afro-American aged—Social conditions.   I. Jackson, James S.
  (James Sidney), 1944-   . II. Chatters, Linda M.   III. Taylor,
  Robert Joseph.
  HQ1064.U5A6342   1993   92-30719
  305.26′08996073—dc20   CIP

     94   95   96   10   9   8   7   6   5   4   3   2

Sage Production Editor: Judith L. Hunter

CONTENTS

FOREWORD

Jacquelyne Johnson Jackson

Just as ethnogerontology in particular and gerontology in general were greatly enriched about two decades ago by James S. Jackson's scholarly emergence, the publication of his and his colleagues' *Aging in Black America* heralds another seminal occasion akin to the early publications of such pioneering gerontologists as James Birren, Wilma Donahue, Carl Eisdorfer, Robert Havighurst, Bernice Neugarten, Ethel Shanas, and Nathan Shock. Concentrated mostly on a cross-national and representative sample of household blacks in the continental United States who were at least 55 years old when the data were soundly collected in 1979 and 1980, *Aging in Black America*'s generally sophisticated theories and empirical findings about the aging and aged conditions of older blacks focus on the five important areas of (a) community, friend, and familial resources; (b) church and religion; (c) impacts of physical and emotional resources on psychological and social functioning; (d) work and retirement; and (e) further research about the social lives of aging and aged blacks.

While *Aging in Black America*'s major conceptual themes strongly emphasize status and role changes and historical or other period effects on individual and cohort life-spans, the editors (James S. Jackson, Linda M. Chatters, and Robert Joseph Taylor) as editors and authors, and their colleagues dutifully keep in mind the cross-sectional nature of their data and, thus, the inherent restrictions of those data in providing any concrete data about "age changes," which are *sine qua non* to a full understanding of aging, including status and role changes accompanying aging.

The only longitudinal data in *Aging in Black America,* reported in the last chapter (17), show proportionate changes between 1980 and 1987 in life satisfaction, help from and frequency of help from church, health satisfaction, health disability, amount of help, voting in presidential and local elections, racial identification, and employment status among persons who were at least 35 years old in 1980. They are intriguing and captivating: I hope that Jackson, Chatters, and Taylor will eventually subject them to more rigorous analyses. For instance, I am curious about which older blacks experienced decreased life satisfaction or church help over time, and how either of those variables related to stability or changes in other available variables.

My acute awareness of James Jackson's (no kin) *Anschauungs-unterrict* (or intuitive method of instruction) and astutely remarkable and ethically responsible record of maximizing his initial and subsesquent research respondents and data to foster ethnogerontologic and gerontologic knowledge and understanding leads me to believe that he will eventually write or edit the very first thoroughly comprehensive and scientifically valid longitudinal study of a nationally representative sample of older Native American blacks in the United States, and perhaps even include representative samples of Native American whites and of majority and minority groups in other developed countries (e.g., Japan's Burakumin and their majority counterparts).

Aging in Black America's strengths are many, including its (a) fairly comprehensive review of the applicable literature; (b) methodical production of empirical findings and typically appropriate and highly rationale discussions of their limitations, including testing such formally simplistic theories as those about the single constructs of *neighboring* for elders or black churches functioning only in a single dimension for their members (some of which have been previously published during the past decade in various refereed journals), and the significant lack of any non sequitur in their discussion or conclusions; (c) heavy concentration on the considerable variability of older blacks, including their different socioeconomic statuses, life-styles, racial identifications, and informal support systems; and (d) wealth of extremely fruitful research leads for social gerontologists and other social scientists (including those who are not in the field of aging).

Many of *Aging in Black America*'s findings, I was pleased to note, support my earliest stated or implied theories and findings about aged Native American blacks, including their considerable sociocultural variability (Jackson, 1967). But James Jackson and his colleagues go far beyond my limited research by providing generalizable and convincing empirical data to show, *inter alia,* that the full understanding of social and related aging among all racial and ethnic groups in the United States in the past, the present, and the future must include an adequate understanding of the multidimensional individual and subgroup aging of Native black Americans within a changing and aging society.

Aging in Black America stresses the special circumstances of contemporary older blacks, who have been racially victimized over their entire life course. In one sense, I, too, share this notion (Jackson, 1991). Yet, perhaps as a sociologist aware of the value of comparative research, I think that any solid determination of the specific circumstances of older Native American blacks that are attributable to them being both black and old as a consequence of their earlier socialization and lifetime conditions (including educational and employment opportunities) must ultimately be compared to such specific circumstances of older Native American whites. That is, I subscribe to no theory, such as the empirically unverified one of double jeopardy, that assumes that just being black and old in the United States sufficiently explains the well-documented racial gaps among the aged (Jackson & Ensley, 1990-1991).

James Jackson and his colleagues also do not make that simplistic assumption, hence their critical emphasis on a life-span approach. While the general absence of racially comparative data in their studies usually prevents them from empirically assessing the special conditions of older blacks vis-à-vis older whites (a notable exception is Chapter 16 by Rose Gibson), they have admirably written the book they said they would write and, in so doing, have made an extremely valuable contribution not only to the ethnogerontologic or gerontologic literature, but also to much of the sociological and related literature on, for example, family, health, religion, and social stratification.

One of their two greatest accomplishments is their empirical demonstration of considerable older black attitudinal and behavioral variability, such as differences in familial support and voting patterns, as well as identification of some factors influencing this diversification. The second is their findings that challenge conventional social scientific wisdom, such as an insignificant relationship between socioeconomic status and religious participation among older blacks. These accomplishments tend to emphasize the multidimensionality of many variables commonly treated as unidimensional within much of the local scientific literature about blacks. Taylor (Chapter 7) also discusses a multidimensional model of measuring religiosity among older blacks.

Aging in Black America edifies well the functions of black churches in the lives of older blacks by showing that they are a central force in providing particularistic support to older blacks (chiefly through such activities as political mobilization, as well as through advice and encouragement, praying, and help during illness), but that older blacks do not use their churches or religions as familial surrogates. Chatters and Taylor also identify some factors affecting the probability of church support for older members. The longitudinal findings also show a decline between 1980 and 1987 in church help and frequency of church help for some older blacks. Thus the extent to which black churches actually aid older blacks needing help is still a considerably mixed and highly variable bag, or, as the authors in *Aging in Black America* might say, a multidimensional phenomenon.

Aging in Black America's last chapter, *virtute et labore,* is its most important, not just because it adequately synthesizes its own findings and its research implications, but also because, when adequately applied and tested, its paradigm of a coherent life-span framework can lead to meaningful explanations about the economic, social, and psychological lives of blacks within their structural and related contexts. As stated earlier, this chapter also contains the only longitudinal findings, all of which should be of special interest to researchers investigating social aging, public policymakers dealing with human services, and service providers assisting older blacks.

For example, the finding of declining informal support to older blacks from their families and friends may support Marjorie Cantor and Virginia Little's (1985) plea for incorporating informal and formal social care in one broad-based system. Neena Chappell (1990) aptly notes that aging populations increase the frequency of social care, giving rise to increased needs for caregivers and public and private programs for them. *Aging in Black America* clearly suggests the need to develop, now and in the decades ahead, better complementary formal and informal social care systems for older blacks.

Public policymakers in particular should heed *Aging in Black America*'s plausible speculations (Chapter 17) about the growing numbers of currently aging (but not old) blacks who are already at risk for impoverished conditions and poor health and related functioning in their old age unless sufficient environmental intervention occurs now to thwart such undesired outcomes. Early negative life-course experiences can be positively reversed with adequate intervention before old age. These positive interventions can also help reduce the public cost of elderly blacks, such as through reduced health care costs. However, in my judgment, any such federal intervention must not concentrate on merely changing the personal behavioral patterns of younger blacks today. I believe that James Jackson and his colleagues correctly emphasize critical changes in the structural environment, including substantially improved education, employment, health, and housing opportunities and outcomes for today's younger blacks. They know that the socio-environmental conditions of each aged individual are influenced by each one's preaged condition. That is, the "father" of an elder is his "younger self."

Stressed above is *Aging in Black America*'s vital importance to ethnogerontologic and social aging specialists, policymakers, and service providers, but its theoretical paradigm and finding also are valuable for many other social scientists who focus on Native American blacks. The pedagogical uses of *Aging in Black America* are enormous: I strongly recommend it as a text for both advanced undergraduate and graduate courses on social aging, and as a supplementary text (or with selected chapters) for undergraduate courses in Introduction to Sociology, Marriage and the Family, Social Stratification, Sociology of Religion, and Race and Ethnic Relations (especially Chapters 13 and 14).

Aging in Black America is the *magnum opus* on older blacks, and its special merit lies in James Jackson's vision of conducting solid research about blacks and his strong scholarly and organization skills in doing so. His work—and that of his colleagues—should serve as an inspiration to all future researchers who are genuinely concerned about "telling it like it is" about the biological, psychological, and sociocultural aging of present and future birth cohorts of highly diversified Native American blacks.

So, *besos los manos* James Jackson, as the mastermind and chief architect of *Aging in Black America* as well as the driving force, since at least 1979, of empirical research about older blacks.

References

Cantor, M., & Little, V. (1985). Aging and social care. In R. H. Binstock & E. Shanas (Eds.), *Handbook of aging and the social sciences* (2nd. ed., pp. 745-781). New York: Van Nostrand Reinhold.

Chappell, N. L. (1990). Aging and social care. In R. H. Binstock & L. K. George, *Handbook of aging and the social sciences* (3rd ed., pp. 438-454). San Diego: Academic Press.

Jackson, J. (1967). Social gerontology and the negro: A review. *The Gerontologist, 7,* 168-178.

Jackson, J. J. (1991). This sho'nuff ain't been no "zombie jamboree." In F. M. Carp (Ed.), *Lives of career women* (pp. 275-298). New York: Insight Books, Plenum.

Jackson, J. J., & Ensley, D. E. (1990-1991). Ethnogerontology's status and complementary and conflicting social and cultural concerns for American minority elders. *Journal of Minority Aging, 12,* 41-78.

PREFACE

This volume continues the work of empirically investigating the economic, political, and social statuses of Americans of African descent. In addition to documenting these statuses, however, these chapters explore the physical, psychological, and social responses of African Americans to their life situations. A previous volume, *Life in Black America,* provided a general overview of the life circumstances of African Americans at the beginning of the 1980s. This volume continues the large integrative reports that provide detailed data analyses on the same national survey. This work utilizes a life-span framework in its focus on the latter part of the adult life course and the interrelationships among physical, social, and psychological aging processes. Selected empirical indicators of these interconnected aging processes are utilized in the analyses on the National Survey of Black Americans data set.

This volume is grounded in a conceptual model that combines role and resource theories. We believe that this framework, stressing the nature and availability of social roles and economic, political, social, and psychological resources, is pivotal in understanding the position of past, present, and future cohorts of African-American elders.

Each chapter provides a brief and selected review of the key literature that describes different aging processes and their interrelationships. Where appropriate, contrasts and comparisons are made with those in the majority group culture, as well as among different social minority and cultural groups. In the final chapter we make explicit a life course framework of adult development and aging in African Americans based on the literature and conclusions drawn in earlier chapters.

The work reported in this volume has been supported by research grants from the National Institute of Mental Health, National Institute on Aging, the Ford and Rockefeller Foundations, and the Carnegie Corporation. Institutional and individual postdoctoral grants were also instrumental in our work and were provided by the National Institute of Mental Health, National Institute on Aging, and the Rockefeller Foundation. We are particularly indebted to Lynn Walker and William Diaz of the Ford Foundation, Bernard Charles of the Carnegie Corporation, and Bruce Williams of the Rockefeller Foundation. Financial and moral support was provided by Steven Withey, then director of the Survey Research Center, Robert Zajonc, then director of the Research Center for Group Dynamics, and Thomas Juster, then director of the Institute for Social Research at the University of Michigan.

We would again like to acknowledge the contribution of Sally Oswald in preparing this manuscript and coordinating the production of this volume and series. She was ably assisted by Ursula Barzey, Keith Hersh, Linda Shepard, Estina Thompson, Myriam Torres, and Monica Wolford. All seven contributed to the analyses and tables reported in this volume.

JAMES S. JACKSON
LINDA M. CHATTERS
ROBERT JOSEPH TAYLOR
The University of Michigan

1

ROLES AND RESOURCES
OF THE BLACK ELDERLY

James S. Jackson
Robert Joseph Taylor
Linda M. Chatters

This volume empirically examines the status and life situations of elderly blacks in the United States. It builds upon the volume *Life in Black America* (J. S. Jackson, 1991), and addresses the special circumstances and strengths of the black American elderly. Although much has been written about the current functioning and status of the black elderly (see, e.g., J. J. Jackson, 1980, 1985; J. S. Jackson, 1988; Manuel, 1982; Stanford, 1983), much of this writing has been speculative, impressionistic, and if empirical, based upon small and restricted samples of black Americans. Thus, much of the available literature about the black elderly has been either extrapolated from the status and situation of nonminority elderly generally or based upon empirical data from small and nonrepresentative samples of black Americans.

This edited volume is unique in at least two respects. First, each chapter is based upon empirical analyses of data from a national survey of the black population (J. S. Jackson, 1991; J. S. Jackson, Tucker, & Gurin, 1987). Therefore, the findings and the generalizations are not as limiting as has been the case in previous studies of this population. Second, the findings presented here have the potential to add to our knowledge and understanding of the situation of black elderly, as well

1

as to debunk many of the myths that have developed about the situation of this ethnic and racial minority population.

Much of the work and research that has been conducted on the black elderly has utilized a victim-centered approach. As a consequence, the focus has been largely on the negative circumstances and situations of the black elderly. Given the demographic and socioeconomic status of the black elderly (J. S. Jackson, Antonucci, & Gibson, 1990a; J. S. Jackson, Burns, & Gibson, in press; Taylor & Chatters, 1988b; Wilson-Ford, 1990), this perspective is perhaps understandable. By and large, however, this typical approach and orientation has failed to increase our understanding about the strengths and overall coping capacity of aging black Americans.

We have entitled this chapter, "Roles and Resources of the Black Elderly," to reflect our approach and our attempt to emphasize those positive aspects of life among older black Americans that contribute to coping capacity and other adaptive behaviors that make the lives of older blacks productive and worthwhile (J. S. Jackson, Antonucci, & Gibson, 1990b). At the same time, we recognize that the black elders of today were born and raised in a largely highly separate and unequal society (Jaynes & Williams, 1989), one in which "separate but equal" (President's Commission on Civil Disorders, 1968) was the credo and two unequal countries, one white, one black, the reality of life for most black Americans. Many would argue that the civil rights struggles over the last 25 to 30 years have actually wrought little change in the day-to-day experiences relating to human growth and development of Americans of African descent (Gurin, Hatchett, & J. S. Jackson, 1989; Jaynes & Williams, 1989). Hence, the title of this volume—*Aging in Black America.*

Due to the paucity of previous findings and the theorizing regarding the conditions of the black elderly, we have used no particular extant theory to organize this book. Because our interest is with the social and behavioral aspects of human development and aging—that is, changes in status and roles across the life span (J. S. Jackson et al., 1990a), we have viewed life course development as a general overarching theme in which to organize the large number of empirical chapters that constitute this volume (Baltes, 1987). Our concern is with the myriad of institutional and informal roles that black Americans assume and the various status conditions that provide resources for successful coping and adaptation (George, 1988).

A second major organizing theme in the present volume has to do with a life-span perspective on black aging (J. S. Jackson et al., 1990a).

The life circumstances of older black Americans are affected, perhaps more than for majority elderly, by their life chances and position in the opportunity structure earlier in their lives (Gibson & J. S. Jackson, 1992; J. S. Jackson, Antonucci, & Gibson, 1990a; J. S. Jackson & Gibson, 1985). The general lack of opportunities and resources (i.e., good jobs, adequate housing, and financial resources) at earlier periods in their lives is a source of many of the more problematic aspects of aging in the later years (J. S. Jackson et al., in press b). Although this life-span focus provides a general organizing theme and perspective on the book, the data set that we are reporting on is cross-sectional in nature (J. S. Jackson et al., 1987). We are therefore unable to examine issues having to do with intraindividual or intracohort change across the individual life-span (J. S. Jackson & Antonucci, 1991a). In most cases, we will be examining current differences among the black elderly population and between older and younger blacks, although an important corollary concern still centers on change across the life-span. This limitation is a methodological one, because as J. J. Jackson (1980) has indicated, no good longitudinal data on minority elderly exist at this time. As a matter of fact, as indicated earlier in this chapter, this is the first quality national cross-sectional data available for use in studying social aging and social gerontological issues within the black population.

Although many scholars and researchers have viewed the study of minority elderly outside of the mainstream research of the elderly and aging in general, we believe that it is important that the study of the black elderly be conceived as contributory to our general understanding of aging phenomena (Barresi, 1987; Driedger & Chappell, 1988; Sokolovsky, 1989). For example, because of clearly demarcated shifts and changes in legal prohibitions and strictures in the case of black Americans (a good example is civil rights legislation), we might expect to find significant historical and cohort effects for relevant behavioral domains. These period or cohort effects may even be more clearly comprehensible for black elderly than those we would expect to find among majority elderly (Hatchett & Nacoste, 1984). This information, derived from the study of the black elderly, may have implications for understanding the operation and the impact of other historical and period effects that may not be as observable within the nonminority aging population. We expect, then, that the results and findings reported in the current volume will have implications not only for greater understanding and comprehension of social aging within black Americans, but also for the aging population more generally (J. S. Jackson, 1988).

Status, Roles, and Resources of Black Americans

In the general aging literature, changes in older age are viewed in terms of loss of status and loss of roles. This is particularly true of those statuses and roles associated with primary institutions (i.e., marriage, parenthood, employment) (Riley, 1985, 1987; Rosow, 1976). In his attempt to comprehend the nature of changes in both statuses and roles, Rosow (1976) differentiated between these two concepts. Under his definition, status represents a formal office or social position that can be designated by name or clear term of reference. A person occupying this position is classified and located within a social structure. A role, however, is made up of the behaviors considered appropriate to any set of rights and duties defined in terms of statuses. With his definitions of role and status, Rosow (1976) developed a typology of four major role types, which he labeled institutional, tenuous, informal, and nonrole. Institutional roles are seen as involving central positions of occupation, family, social class, race, ethnicity, religious affiliation, and so on. Within the institutional role types, role expectations are viewed as directly linked to a definite social status. The tenuous role type is viewed as the case of definite social positions without substantive roles. Rosow (1976) offered as examples of this situation titular positions or offices that are honorific or nominal, as well as amorphous roles, which are exemplified by long-term unemployment and lack of any work history. Tenuous roles are also seen in situations of role attrition, where there is significant shrinkage within roles. Rosow (1976) noted that this may be particularly problematic as people age. Situations in which there is a retention of statuses without any particular functions he viewed as problematic for these tenuous roles. The informal roles involve role behaviors that are not connected with any particular status or position. These are seen as serving significant group functions, both positive and negative. The final category of nonrole is viewed as a situation in which there is no status position and also no expectations of behavior forming a role. Rosow (1976) viewed this category as including particular idiosyncratic behavior, personal style, and personality elements.

Although Rosow (1976) included marginal individuals under the tenuous role definition, we can conceive of marginal individuals fitting under the nonrole category, lacking both social status and clear behavioral expectations. A number of marginal categories, particularly related to oppressed minorities, could be viewed as fitting within this category. In Rosow's (1976) categorization of statuses and roles, they are viewed both as potentially independent and as having significant impact upon individual outcomes.

Our concern in the present volume is how the presence or absence of major statuses impact upon individual well-being. Similarly, we are concerned with how certain types of institutionalized and informal roles, that is, institutionalized roles of worker and family member, as well as more informal roles, such as confidant and neighbor, may impact upon individual outcomes (Burton & Dilworth-Anderson, 1991; J. S. Jackson et al., in press b).

For the most part, aging has been viewed as a process of a reduction in social and economic status, as well as a loss of roles. Much of the literature has been conceived in terms of how dwindling resources and dwindling expectations of behavior occur and how these particular occurrences impact upon the behavior of elderly individuals. In many ways, race has been considered to be a status or a role placement that impacts upon both life chances and behavior (Allen & Britt, 1983; Riley, 1985; Streib, 1985). Our purpose in studying black American elderly is to examine how various statuses and roles within that population impact upon the life circumstances and situations of black Americans in old age. In this regard, we are concerned with the continuities and discontinuities in statuses and roles across the life span and their impact upon the circumstances and situations of black Americans in old age. Because of the focus previously on race as either a status or a role or categorization that places one within the general stratification system (Streib, 1985), much less attention has focused on how statuses and roles within race groups impact upon individual behavior and social standing.

We believe that the statuses and roles that black Americans demonstrate in older age are for the most part continuous with the statuses and roles available to them at younger ages (Barresi, 1987; J. S. Jackson et al., 1990a; J. S. Jackson & Gibson, 1985). Thus, poor jobs and low income during postadolescence and young adulthood will be reflected in poor job histories across the life span, which is again reflected in lowered retirement opportunities and resources in old age (Taylor & Chatters, 1988b; Wilson-Ford, 1990). In a similar manner, the lack of educational opportunities early in life may continue to impact at all points of the life span, culminating in lowered opportunities in old age. Similar arguments could be drawn for many of the major statuses and status positions in other spheres of life as well (Riley, 1987). Thus, those statuses that serve as important resources for individual utilization in terms of increased opportunities are not available to black Americans at early points in the life course or are available in such impoverished form that they do not serve a useful function.

Because these formal institutionalized statuses and roles may not be available to black Americans in any abundance during early years, individuals and groups (such as the family) may out of necessity turn to more informal sources for succor and support. Thus, it has been argued previously that the black family and other informal community resources play important roles for blacks throughout their life span and into older age (J. J. Jackson, 1980). Many have argued from a policy perspective that these institutionalized roles and statuses play an important part in the survival of individual black Americans. Other writers have suggested that they do not necessarily replace more formal benefits, rights, and privileges acquired by nonminority elderly (e.g., George, 1988). And yet, these informal roles and statuses may play an important part in the quality of the lives of black aging individuals.

One final note should be made regarding the life span perspective in examining psychological and social aging among the black elderly. Both the double jeopardy hypotheses and its variants (e.g., Bengtson, 1979; Dowd & Bengtson, 1978; Markides, Liang, & J. S. Jackson, 1990), as well as conceptualizations that emphasize a resource availability approach to the study of the lives of black elderly, are static in conception (Allen & Britt, 1983; Bengtson, 1979). Although we do not fully understand how, it is clear that the lifetime experiences of low status and impoverished roles may interact to affect psychological and social aging and impact upon the life circumstances and social situations of the black elderly in older age. It is not merely the additive combination of being black as a low-status position and having poor resources that lead to negative outcomes in older age. It is the presence of systematic forces and poor opportunity structure circumstances that are present in young adulthood and middle age that lead to the set of statuses and roles that are available to elderly black. These in turn influence major life outcomes and events in old age (J. S. Jackson, Antonucci, & Gibson, 1990a; Markides et al., 1990; Wilson-Ford, 1990).

Data Base for This Volume

The data for the individual chapters presented in this volume are all from the National Survey of Black Americans (J. S. Jackson et al.,

1987). This survey, conducted in 1979 and 1980, is based upon a cross-section sample of the black American population 18 years of age and older, residing in individual households and self-identified black. The total sample consists of 2,107 individuals interviewed individually by black interviewers in their households. These 2,107 interviews represent nearly a 70% response rate. Although more detailed information on the sample and approach to this study are presented elsewhere (J. S. Jackson, 1991; J. S. Jackson et al., 1987; Taylor, 1986), a brief description of the sample and study are presented below.

Black Elderly Subsample Survey Description and Demographic Overview

The analyses were conducted on the National Survey of Black Americans (NSBA), the first data set utilizing a nationally representative cross section of the adult (18 years and older) black population living in the continental United States (J. S. Jackson et al., 1987). The sample was drawn according to a multistage area probability procedure designed to assure that every black household had the same probability of being selected for the study. Based on the 1970 Census distribution of the black population, 76 primary areas were selected for interviewing. These sites were stratified according to racial composition, and smaller geographical areas, called "clusters," were randomly chosen. Next, professionally trained interviewers went into each cluster and listed every habitable household. Finally, within each selected black household, one person was randomly chosen to be interviewed. This sampling procedure resulted in 2,107 completed interviews, conducted in 1979 and 1980, representing a response rate of nearly 70%. The analyses in this volume are based largely on the 581 respondents who were 55 years of age and older. Chapter 13 (Brown and Barnes-Nacoste) uses the entire age range of the NSBA sample; Chapter 5 (Chatters and Taylor) uses respondents who were interviewed in both the original NSBA and reinterviewed as part of the Three Generation Family Study.

As shown in Table 1.1, respondents ranged in age from 55 years to 101 years, with a mean age of 67 years; 41.1% were between the ages of 55 and 64 years; another 39.6% were 65 to 74; and the remaining 19.3% of the sample were 75 years of age and above. Women comprised slightly less than two thirds of this older sample. Respondents were categorized as married and common law (38.9%), divorced (7.8%), separated (9.2%), widowed (40.9%), or never married (3.2%). Reflecting

Table 1.1 Demographic Distribution of Respondents Aged 55 Years and Above

Demographic Variables	(N)	%
Age		
55-64	240	41.1
65-74	230	39.6
75+	111	19.3
Total	581	100.0
Gender		
Male	215	37.0
Female	366	63.0
Total	581	100.0
Marital Status		
Married and common law	223	38.9
Divorced	45	7.8
Separated	53	9.2
Widowed	237	40.9
Never married	20	3.2
Total	578	100.0
Education		
0 to 6 years	198	34.7
7 to 11 years	226	39.7
High school graduate	146	25.6
Total	570	100.0
Income		
Under $5,000	120	25.2
$5,000 to $6,999	101	21.3
$7,000 to $11,999	121	25.5
$12,000+	133	28.0
Total	475	100.0
Poverty		
Below/equal poverty	148	31.0
Above poverty	329	69.0
Total	477	100.0
Employment Status		
Working	186	32.1
Not working	393	67.9
Total	579	100.0
Urbanicity		
Urban	419	72.1
Rural	162	27.9
Total	581	100.0
Region		
Northeast	96	16.5
North Central	111	19.1
South	344	59.2
West	30	5.2
Total	581	100.0

NOTE: Missing data on several of the demographic factors resulted in frequencies of less than 581.

their low-income status, over 25.2% of the respondents had a total family income of less than $5,000 a year. Almost one fourth of the respondents had a family income between $5,000 and $6,999 a year. In addition, 28.6% of the elderly respondents had an income of $12,000 and over. The average family income was approximately $8,000.

Respondents in this sample had few years of formal education, on average only 8 years. A quarter of the sample had at least a high school diploma, 34.7% had 6 years or less of formal education, and 39.7% had 7 to 11 years. Of those with a high school degree or more, 9.5% had attended college or received a college degree. Two thirds (67.9%) of the respondents were not currently working. In all, 72.1% of the sample resided in urban areas and 27.9% resided in rural areas. Over half (59.2%) of the respondents resided in the South, 19.1% resided in the North Central region, 16.5% in the Northeast, while only 5.2% resided in the West.

In summary, there are two major, unique features of the National Survey of Black Americans. First, the sample is self-weighting, based upon the distribution of the black population. Prior to this study, a representative sample had never been attempted on the entire black population in a national study. The sampling design and outcome for the study clearly indicate that we were successful in meeting the goals of obtaining a representative sample of black Americans, regardless of geographical location. The second major contribution of this study to our understanding of black American behavior relates to the lengthy interview schedule, which lasted approximately an average of 2-1/2 hours. This interview covered major topics of neighborhood life, religious and church affiliation, family and friends, work and retirement, health and health status, mental health status, group and self-identification, and traditional major demographic and socioeconomic status variables. The questionnaire itself was based upon several qualitative and ethnographic approaches to concept and construct development that entailed over 2 years of work. It is clear from analyses that have been conducted thus far that the interview material has provided a rich source of data and information for studying the roles and resources of the black elderly.

Orientation to This Volume

This book is divided into five sections. These sections reflect major substantive issues related to psychological and social dimensions of aging among black Americans. Although many of these categories would undoubtedly be included in the study of aging in any population group, some of the chapters within these headings are peculiar to the life situation and circumstances of black Americans. Section I focuses on an examination of community, friend, and family resources. In Chapter 2 Rukmalie Jayakody examines the structural and functional dimensions of an important citadel of the black elderly, neighborhoods and neighboring. She demonstrates that behavioral and perceptual neighboring form two separate dimensions, the former related to social support received and the latter related to reducing feelings of loneliness and isolation. John L. McAdoo in Chapter 3 continues the analysis of community effects, adding a slightly more ominous but ever-present dimension of life for the black elderly, crime and perceived safety within black neighborhoods. He focuses on an analysis of the ways community structure and social interaction and integration impact upon the black elderly. He presents criminal activity and community influences as major determinants of the quality of life within the immediate environment of the black elderly and specifically examines the way perceptions of neighborhood quality of life and social integration influence individual aspects of life, primarily self-esteem and life satisfaction.

In Chapter 4, Robert Joseph Taylor, Verna M. Keith, and M. Belinda Tucker address the structure of the family and gender and friendship roles of the black elderly. Their purpose is to provide a description of family structure nationally and the extent of attachment of black elderly within these different types of family patterning. As indicated by several writers (Cantor, 1979; J. J. Jackson, 1980, 1985; McAdoo, 1987; Taylor, Chatters, Tucker, & Lewis, 1990), the black family has served as perhaps the single most important resource for the positive development of individual black Americans (Dressler, 1985) Although similarities among men and women abound (e.g., endorsement of gender equality) differences exist in such things as actual performance of household tasks and ideal marital circumstances. Most important, the analyses in Chapter 4 reveal that older black Americans are both major contributors to the family and family life as well as major beneficiaries of the resources within the family (Chatters & Taylor, 1990; Taylor & Chatters, 1991).

Linda M. Chatters and Robert Joseph Taylor examine the intergenerational exchanges and functions of family networks in Chapter 5. As with the structural aspects of the analysis in the previous chapter, the concern in Chapter 5 is on examining how structural characteristics relate to family functions and perceived exchanges among parents and their adult children. The literature has long documented in small anthropological research (e.g., Stack, 1974) how exchanges among family generation positions provide an important source of succor and are major resources in the livelihood of black Americans (Taylor, 1985). The analysis in this chapter provides a great deal of support for prior research, but also reveals important gender and marital role differences in the giving and receipt of intergenerational assistance.

The last chapter in this section, Chapter 6, turns to the important implications of gender roles and intimate relationships among older black Americans. Eleanor Engram and Shirley A. Lockery note the paucity of research on intimate relationships among African Americans generally, but especially among those in their older decades. They attempt to address many of the myths and negative stereotypes that are held about black intimacy and sex roles within their examination of the division of labor within the context and functioning of the family, as well as how gender may impact upon the types of exchanges and intimate resources available in older age for black Americans.

The two chapters in Section II focus on the nature and role of the church and religion in the lives of older blacks. As noted previously by many authors (Chatters & Taylor, 1989; J. J. Jackson, 1980, 1985; Manuel, 1982; Taylor & Chatters, 1986a, 1986b, 1988a), the church and religious observance have played a critical function in the life and development of black Americans (J. S. Jackson, 1991). In fact, some have argued that the church is the single most important formal institution within the black community (Taylor & Chatters, 1986a). In Chapter 7, Robert Joseph Taylor examines the role and nature of the church among older black Americans. In this structural analysis he documents church attendance patterns and the functioning and nature of the black church and religious observance. His findings support those reported in many previous smaller and less comprehensive research studies. He concludes that religious institutions play a critical role in the life of older blacks, but that a considerable amount of religious participation and attitudinal heterogeneity exists in the nature of how these roles are executed. He suggests that religiosity is multidimensional in its structure and its functional relationships in reducing stress, improving well-being, and facilitating instrumental support. Jacqueline M. Smith in Chapter 8 continues and expands on the structural and functional themes presented in the prior chapter. Her analyses examine how the church in the context of other institutions (e.g., the family) and status positions functions to provide supportive networks and useful roles for older individuals. Her results provide both support for prior findings (e.g., the importance of gender), as well as a lack of support for others (e.g., a facilitating role of the family or socioeconomic status).

Section III covers the role of physical and emotional resources in the psychological and social life of the black elderly. Physical and emotional resources are conceived as both outcomes as well as resources available for the black elderly that may have positive or negative influences on the conditions of their lives. In Chapter 9, Mary McKinney Edmonds provides a descriptive account of the physical health status of the black elderly. She conceptualizes conditions of individual life mastery, such as locus of control and life satisfaction, among different age groups as independent variables affecting and influencing perceived health status, including both doctor-reported illnesses as well as self-assessments of health. This descriptive account of the current health status and functioning of older black Americans is supportive of prior findings (e.g., J. S. Jackson, 1988). Edmonds finds widespread serious chronic conditions, significant numbers who perceive barriers to health care, and somewhat paradoxically high levels of health satisfaction. In Chapter 10, Linda M. Chatters focuses on how functional disability and self-reported physical health problems influence perceived stress and the well-being of the elderly. She finds that good health and the absence of health disability serve as resources that moderate the psychological functioning and personal well-being perceptions of the elderly. Complementing the focus of the preceding chapter, Ruth L. Greene, James S. Jackson, and Harold W. Neighbors in Chapter 11 address the mental health status, emotional resources, and help-seeking behavior of older blacks. Their overarching concern is in describing the current mental health status of the black elderly and how psychological conditions are related to other major status dimensions, such as age, income, education, and gender. Chapter 11 concludes with an examination of how mental health status and major status dimensions are related to seeking help from professionals and non-professionals in reaction to significant personal problems. The findings provide an important descriptive profile of how help-seeking behavior is differentiated among a variety of statuses and role behaviors of the black elderly.

With Section IV we turn to an examination of political participation and group identification. Robert J. Smith and Michael C. Thornton in Chapter 12 examine the nature of group identification among the black elderly. Several years ago Manuel (1982) noted the lack of scientific attention to the definition of what constitutes minority status and particularly black group status among the elderly. Recent work has addressed this deficiency (e.g., Broman, Neighbors, & J. S. Jackson, 1988), showing that group identification can serve as an important personal and group resource in older age. The present chapter attempts to document the distribution of varying measures of race identification and how they relate to education, income, and gender among the black elderly. Smith and Thornton conclude that the current cohort of black elderly constitute a very heterogenous group differing widely on the relationship of the major status variables to multiple assessments of group identification. In Chapter 13, Ronald E. Brown and Rupert W. Barnes-Nacoste build on the findings in Chapter 12 in examining voting behavior, one of the major social participatory variables in previous studies of the elderly (Bengtson, Cutler, Mangen, & Marshall, 1985), but one that has not been thoroughly addressed among black Americans (Brown, 1984; George, 1988). But as J. J. Jackson (1980) indicated, the political participation of minority elderly is of critical concern, affecting the development of relevant social and political programs that may influence the lives and livelihood of current and subsequent cohorts of elderly individuals (George, 1988). Brown and Barnes-Nacoste view political participation as a valued activity on the part of the black elderly, and their concern is with what factors (particularly group identification and social and economic status) relate to positive participation in the electoral process. The major outcome variables of interest are voting and other political activities, such as campaigning and contacting public officials. Their results provide support for their thesis that one effect of severe racial socialization conditions among this cohort of elderly blacks results in the formation of a strong sense of group solidarity that translates into active political participation. In Chapter 14 Robert Joseph Taylor and Michael C. Thornton build on the preceding two chapters to focus their attention narrowly on how one historically important participatory dimension, religiosity, relates to political participation, notably voting. Their results indicate that religiosity plays a significant role in political participation, independently of the effects of status position. Particularly important are the effects of church attendance and church membership in leading to increased participation, in comparison to the weaker effects of more devotional aspects of religious expression.

Section V focuses on the role and function of work and retirement. As many have noted (Gibson, 1991; J. S. Jackson & Gibson, 1985), disability and poor job histories often lead to relatively early detachment from the labor force, but the lack of financial and other social resources often results in later formal retirement from paid work on the part of the black elderly. Lerita M. Coleman in Chapter 15 examines those variables that are related to the current work status of the black elderly. Her analyses address the nature of the work that the black elderly are involved in and how work status relates to sociodemographic and socioeconomic status variables. She discusses some of the barriers to full productive participation and concludes that work constitutes an important and often untapped resource for the black elderly, providing meaningful personal and group productive roles. Finally, in Chapter 16, Rose C. Gibson explores the retirement status of the black elderly. Although retirement is one of the major processes studied in social gerontology (George, 1988; J. J. Jackson, 1980), very little is known about the nature of retirement in racial and ethnic minority populations (see, e. g., Gibson, 1987; 1991; J. S. Jackson & Gibson, 1985). Gibson examines the patterns of retirement and the major socioeconomic and social status variables that are related to the retirement decision and individual assessment of the quality of retirement. Her findings indicate that the lifetime work experiences of black Americans affect self-definitions of retirement, leading to a unique experience of what has traditionally been studied as part of the retirement decision, event, and process.

In the final chapter (Chapter 17), we summarize the substantive chapters that have gone before within a life course and cohort framework. In this chapter we draw conclusions regarding psychological and social dimensions of aging—pointing out the major areas where the data support previous speculations, as well as major diversions, and how new cohorts of the black elderly and current and future period events may influence the conclusions that we draw. Finally, we end with an assessment of directions for future research that may contribute to a better understanding of social gerontology of the black American elderly.

Summary

As indicated previously, the major purpose of this book is to examine empirically psychological and social dimensions of aging among black American elderly. We noted earlier that although there has been much speculation, particularly over the last decade, regarding the conditions and circumstances of life for black elderly (J. J. Jackson, 1980; J. S.

Jackson, 1988), few systematic high-quality data have been available. Empirical studies have, for the most part, been based upon small, nonrepresentative samples or parts of comparative efforts in which the number of black Americans available for analysis has been limited.

The current volume provides a coherent, related collection of papers that bring to bear sophisticated analyses on a representative, relatively large sample of the black American older population. As described earlier, the NSBA data set, because of its size, scope, and national character, permits detailed empirical examination of many psychological and social factors considered to be important in previous writings and less extensive empirical studies and related to aging in racial and ethnic minority groups.

In sum, we believe that this book provides a systematic overview of the multiple statuses of older black Americans and the important roles and resources that are available and may influence their quality of life, health, and functioning. It is our hope that by bringing high-quality data and sophisticated analyses to bear upon what have been largely speculative accounts, we can encourage better and more refined empirical data collections and analyses. We believe that such efforts may ultimately lead to the development of widely accepted and useful theoretical frameworks for understanding the psychological and social aging processes among black Americans.

References

Allen, L. R., & Britt, D. W. (1983). Social class and mental health: The impact of resources and feedback. In R. D. Felner, L. A. Jason, J. N. Moritsugu, & S. Farber (Eds.), *Preventive psychology* (pp. 149-161). Elmsford, NY: Pergamon.

Baltes, P. B. (1987). Theoretical propositions of life-span developmental psychology: On the dynamics between growth and decline. *Developmental Psychology, 23,* 611-626.

Barresi. C. M. (1987). Ethnic aging and the life course. In D. E. Gelfand & C. M. Barresi (Eds.), *Ethnic dimensions of aging* (pp. 18-34). New York: Springer.

Bengtson, V. L. (1979). Ethnicity and aging: Problems and issues in current social science inquiry. In D. E. Gelfand & A. J. Kutzik (Eds.), *Ethnicity and aging: Theory, research and policy* (pp. 9-31). New York: Springer.

Bengtson, V. L., Cutler, N., Mangen, D., & Marshall, V. (1985). Generations, cohorts and relations between age groups. In R. B. Binstock & E. Shanas (Eds.), *Handbook of aging and the social sciences* (pp. 304-338). New York: Van Nostrand Reinhold.

Broman, C. L., Neighbors, H. W., & Jackson, J. S. (1988). Racial group identification among black adults. *Social Forces, 67,* 146-158.

Brown, R. E. (1984). *Determinants of black political participation.* Unpublished doctoral dissertation, University of Michigan, Ann Arbor.

Burton, L. M., & Dilworth-Anderson, P. (1991). The intergenerational family roles of aged black Americans. In S. P. Pfeifer, & M. B. Sussman (Eds.), *Families: Intergenerational and generational connections* (pp. 311-330). New York: Haworth.

Cantor, M. H. (1979). Neighbors and friends: An overlooked resource in the informal support system. *Research on Aging, 1*, 434-463.

Chatters, L. M., & Taylor, R. J. (1989). Age differences in religious participation among black adults. *Journal of Gerontology: Social Sciences, 44*, S183-S189.

Chatters, L. M., & Taylor, R. J. (1990). Social integration among aging blacks. In Z. Harel, E. McKinney, & M. Williams (Eds.), *Understanding and serving the black aged* (pp. 82-99). Newbury Park, CA: Sage.

Dowd, J., & Bengtson, V. L. (1978). Aging in minority populations: An examination of the double jeopardy hypothesis. *Journal of Gerontology, 33*(3), 427-436.

Dressler, W. (1985). Extended family relationships, social support, and mental health in a Southern black community. *Journal of Health and Social Behavior, 26*, 39-48.

Driedger. L., & Chappell, N. (1988). *Aging and ethnicity: Toward an interface.* Toronto, CA: Butterworths.

George, L. K. (1988). Social participation in later life: Black-white differences. In J. S. Jackson (Ed.), *The black American elderly: Research on physical and psychosocial health* (pp. 99-126). New York: Springer.

Gibson, R. C. (1987). Reconceptualizing retirement for black Americans. *The Gerontologist, 27*(6), 691-698.

Gibson, R. C. (1991). The subjective retirement of black Americans. *Journal of Gerontology: Social Sciences, 46*, S204-S209.

Gibson, R. C., & Jackson, J. S. (1992). The black oldest old: Health, physical functioning and informal supports. In R. Suzman & D. Willis (Eds.), *The oldest old* (pp. 505-515). New York: Oxford University Press.

Gurin, P., Hatchett, S. J., & Jackson, J. S. (1989). *Hope and independence: Blacks' response to electoral and party politics.* New York: Russell Sage.

Hatchett, S. J., & Nacoste, R. W. (1984). *Exposure to desegregated schooling: Profiling the experience of black Americans.* Unpublished manuscript, University of Michigan, Institute for Social Research, Ann Arbor.

Jackson, J. J. (1980). *Minorities and aging.* Belmont, CA: Wadsworth.

Jackson, J. J. (1985). Race, national origin, ethnicity, and aging. In R. B. Binstock & E. Shanas (Eds.), *Handbook of aging and the social sciences* (pp. 264-303). New York: Van Nostrand Reinhold.

Jackson, J. S. (Ed.). (1988). *The black American elderly: Research on physical and psychosocial health.* New York: Springer.

Jackson, J. S. (Ed.). (1991). *Life in black America.* Newbury Park, CA: Sage Publications.

Jackson, J. S., & Antonucci, T. C. (1991). Social support processes in the health and effective functioning of the elderly. In M. L. Wykle (Ed.), *Stress and health among the elderly* (pp. 72-95). New York: Springer.

Jackson, J. S., & Antonucci, T. C. (in press). Survey research methodology and life-span human development. In S. H. Cohen & H. W. Reese (Eds.), *Life-span developmental psychology: Methodological innovations.* Hillsdale, NJ: Lawrence Erlbaum.

Jackson, J. S., Antonucci, T. C., & Gibson, R. C. (1990a). Cultural, racial, and ethnic minority influences on aging. In J. E. Birren & K. W. Schaie (Eds.), *Handbook of the psychology of aging* (3rd ed., pp. 103-123). New York: Academic Press.

Jackson, J. S., Antonucci, T.C., & Gibson, R. C. (1990b). Social relations, productive activities, and coping with stress in late life. In M.A.P. Stephens, J. H. Crowther, S. E. Hobfoll, & D. L. Tennenbaum (Eds.), *Stress and coping in later life families* (pp. 193-209). Washington, DC: Hemisphere.

Jackson, J. S., Antonucci, T. C., & Gibson, R. C. (in press). Cultural, ethnic, and racial influences on aging productively. In S. A. Bass, F. G. Caro, & Y. P. Chen (Eds.), *Achieving a productive aging society.* Westport, CT: Greenwood.

Jackson, J. S., Burns, C. J., & Gibson, R. C. (1992). An overview of geriatric care in ethnic and racial minority groups. In E. Calkins, A. B. Ford, & P. R. Katz (Eds.), *Practice of geriatrics* (2nd ed., pp. 57-64). Philadelphia: Harcourt Brace Jovanovich.

Jackson, J. S., & Gibson, R. C. (1985). Work and retirement among black elderly. In Z. Blau (Ed.), *Work, retirement, and social policy* (pp. 193-222). Greenwich, CT: JAI.

Jackson, J. S., Tucker, M. B., & Gurin, G. (1987). *National survey of black Americans, 1979-1980.* Ann Arbor, MI: Inter-University Consortium for Political and Social Research.

Jaynes, G. D., & Williams, R. M., Jr. (Eds.). (1989). *A common destiny: Blacks and American society.* Washington, DC: National Academy Press.

Manuel, R. C. (Ed.). (1982). *Minority aging: Sociological and social psychological issues.* Westport, CT: Greenwood.

Markides, K. S., Liang, J., & Jackson, J. S. (1990). Race, ethnicity, and aging: Conceptual and methodological issues. In L. K. George & R. H. Binstock (Eds.), *Handbook of aging and the social sciences* (3rd ed., pp. 112-129). New York: Academic Press.

McAdoo, H. P. (1988). *Black families.* (2nd ed.) Beverly Hills: Sage.

Report of the President's Commission on Civil Disorders. (1968). New York: Bantam.

Riley, M. W. (1985). Age strata in social systems. In R. H. Binstock & E. Shanas (Eds.), *Handbook of aging and social science* (2nd ed., pp. 369-411). New York: Van Nostrand Reinhold.

Riley, M. W. (1987). On the significance of age in sociology. *American Sociological Review, 52,* 1-14.

Rosow, I. (1976). Status and role change through the life span. In R.B. Binstock & E. Shanas (Eds.), *Handbook of aging and the social sciences* (pp. 457-482). New York: Van Nostrand Reinhold.

Sokolovsky, J. (1989). Bringing culture back home: Ethnicity, aging and family support. In J. Sokolovsky (Ed.), *The cultural context of aging* (pp. 201-211). New York: Bergin & Garvey.

Stack, C. (1974). *All our kin.* New York: Harper & Row.

Stanford, E. P. (1983). A minority perspective. *The Gerontologist, 23,* 215.

Streib, G. F. (1985). Social stratification and aging. In R. H. Binstock & E. Shanas (Eds.), *Handbook of aging and the social sciences* (2nd ed., pp. 339-368). New York: Van Nostrand Reinhold.

Taylor, R. J. (1985). The extended family as a source of support to elderly blacks. *The Gerontologist, 25*(5), 488-495.

Taylor, R. J. (1986). Receipt of support from family among black Americans: Demographic and familial differences. *Journal of Marriage and the Family, 48,* 67-77.

Taylor, R. J., & Chatters, L. M. (1986a). Church based informal support among elderly blacks. *The Gerontologist, 26,* 637-642.

Taylor, R. J., & Chatters, L. M. (1986b). Patterns of informal support to elderly black adults: Family, friends, and church members. *Social Work, 31,* 432-438.

Taylor, R. J., & Chatters, L. M. (1988a). Church members as a source of informal social support. *Review of Religious Research, 30,* 193-203.

Taylor, R. J., & Chatters, L. M. (1988b). Correlates of education, income, and poverty among aged blacks. *The Gerontologist, 28,* 435-441.

Taylor, R. J., & Chatters, L. M. (1991). Extended family networks of older black adults. *Journal of Gerontology: Social Sciences, 46, S210-S217.*

Taylor, R. J., Chatters, L. M., Tucker, M. B., & Lewis, E. (1990). Developments in research on black families: A decade in review. *Journal of Marriage and the Family, 52,* 993-1014.

Wilson-Ford, V. (1990). Poverty among black elderly women. *Journal of Women and Aging, 2*(4), 5-20.

SECTION I

Community, Friends, and Family

2

NEIGHBORHOODS AND NEIGHBOR RELATIONS

Rukmalie Jayakody

Neighborhood primary groups play an important role in individuals' lives (Fellin & Litwak, 1968) and provide a unique set of functions not met by families, friends, or formal organizations. These functional roles include the neighborhood as a center for interpersonal influence, a source of mutual aid, an organizational base for formal and informal organizations, a reference group and social context, and a status arena (Warren, 1971; see Litwak & Szelenyi, 1969, for further discussion). Because of their physical proximity, neighbors are in a position to provide personal advice, psychological support, and help on an emergency basis (Fellin & Litwak, 1968). Neighbors, in contrast to family, can be expected to help with tasks requiring speed in assistance or knowledge of the spatial area (Cantor, 1979a; Unger & Wandersman, 1985; Wellman & Leighton, 1979). For instance, many crisis situations, such as baby-sitting, advice, or emergency first aid, can be handled by neighbors.

Neighborhoods and Elderly Adults

Neighborhoods provide "proximity anchored social networks" (Olson, 1982). For people who are not mobile, such as the elderly, children, and low-income persons (due to lack of access to cars and public transportation), the proximity afforded by neighborhood contact is essential for friendship and companionship (Wireman, 1984). With the elderly's decrease in mobility, neighbors become particularly important, both as a source of primary interaction and as a form of localized informal support. Except in higher socioeconomic strata, the elderly are inclined to be neighborhood bound (Cantor, 1975) and their friends tend to be people located in the same neighborhood (Cantor, 1979a). Several studies confirm the importance of neighborhoods for elderly adults. A survey conducted in Australia found that 74% of the sample had daily contact with neighbors (Prinsley & Cameron, 1979). In a neighborhood where elderly residents have known each other for several years, closely knit networks of mutual assistance and support among the oldest old residents were present (Rosel, 1983). Sixty percent of the sample of elderly residents in the inner-city areas of New York City indicated their neighbors provided assistance on a reciprocal basis (Cantor, 1979a). Because the elderly are neighborhood bound, socialization with neighbors assumes greater importance. Neighbors provide an important primary contact for the elderly that is different from their contact with kin.

In addition to age, race gains special importance in neighboring. Neighborhoods play a more significant role in the lives of blacks than whites (Warren, 1975). Blacks are more likely than whites to view their neighborhood as: (a) a center for interpersonal influence, (b) a social context or reference group, and (c) an interaction arena (Warren, 1975). In addition, high levels of residential segregation (Massey, 1990; Massey & Denton, 1988) result in blacks living in more racially homogeneous areas than members of other racial groups (White, 1987). This segregation and social differentiation from the city provides an additional basis for neighborhood association (Suttles, 1968) and a "community of interest" might be created based on the shared racial status (Wireman, 1984).

Neighbor Relations

The term *neighboring* is used to refer to the relationships and interactions occurring between people living in spatial proximity of one another. Neighboring consists of the activities that people carry out in their role as neighbors (Keller, 1968). Although in the past this term has been used only to refer to active neighbor associations (such as visiting), I argue that passive neighbor relations exist as well.

Perceptual and Behavioral Neighboring Neighboring is a construct consisting of two dimensions (Mann, 1954), which I will term *perceptual* and *behavioral* neighboring. Perceptual neighboring is measured by the extent to which one knows one's neighbors. It is a passive form of neighboring indicating a sense of caring and goodwill toward neighbors, but it does not necessarily involve visiting or companionship. Perceptual neighboring is important because when need arises, especially in times of crisis, assistance from neighbors may be requested or will be volunteered. Behavioral neighboring includes active associations and overt forms of social relationships, such as visiting. Perceptual and behavioral neighboring occur in varying degrees. A low degree of both perceptual and behavioral neighboring results in a lack of social relationships among neighbors, and even in times of crisis help from neighbors might be unavailable. A high degree of perceptual and behavioral neighboring leads to a great deal of interaction, mutual aid, and conversation.

Neighboring Among Elderly Black Americans

Neighborhood relationships among black Americans, particularly elderly black Americans, is a neglected area of research. Although the neighborhood plays an important role in elderly black Americans' lives, research has yet to examine the elements that predict neighboring among this group. Research has not differentiated between perceptual and behavioral neighboring, but studies conducted on neighboring as a single concept, conducted on mostly white and all-age samples, provide some guidance as to what factors will be important. There are three sets of variables impacting neighboring: (a) structural factors, (b) neighborhood aspects, and (c) demographic factors.

Structural Factors The type of residential living unit is a major discriminator among the levels of involvement in a neighborhood (Riger & Lavrakas, 1981). Persons living in single-family houses are more likely to be involved in their neighborhood, whereas those living in multiunit dwellings tend to be less involved. Additionally, persons living in single-family detached homes will experience fewer problems with neighbors with boundary control or privacy. Thus, they will have positive feelings toward neighbors and interact on a more frequent basis (Silverman, 1986). Whether people own or rent their housing unit is another important predictor of neighboring; home owners tend to neighbor more than renters (Ahlbrandt, 1984).

Neighborhood Factors Neighborhood factors can be important predictors of interaction among neighbors (Silverman, 1986). Length of residence (Ahlbrandt, 1984; McGahan, 1972; Riger & Lavrakas, 1981) and homogeneity among neighbors are a decisive source of positive neighboring (Gans, 1962). People living in ethnically homogeneous neighborhoods are more likely to trust their neighbors and feel closer to them, and thus neighbor more frequently (Silverman, 1986). Fear of crime can severely restrict mobility and neighborhood use, thereby hindering neighbor interactions (Braungart, Hoyer, & Braungart, 1979; Cantor, 1979b).

Demographics The impact of various demographic factors on neighboring is ambiguous. Although some research reports married couples to neighbor more (Nohara, 1968; Tomeh, 1964), other studies found people living alone neighbor more frequently (Cantor, 1979a; Kohen, 1983; McGahan, 1972). Inconclusive results exist for socioeconomic status as well. An association between socioeconomic status and neighboring was found by some (Ahlbrandt, 1984; Fellin & Litwak, 1968; Hallman, 1984), but others found a weak (Philliber, 1976) or no correlation (Warren, 1975). Upper classes are expected to have less neighbor contact, as they have more extensive nonspatial relationships. The importance of gender on neighboring is also unclear. Several studies found no association (Nohara, 1968; Tomeh, 1976), but Bulmner (1986) and Kohen (1983) found women to neighbor more than men. Most research reports a negative relationship between urbanicity and neighboring (e.g., see Greider & Krannich, 1985; Keller, 1968; Key, 1965), but Silverman (1986) argues that urbanicity has no direct effect on neighboring.

The majority of neighborhood and neighboring research utilizes case examples or historical reviews of individual cities (Cantor, 1979a, 1979b; Fischer, 1982; Liebow, 1967; Warren, 1975; Whyte, 1955; Zito, 1974). An exception is White (1987), who provided a useful demographic description of U.S. neighborhoods based on the 1980 census. The present research utilizes a national probability sample to provide a general picture of neighboring among elderly black adults.

Hypotheses

Although prior research found inconclusive findings for the effect of marital status on neighboring (Cantor, 1979a; Kohen, 1983; McGahan, 1972; Nohara, 1968; Tomeh, 1964), I believe it to be an important predictor. Patterns of contact and interaction can be strongly affected by marital status. Whereas other adult roles become less salient with age, marital status continues to be a major organizing force in the lives of the elderly (Kohen, 1983). It is predicted that married people will interact with and know their neighbors more than people of other marital statuses. It can be argued that a married couple has two people interacting with others, which would increase each person's circle of acquaintances. Many forms of visiting occur in a couple context. For instance, a married couple might go over to their neighbors' house to play cards or participate in another type of couple activity. Marriage is a socially accepted role and provides the basis for many types of relationships. Marriage might be the basis for the continuance of a relationship developed over time by both husband and wife. The death of a spouse could produce a change in the relationship.

Both perceptual and behavioral neighboring are important to elderly adults. Although behavioral neighboring (visiting neighbors) might indicate the existence of an informal support network, perceptual neighboring (knowing neighbors) could be important in reducing feelings of loneliness and isolation. The following analysis examines the role of marital status on both perceptual and behavioral neighboring. In addition, other possible predictors of both neighboring constructs will be explored.

Methods

Sample and Dependent Measures

This analysis is based on a subsample of the National Survey of Black Americans (NSBA). It includes the responses of those study participants 55 years of age and older at the time of the interview ($N = 581$). Behavioral neighboring was measured by the question: "How often do you get together with any of your neighbors—that is, either visiting at each other's homes or going places together? Would you say nearly every day, at least once a week, a few times a month, at least once a month, a few times a year, or never?" The question measuring perceptual neighboring was: "How many of your neighbors do you know well enough to visit or call on? Would you say you have many, some, a few, or none that you know well enough to visit or call on?"

Independent Measures

Three sets of independent measures, structural aspects, neighborhood aspects, and demographic variables, including marital status, are utilized in this analysis.

Structural Aspects Structural aspects measure the physical makeup of the community either promoting or hindering neighbor interactions. One component is the type of residential living unit, apartments, town houses, single-family detached homes, or other housing type (mobile home, trailer, row house, other). This information is not part of the survey but was obtained from the cover sheet for the questionnaire filled out by the interviewer. Owning or renting the unit of dwelling, another component of structural aspects, will also be examined.

Neighborhood Aspects Neighborhood conditions that can affect the frequency of neighboring include neighborhood satisfaction, length of residence in the neighborhood, and frequency of physical assaults or muggings occurring in the neighborhood. Racial homogeneity—the number of blacks residing in the respondent's neighborhood—is also examined. Table 2.1 presents the distributions for both neighborhood and structural aspects.

Demographic Variables The demographic variables utilized in this study include marital status, education, income, gender, degree of urbanicity, and region of the country.

Results

Perceptual Neighboring

Overwhelmingly, the elderly blacks in this sample were familiar with their neighbors. Only 8.3% indicated they did not know any of their neighbors. Forty-seven percent reported knowing a few neighbors, 18% knew some, and 27% knew many of their neighbors. The results of the regression analysis for the number of neighbors known on the structural aspects, neighborhood aspects, and demographic characteristics are presented in Table 2.2 (Model 1). This model explained 12% of the variance ($R^2 = .119$, $F_{(16,464)} = 3.921$, $p < .001$). Length of residence in the neighborhood and neighborhood satisfaction were the only two variables significantly associated with perceptual neighboring. Analysis exclusively on the married respondents reveals that neighborhood satisfaction was the only variable significantly related to the number of neighbors known ($R^2 = .130$, $F_{(14,186)} = 2.154$, $p < .01$). Among the widowed respondents, length of residence in the neighborhood was the only variable significantly related to perceptual neighboring. This model explained 18% of the variance in perceptual neighboring ($R^2 = .184$, $F_{(14,176)} = 2.830$, $p < .001$).

Behavioral Neighboring

Over half the sample reported visiting their neighbors at least a few times a month. Fifteen percent of the respondents never visited their neighbors, 20% visited a few times a year, 8% visited once a month, 20% visited two to three times a month, 27% visited one to three times a week, and 10% reported visiting their neighbors at least every day. The regression coefficients for the frequency of visiting neighbors regressed on structural aspects, neighborhood aspects, and demographic characteristics are presented in Table 2.3 (Model 1) and explained 11% of the variance ($R^2 = .105$, $F_{(16,428)} = 3.123$, $p < .001$). Although no variables were significantly associated with visiting neighbors, several bordered significance ($p < .10$). Respondents living in another housing type (mobile home, trailer, row house, or other) tend to visit their neighbors more frequently than those living in single-family detached homes. Education was negatively associated with frequency of behavioral neighboring: The higher a respondent's education, the less interaction he or she had with neighbors. Region of the country also has an impact on visiting neighbors. Both the North Central and the West are negatively associated with behavioral neighboring. In addition, widows appear to visit their neighbors on a more frequent basis than married respondents. The model for married respondents (Table 2.3, Model 2) explained 25% of the variance ($R^2 = .245$, $F_{(14,170)} = 3.712$, $p < .001$) for the frequency of visiting neighbors. Neighborhood satisfaction was positively associated with behavioral neighboring, whereas urbanicity showed a negative relationship.

Summary and Discussion

The "pervasive ignorance of neighbors" found by Zito (1974) did not hold for this sample. The majority of black elderly both know and visit their neighbors. Although support was not examined, this research indicates that neighbors are an important resource to the elderly and neighbor relations are not characterized by impersonality (Durkheim, 1933) or a lack of association (Key, 1965). Two major findings arise from the present research. First, this study indicates marital status differences in both perceptual and behavioral neighboring. No single independent variable was significantly associated with either perceptual or behavioral neighboring over different marital statuses on a consistent basis. Second, the findings demonstrate that neighboring is not a single construct, but consists of two dimensions. Variables that were significant in predicting one dimension of neighboring were not significant for the other dimension.

Marital Status Differences

There were no consistent differences in either perceptual or behavioral neighboring. The predictors explained the greatest amount of variance in the widowed sample for perceptual neighboring and in the married sample for behavioral neighboring. Additionally, the predictors did not explain any variance in perceptual neighboring for the other marital statuses (never married, separated, and divorced), and no variance in behavioral neighboring for the widowed and other statuses. This indicates that patterns of neighboring are not identical over different marital statuses. Interesting results appear for the widowed respondents. The hypothesis that the widowed behaviorally neighbor less than the married was not substantiated. Although the widowed have the greatest frequency of neighbor interactions (highest degree of behavioral neighboring), they knew fewer of their neighbors than married respondents (lower degree of perceptual neighboring). As hypothesized, the married perceptually neighbored more than the other marital statuses. The married have a wider realm of acquaintances because there are two people in the couple making and sustaining relationships. With the death of a spouse, there is a decrease in the making of new contacts. Also, couple-orientated relationships established when the spouse was alive become less salient and can break off, leaving the widow with a smaller circle of acquaintances.

The finding that widowed respondents interact with this smaller circle on a more frequent basis than do their married counterparts might be explained by widows turning to their neighbors as a replacement for support and companionship previously received from their spouse.

Other work indicates widows have a greater intimacy with friends than the married (Powers & Bultena, 1976) and friendship increases between the 1st and 4th year of bereavement (Ferraro, Mutran, & Barresi, 1984). Widows take more responsibility for their relationships and are more aware of the need to become connected to others (Heinemann & Evans, 1990). Their added sense of responsibility for relationships might mean that they choose to end tenuous relationships and place more effort in fostering and sustaining close relationships. Consequently, this research in conjunction with present findings indicates that although the widowed have a smaller circle of acquaintances, they rely heavily on this group.

An alternative explanation for the marital statuses differences is varying degrees of neighborhood importance. Whereas the married seem to have retained networks detached from a specific locality or have "personal portable communities" (Crump, 1977), this does not seem true for the widowed. Widows appear to have the greatest reduction in life space and are neighborhood bound more than persons of other marital statuses. Transportation could be a central explanation for this life space reduction. The majority of elderly widows are women, and many elderly women never drove and lose mobility when their husband dies. Or the elderly might stop or limit their driving because of costs of gasoline and car maintenance. They might also reduce driving because of uneasiness at venturing alone into unfamiliar territory. This reduction in life space means that the neighborhood as a place of interaction is especially important in providing friendship and companionship for widows. Interestingly, although the predictors examined explained the greatest amount of variance in perceptual neighboring for the widowed sample, little is known about behavioral neighboring among this group.

Two possible explanations exist for the lack of findings among the nonmarried. One possibility is that the reduction in life space and the centrality of the neighborhood as a basis of association do not apply to the never married, separated, and divorced. They might have formed strong ties with friends outside their immediate spatiality. Given the high number of the elderly who are either married or widowed (over 80% in this sample), those who are not married might feel a need to look for others like themselves. For them, locality is not the basis of association. Instead, they look for those with similar marital histories. Additionally, they are accustomed to being independent and might have retained their mobility by continuing to drive or by utilizing public transportation.

A second possible explanation is that people in these marital statuses experience a high degree of social isolation. In a longitudinal examination of the social contacts of unmarried older persons, Keith (1989) found that 36% of those divorced had not maintained contacts with friends, whereas 22% of those never married had no contact with friends. Divorced respondents may have limited interaction with neighbors because of perceived discrimination and alienation based on their divorced status (Kitson, Lopata, Holmes, & Mayering, 1980). These feelings of alienation could be true for the separated and never married as well.

Other Findings

The present research showed that the level of crime, measured by the frequency of muggings in the neighborhood, had no significant effect on either perceptual or behavioral neighboring. This is not to say that crime is not an important factor in the life of the elderly. As shown in Table 2.1, only 45% of the respondents indicated that muggings never or hardly ever occurred in their neighborhood. That frequency of muggings is not a significant predictor of neighboring indicates the resourcefulness of elderly blacks and the adaptions they make to their environment. Rather than letting crime stop them from neighboring, they seem to be finding ways around the problem. It is possible that the elderly visit their neighbors during the morning, when the level of crime is low, or form some other adaptive technique to continue their relationships with those around them. This findings is interesting, considering previous research that found the elderly to be more afraid of crime than other age groups (Braungart, Hoyer, & Braungart, 1979). Although crime is a problem, they are not letting their fear cripple their activities.

As presented in Table 2.2, satisfaction with the neighborhood is significantly associated with the number of neighbors known for the married sample. If there is a high level of neighborhood satisfaction, neighbors are open to interaction and association. If people are not happy with their neighborhood, they might be unfriendly to those they meet, discouraging associations from developing. Additionally, for the widowed sample, length of residence in the neighborhood was significant in predicting perceptual neighboring. This fits in with the previously discussed hypotheses on widows. Residing in a neighborhood for an extended time, they have had more opportunity to meet and interact with their neighbors. Additionally, they might have met many

Table 2.1 Structural and Neighborhood Aspects Distribution of Respondents Aged 55 and Older

Structural Aspects	(N)	%
Housing Type		
Single-family house	401	69.4
Apartment	138	23.9
Other housing	39	6.7
Total	578	100.0
Own or Rent Housing		
Own	361	64.6
Rent	198	35.4
Total	559	100.0
Neighborhood Aspects	(N)	%
Length of Residence		
Less than 2 years	11	2.1
2 to 5 years	47	8.9
5 to 10 years	136	25.7
More than 10 years	336	63.3
Total	530	100.0
Racial Composition		
Mostly white	35	6.3
Half black	61	11.0
Mostly black	183	32.9
All black	278	49.8
Total	557	100.0
Muggings in Neighborhood		
Never	98	17.3
Hardly ever	158	27.8
Not too often	183	32.2
Fairly often	70	12.3
Very often	59	10.4
Total	568	100.0
Neighborhood Satisfaction		
Very good	276	47.7
Fairly good	261	45.2
Fairly bad	24	4.2
Very bad	17	2.9
Total	578	100.0

NOTE: Missing data on some of the demographic variables results in Ns of less than 581.

of their neighbors while their spouse was still alive, and although they may not interact, the acquaintance is a potential resource in times of need.

Table 2.2 Regression Coefficients for the Structural Aspects, Neighborhood Aspects, and Demographic Variables on Perceptual Neighboring

Predictors[1]	Model 1 b	Model 1 se	Model 2 b	Model 2 se	Model 3 b	Model 3 se	Model 4 b	Model 4 se
Intercept	1.681***	.436	1.089	.725	2.45***	.677	1.35	.964
Structural Aspects								
Apt.	−.194	.134	−.255	.228	−.288	.211	.070	.312
Other	−.048	.169	−.087	.079	.236	.307	−.266	.369
Own/rent	.047	.113	.072	.194	−.046	.187	.082	.245
Neighborhood Aspects								
Length of residence	.146**	.059	.131	.097	.209*	.101	.104	.130
Muggings	−.019	.040	−.037	.071	−.068	.059	.075	.104
Satisfaction	.273***	.067	.322**	.121	.184#	.102	.308	.150
Homogeneity	−.040	.049	.081	.080	−.127	.080	−.058	.116
Demographic Variables								
Education	−.012	.056	.071	.084	−.104	.104	−.074	.128
Income	−.007	.013	−.004	.021	−.022	.022	.009	.027
Urbanicity								
Urban	−.155	.109	−.251	.183	−.156	.167	−.037	.300
Region								
Northeast	.002	.139	.240	.222	−.124	.229	−.320	.322
North Central	−.161	.122	−.022	.208	−.230	.191	−.294	.284
West	.182	.211	.375	.300	.109	.438	−.356	.488
Sex								
Male	−.056	.093	−.162	.141	.086	.174	−.017	.207
Marital Status								
Widow	−.020	.106						
Other	−.036	.125						
R^2	.119***		.130*		.184***		.0	

NOTE: b = unstandardized coefficient; se = standard error
1. Several of the predictors in this analysis were represented by dummy variables:
Structural housing: single detached, apartment, other—single detached excluded category
   Own or rent: 1 = own, 0 = rent
   Urbanicity: 1 = urban, 0 = rural
   Region: Northeast, North Central, South, West—South excluded category
   Sex: 1 = male, 0 = females
   Marital status: married, widowed, other—married excluded category
#$p < .10$; *$p < .05$; **$p < .01$; ***$p < .001$.

Widowhood, along with type of housing, education, and region, all bordered significance as predictors of behavioral neighboring. Contrary to previous findings (Riger & Lavrakas, 1981), persons living in mobile homes, trailers, and row houses visit their neighbors more than do people living in single-family detached homes. These findings also show a negative relationship between education and behavioral neighboring. That is, as levels of education increase, visiting neighbors decreases. Possibly, increased levels of education indicate more portability of networks and less reliance on the neighborhood as a center of association. Higher levels of education could bring participation in associations or groups located outside the neighborhood. No significant associations were found between income and behavioral neighboring for the overall sample, but a significant negative relationship did exist for the married respondents. Like education, income brings increased mobility and less reliance on neighborhood contacts for companionship.

No previous research has investigated the effects of region on neighbor relations. As presented in Table 2.3, the current work shows people residing in the South visit their neighbors more than those residing in other regions of the country. The findings suggest that the South may possess a unique set of cultural values that encourage visiting among the elderly (Chatters, Taylor, & Jackson, 1985). Additionally, in the married sample, urbanicity is negatively associated with behavioral neighboring. This is in keeping with previous findings (Greider & Krannich, 1985; Key, 1965) as well as with theories of the declining importance of the neighborhood in modern industrial society (Redfield, 1947; Wirth, 1938).

Conclusion

The present research has shown that perceptual and behavioral neighboring are two separate neighboring dimensions. Both dimensions are important to understanding the role neighborhoods and neighbors play in the lives of elderly blacks. Whereas behavioral neighboring is important for social support, perceptual neighboring is important in reducing feelings of loneliness and isolation.

Neighbors are an important component in the informal nonkin support system of the elderly and may enhance the ability of older people to remain in their community. Especially for childless elderly, friends and neighbors substitute for primary social support. Even for older people with children, there are important socialization and support tasks that only neighbors can fulfill (Cantor, 1979a). Elderly adults must have both large-scale formal organizations and small primary groups, such

Table 2.3 Regression Coefficients for the Structural Aspects, Neighborhood Aspects, and Demographic Variables on Behavioral Neighboring

Predictors[1]	Model 1		Model 2		Model 3		Model 4	
	b	se	b	se	b	se	b	se
Intercept	3.78***	.805	3.00	1.21	3.86	1.29	3.91	1.85
Structural Aspects								
Apt.	−.087	.246	−.476	.382	−.281	.406	.984	.572
Other	.522#	.305	.358	.440	.192	.569	1.26	.694
Own/rent	−.286	.207	−.059	.327	−.755	.355	.487	.440
Neighborhood Aspects								
Length of residence	−.031	.109	−.196	.163	−.115	.196	.209	.237
Muggings	.009	.072	.015	.116	−.001	.113	.018	.191
Satisfaction	.134	.127	.460*	.207	.038	.206	−.071	.301
Homogeneity	.046	.088	.189	.128	.025	.154	−.242	.208
Demographic Variables								
Education	−.123#	.102	−.072	.133	−.007	.217	−.647	.223
Income	−.021	.023	−.062#	.035	.031	.043	−.019	.047
Urbanicity								
Urban	−.276	.194	−.651*	.296	−.103	.313	.615	.539
Region								
Northeast	−.384	.251	.164	.357	−.786	.451	−.772	.576
North Central	−.414#	.224	−.424	.336	−.620	.380	−.139	.534
West	−.652#	.379	−.861#	.485	−.421	.812	−.337	.866
Sex								
Male	−.093	.170	.080	.233	−.446	.339	−.064	.375
Marital Status								
Widow	.373#	.195						
Other	.128	.227						
R^2	.105***		.235***		.0		.0	

NOTE: b = unstandardized coefficient; se = standard error
1. Several of the predictors in this analysis were represented by dummy variables:
Structural housing: single detached, apartment, other—single detached excluded category
  Own or rent: 1 = own, 0 = rent
  Urbanicity: 1 = urban, 0 = rural
  Region: Northeast, North Central, South, West—South excluded category
  Sex: 1 = male, 0 = females
  Marital status: married, widowed, other—married excluded category
#$p<.10$; *$p<.05$; **$p<.01$; ***$p<.001$.

as family, neighbors, and friends, to manage the tasks of daily life (Litwak, 1985). The results of the present research reveal neighbors and neighborhoods remain salient in the lives of older blacks.

Although neighbors are an important primary association for elderly adults, this research has shown the paucity of available information on the topic. The current study, in addition to providing two different dimensions of neighboring, has also shown the existence of marital status differences. Future research needs to examine the supportive role of neighbors in the lives of elderly adults, and elderly black adults in particular.

References

Ahlbrandt, R. (1984). *Neighborhoods, people and community*. New York: Plenum.

Braungart, M., Hoyer, W., & Braungart, R. (1979). Fear of crime among the elderly. In A. Goldstein, W. Hoyer, & P. Monti (Eds.), *Police and the elderly* (pp. 15-29). New York: Pergamon.

Bulmner, M. (1986). *Neighbors: The work of Philip Abrams*. London: Cambridge University Press.

Cantor, M. H. (1975). Life space and the social support systems of the inner city elderly of New York City. *The Gerontologist, 15*, 23-27.

Cantor, M. H. (1979a). Neighbors and friends: An overlooked resource in the informal support system. *Research on Aging, 1*, 434-463.

Cantor, M. H. (1979b). The informal support system of New York's inner-city elderly: Is ethnicity a factor? In D. E. Gelfand & A. J. Kutzik (Eds.), *Ethnicity and aging: Theory, research, and policy* (pp. 153-174). New York: Springer.

Chatters, L. M., Taylor, R. J., & Jackson, J. S. (1985). Size and composition of the informal helper networks of elderly blacks. *Journal of Gerontology, 40*, 605-614.

Crump, B. (1977, September 5-9). *The portability of urban ties*. Paper presented at the meeting of the American Sociological Association, Chicago.

Durkheim, E. (1933). *The division of labor in society*. New York: Macmillan.

Fellin, P., & Litwak, E. (1968). The neighborhood in urban American society. *Social Work, 13*, 72-80.

Ferraro, K. F., Mutran, E., & Barresi, C. M. (1984). Widowhood, health, and friendship support in later life. *Journal of Health and Social Behavior, 25*, 245-259.

Fischer, C. S. (1982). *To dwell among friends*. Chicago: University of Chicago Press.

Gans, H. (1962). *The urban village*. New York: Free Press.

Greider, T., & Krannich, R. S. (1985). Neighboring patterns, social support, and rapid growth: A comparison analysis from three western communities. *Sociological Perspectives, 28*(1), 51-70.

Hallman, H. W. (1984). *Neighborhoods: Their place in urban life*. Beverly Hills, CA: Sage.

Heinemann, G. D., & Evans. P. L. (1990). Widowhood: Loss, change, and adaption. In T. H. Brubaker (Ed.), *Family relationships in later life* (pp. 142-168). Newbury Park, CA: Sage.

Keith, P. M. (1989). *The unmarried in later life*. New York: Praeger.

Keller, S. (1968). *The urban neighborhood: A sociological perspective*. New York: Random House.

Key, W. (1965). Urbanism and neighboring. *Sociological Quarterly, 6,* 379-385.

Kitson, G., Lopata, H., Holmes, W., & Mayering, S. (1980). Divorcees and widows: Similarities and differences. *American Journal of Orthopsychiatry, 50,* 291-301.

Kohen, J. A. (1983). Old but not alone: Informal social supports among the elderly by marital status and sex. *The Gerontologist, 23*(1), 57-63.

Liebow, E. (1967). *Tally's corner: A study of negro street corner men.* Boston: Little, Brown.

Litwak, E. (1985). *Helping the elderly: The complementary roles of informal networks and formal systems.* New York: Guilford.

Litwak, E., & Szelenyi, I. (1969). Primary group structures and their functions: Kin, neighbors, and friends. *American Sociological Review, 34,* 465-481.

Mann, P. (1954). The concept of neighborliness. *American Journal of Sociology, 60,* 163-168.

Massey, D. S. (1990). American apartheid: Segregation and the making of the underclass. *American Journal of Sociology, 96*(2), 329-357.

Massey, D. S., & Denton, N. (1988). Suburbanization and segregation in U.S. metropolitan areas. *American Journal of Sociology, 94,* 592-626.

McGahan, P. (1972). The neighbor role and neighboring in a highly urban area. *Sociological Quarterly, 13*(3), 397-408.

Nohara, S. (1968). Social context and neighborliness: The negro in St. Louis. In S. S. Greer, D. McElrath, M. W. Miner, & P. Oleans (Eds.), *The new urbanization.* New York: St. Martin's.

Olson, P. (1982). Urban neighborhood research: Its development and current focus. *Urban Affairs Quarterly, 17*(4), 491-519.

Powers, E. A., & Bultena, D. L. (1976). Sex differences in intimate friendships of old age. *Journal of Marriage and the Family, 38*(4), 739-747.

Philliber, W. (1976). Prior training, opportunity and vested interest as factors influencing neighborhood integration. *Pacific Sociological Review, 19,* 231-244.

Prinsley, D., & Cameron, K. (1979). Old people living alone—Is organized observation necessary? *Australian Journal of Social Issues, 14*(4), 297-300.

Redfield, R. (1947). The folk society. *American Journal of Sociology, 52,* 293-308.

Riger, S., & Lavrakas, P. (1981). Community ties: Patterns of attachment and social interaction in urban neighborhoods. *American Journal of Community Psychology, 9,* 55-66.

Rosel, N. (1983). The hub of a wheel: A neighborhood support network. *International Journal of Aging and Human Development, 16*(3), 193-200.

Silverman, C. J. (1986). Neighboring and urbanism. *Urban Affairs Quarterly, 22*(2), 312-328.

Suttles, G. (1968). *The social order of the slum.* Chicago: University of Chicago Press.

Tomeh, A. (1976). Informal group participation and residence patterns. *American Journal of Sociology, 70,* 28-35.

Unger, D., & Wandersman, A. (1985). The importance of neighbors: The social, cognitive, and affective components of neighboring. *American Journal of Community Psychology, 13*(2), 1139-1169.

Warren, D. I. (1971). Neighboring in urban areas. In *The Encyclopedia of Social Work* (*16*[1], pp. 872-882). New York: National Association of Social Workers.

Warren, D. I. (1975). *Black neighborhoods: An assessment of community power.* Ann Arbor: University of Michigan Press.

Wellman, B., & Leighton, B. (1979). Networks, neighbors, and communities: Approaches to the study of the community question. *Urban Affairs Quarterly, 14*(3), 363-390.

White, M. J. (1987). *American neighborhoods and residential differentiation.* New York: Russell Sage.

Whyte, W. F. (1955). *Street corner society.* Chicago: University of Chicago Press.

Wireman, P. (1984). *Urban neighborhoods, networks and families: New forms for old values.* Lexington, MA: Lexington.

Wirth, L. (1938). Urbanism as a way of life. *American Journal of Sociology, 44,* 3-24.

Zito, J. M. (1974). Anonymity and neighboring in an urban, high rise complex. *Urban Life and Culture, 3*(3), 243-262.

3

CRIME STRESS, SELF-ESTEEM, AND LIFE SATISFACTION

John L. McAdoo

This chapter explores the effects of crime stress on the self-esteem and life satisfaction of the black elderly. We wished to determine the degree to which the elderly sample in the National Survey of Black Americans (NSBA) perceived community security as a strong mediator of crime stress. We were also interested in learning the impact of crime stress, controlling for community and demographic variables, on self-esteem and life satisfaction.

Background

The evidence from national surveys on criminal victimization indicates that the elderly are generally subject to less victimization (Antunes, Cook, Cook, & Skogan, 1977; Cook, Skogan, Cook, & Antunes, 1978; Hindelang, 1976; Hochstedler, 1977). Liang and Sengstock (1981) in reviewing national crime statistics found that the elderly are victims of such crimes as rape, robbery, and assault at an annual rate of 9 per thousand whereas the rate for the general population is 32 per thousand. They noted that the risk of victimization of elderly black males may be 14 times higher than the risk of victimization of white females.

McNeely (1983) in analyzing statistics from the most recent national crime survey noted that the concern for the safety of the black elderly is warranted. Black elderly females living in areas that are 76% to 100% black have a personal victimization rate of 36.1 per thousand population, almost exactly the same as the personal victimization rate of the general population. Black older men were found to have the highest rate of household victimization, almost 40% higher than older white men. McNeely concluded that elderly blacks are justified in their fear of crime. That their relatively high risk of exposure to personal property offenses continues throughout a period in their lives in which physical and earning capacities are diminished legitimates their concern. National studies (Harris & Associates, 1975) have also reported that a large number of elderly respondents rate fear of crime as their most serious problem.

Crime stress or fear of crime is an intrapsychic response to a perceived or real threat to one's feelings of well-being in which the person changes his or her behavior. Crime stress exists where perceptions of risk of victimization and feelings of vulnerability are high, and older persons restrict their freedom of movement and limit their social and recreational activities. The consequences of high crime stress may be an increase in personal dissatisfaction, feelings of alienation and isolation, and a lower quality of life (Goldsmith & Tomas, 1974; Lebowitz, 1975). Several studies have noted that crime stress exists in older subjects to such a high degree that these persons limit their activities, refuse to go places, and limit their mobility and participation in community activities (Cunningham, 1973; Gubrium, 1973; McAdoo, 1978).

Sundeen and Mathieu (1976) found that urban elderly tended to have fewer connections with individuals and support systems, reported feeling vulnerable to victimization during the daylight hours as well as at night, had a lower likelihood of being able to depend upon informal networks for protection, and had a lower evaluation of the effectiveness of the police to protect them.

Studies of the impact of crime noted that elderly victims of criminal activity experienced increased amounts of stress and psychological problems as a result of that process. The study also noted a decrease in well-being, joy, and contentment and an increase in anxiety, fear, guilt, and depression among the elderly sample. Not only did these elderly exhibit a significant degree of crime stress, but relatives, friends, and neighbors who attempted to provide support and help to them also suffered some degree of crime stress and psychological problems (Cunningham, 1973; Hochstedler, 1977; Lebowitz, 1975; Skogan & Maxfield, 1981).

Crime stress among the elderly appears to vary in its intensity according to demographic characteristics. Black women were found to have the highest degree of crime stress, followed by black men, white women, and white men. A number of studies have noted that crime stress is higher in neighborhoods reporting higher official crime rates. For the elderly no residence status differences were noted, as those living in cities, suburbs, and retirement communities had equally high crime stress (Clements & Kleiman, 1976; Furstenberg, 1971; Lebowitz, 1975; Skogan, 1981; Skogan & Maxfield, 1981; Sundeen & Mathieu, 1976).

Very few studies have been done on the impact of crime stress on the self-esteem and satisfaction with life of older black Americans. McAdoo (1978, 1983) found that the subjects in his Washington, D.C., samples exhibited the same degree of crime stress found in other studies. In addition they reported a negative evaluation of the community protection afforded to them. In spite of their high levels of crime stress, these subjects felt good about themselves, had high morale, and were generally satisfied with their lives.

McAdoo (1978) argued that his subjects were able to compartmentalize their high levels of crime stress. It was equally clear, however, that they significantly reduced their social interaction with kin and friends in order to control their feelings of vulnerability. Crime stress for the black elderly would appear to have enormous implications for the quality of their lives (Garofalo, 1979), and it would appear that we need to evaluate perceptions of community safety in evaluating the effect of crime stress on black older persons' self-esteem and satisfaction with life. In summary, previous research generally indicates that elderly black Americans are highly vulnerable and experience a significant amount of crime stress regardless of geographic region. Elderly respondents who are female, live in cities, and are poor experience the greatest degree of crime stress. Very few studies have evaluated the impact of crime stress on the black elders' self-esteem and their satisfaction with life.

The questions asked in this study are: (a) What is the effect of crime stress on the elderly respondents' self-esteem? (b) What impact does crime stress have on the elderly respondents' satisfaction with life? and (c) To what degree does satisfaction with community protection influence the elderly respondents' satisfaction with life?

Method

Independent Variables

Crime Stress Responses to the questions of frequency of problems with muggings, burglaries, assaults, or similar crimes were listed as a measure of crime stress. Responses were rated on a 5-point scale: very often, fairly often, not too often, hardly ever, and never. Those respondents who perceived that the problems occurred very often were identified as people with high crime stress.

Community Protection Responses to a question of level of satisfaction with the police protection was used as a measure of satisfaction with community protection. The responses were rated on a 4-point scale from very satisfied to very dissatisfied.

Community Satisfaction Responses to a question pertaining to feelings about the neighborhood were tabulated on a 4-point scale: very good, fairly good, fairly bad, and very bad.

Condition of Home Determination of condition of home was based upon a questionnaire filled out by the interviewers, who were asked to rate whether the home needed major, minor, or no repairs.

Conditions of the Community The interviewers were requested to fill out a questionnaire related to the conditions of the home in the community and the ratings were the same as for the individual respondent's home.

Types of Dwellings in the Neighborhood A variable was included that rated the types of dwellings that were close to the subjects' homes. The interviewers were asked to respond in a dichotomy fashion to questions related to multiple housing units, single boarded-up housing, and/or abandoned dwellings.

Dependent Variables

Self-esteem A modified version the Rosenberg self-esteem scale was used to determine the elderly respondents' self-esteem score.

Life Satisfaction Respondents were asked a question related to the degree that they were satisfied with their life as a whole. The responses were rated on a 4-point scale from very satisfied to very dissatisfied.

Analysis Procedure

Both bivariate and multivariate analyses were utilized in a two-stage process in examining the predictors and correlates of crime stress. Multiple classification analysis (MCA) was utilized to investigate the determinants of crime stress and the effects of crime stress, controlling for certain demographic variables on the self-esteem and life satisfaction variables. MCA (Andrews, Morgan, Sonquist, & Klem, 1974) is a form of multiple regression analysis that allows an investigation of effects of crime stress before (eta coefficient) and after (beta coefficient), partialing out the effects of control variables. Because the independent variables are always treated as sets of classes or categories, one of the major features of MCA is that the independent variables can be nominal (categories), ordinal (ranking), or interval (classes of a numerical variable) scaled variables.

Results

The majority of respondents reported moderate levels of crime stress (59%), another 17% claimed to have very little stress, and 10% of the sample reported extremely high stress levels. A majority of the older respondents were either very satisfied (42%) or somewhat satisfied (33%) with the protection they received from the police. Eighty-one (14%) reported that they were somewhat dissatisfied, and only 10% of the sample claimed to be very dissatisfied with the police protection. Ninety-three percent of the sample reported that they were satisfied with their community, with 47.8% of the respondents rating their community a very good place to live and 45% of the respondents rating their community as a fairly good place to live. Only 4% of the respondents reported that their community was a fairly bad place to live, and less than 3% of the respondents reported that their community was a very bad place to live.

The majority of the older persons' homes seem to be in good repair, with the observers noting that 45% of the homes needed no repairs and 40% of the homes needed only minor repairs. Only eighty-four (14.8%)

Table 3.1 Multiple Classification Analysis of Crime Stress on Selected Community
and Demographic Variables

Variable	Class Mean	Adjusted Mean	Eta^2	Beta
Age in Years			.01	.08
55-64	2.82	2.82		
65-75	2.80	2.79		
75+	2.55	2.58		
Sex			.00	.07
Male	2.83	2.86		
Female	2.72	2.70		
Marital Status			.01	.09
Married	2.74	2.74		
Divorced	3.16	2.96		
Separated	2.61	2.56		
Widowed	2.76	2.81		
Single	2.57	2.44		
Education			.02	.05
0 to 6 years	2.56	2.69		
7 to 11 years	2.80	2.76		
12+ years	2.96	2.85		
Income			.01	.06
$ 0 to $2,999	2.66	2.82		
$3,000 to $4,999	2.82	2.81		
$5,000 to $9,999	2.81	2.64		
$10,000 +	2.88	2.69		
Urbanicity			.06	.12
Urban	3.07	2.91		
Rural	2.49	2.63		
Region			.04	.06
Northeast	3.13	2.85		
North Central	2.94	2.74		
South	2.58	2.73		
West	3.09	2.94		
Police Protection			.12	.19
Very satisfied	2.37	2.51		
Somewhat satisfied	2.83	2.71		
Somewhat dissatisfied	3.61	3.37		
Very dissatisfied	3.61	3.37		
Community Satisfaction			.11	.10
Very good	2.38	2.54		
Fairly good	2.98	2.89		
Fairly bad	3.77	2.36		
Very bad	3.43	3.01		

continued

Table 3.1 Continued

Variable	Class Mean	Adjusted Mean	Eta^2	Beta
Condition of Own Home				
Needs major repairs	2.70	2.65	.01	.08
Needs minor repairs	2.64	2.74		
No repairs needed	2.86	2.86		
Condition of Community Homes				
Need major repairs	2.89	2.91	.01	.01
Need minor repairs	2.66	2.68		
No repairs needed	2.61	2.57		
Living in Multiple Dwelling				
Yes	3.09	2.92	.03	.09
No	2.75	2.80		
Living in Single Dwelling				
Yes	2.24	2.77	.00	.02
No	2.94	2.69		
A Lot of Abandoned Homes				
Yes	2.88	2.72	.00	.02
No	2.73	2.77		

of the homes of those interviewed appeared to need major repairs. This was also true of those homes in the neighborhood, with over two thirds of the homes in the neighborhood needing minor (47%) or no (29.7%) repairs, whereas 23% of the homes (129) were in need of major repairs.

Following previous research studies that examined the impact of community factors in crime stress, the MCA model included demographic and community predictors: age, sex, marital status, education, income, urbanicity and region, community satisfaction, police satisfaction, condition of home and community, and type of dwelling (Table 3.1). This model was significant at the $p < .01$ level, $F_{42,393} = 2.91$ and explains 18% (adjusted) of the variance in crime stress. The most influential predictors in contributing to the explained variation in crime stress when the other demographic and community variables are held constant are police satisfaction (beta = .19), community satisfaction (beta = .19), and urbanicity (beta = .12).

Elderly respondents who expressed the greatest dissatisfaction with police protection and dissatisfaction with their community had the highest levels of crime stress. Those respondents who were satisfied with police protection and satisfied with their communities had lower

Table 3.2 Multiple Classification Analysis of the Relationship Between Crime Stress and Self-Esteem (Model 1) and Life Satisfaction (Model 2) Controlling for Community and Demographic Variables

Variable	Class Mean	Adjusted Mean	Eta^2	Beta	R^2
Model 1 Self-Esteem					
Crime Stress					
Very often	20.93	21.12	.01	.10	.02
Fairly often	21.59	21.57			
Not too often	21.37	21.30			
Hardly ever	21.69	21.74			
Never	21.16	21.12			
Model 2 Life Satisfaction					
Crime Stress					
Very often	2.95	3.19	.06	.18	.16
Fairly often	3.04	3.14			
Not too often	3.28	3.24			
Hardly ever	3.55	3.50			
Never	3.24	3.17			

amounts of crime stress. Elderly respondents living in rural areas reported significantly lower amounts of crime stress. Although region was found to be a moderate predictor of stress, those elderly respondents living in the South and North Central were lower in their level of crime stress than those living in the Northeast and the West.

Elderly respondents living in areas where there were single-family dwellings expressed lower crime stress than did those living in areas where there were multiunit dwellings. The respondents living in communities where no or very little repairs were needed had lower stress than those who lived in communities where major repairs were needed. The subjects with homes that needed minor repairs exhibited lower crime stress than those with homes needing major repairs or no repairs at all.

Table 3.2 presents the results of the MCA model on the relationship of crime stress on (a) self-esteem and (b) life satisfaction, controlling for the community and demographic variables. Crime stress had no significant impact on self-esteem. Crime stress, however, significantly impacted life satisfaction. Respondents with lower levels of crime stress generally had higher levels of life satisfaction.

Summary

In contrast to other studies (McAdoo, 1978), the respondents in this study had relatively low levels of crime stress. They were satisfied with their community and the police protection offered to them. They lived in communities where the homes were in relatively good condition, and for the majority of the subjects, their homes needed little more than minor repairs. Over half of the subjects lived in the South and were found to have the lowest levels of crime stress. Black elders who lived in urban areas were found to be the most dissatisfied with police protection and their community, and they exhibited the highest degree of crime stress.

The patterns of findings did not differ markedly from the literature. Females were found to be lower in crime stress than males and those respondents who were either married or widowed were also found to be lower in crime stress. The older respondents who exhibited the lowest education level were also lower in crime stress, but the differences were not significant. Those respondents living in the Northeast were found to have higher levels of crime stress than respondents living in other regions except the West.

The level of crime stress did not significantly influence the way these respondents felt about themselves. The black respondents in this sample exhibited generally high self-esteem regardless of level of stress. No demographic or community status differences were observed in this study, although black elderly respondents who had high levels of stress felt the most positive about their satisfaction with life. Higher levels of crime stress were found to be significantly related to lower life satisfaction.

McAdoo (1978) suggested that the black urban elderly are able to compartmentalize their high levels of crime stress and maintain their positive self-esteem. Self-esteem is seen as a relatively stable personality trait that is not easily influenced by situational factors. The older respondents are able to recognize the kinds of situational factors that may cause them stress and move to control them by limiting their activities and taking precautions that reduce their risk of victimization.

We find the older respondents' high degree of satisfaction with community protection, if true, encouraging. This could suggest that police are more visible and seen as a positive detriment to criminal activity. High satisfaction with community may be related to satisfaction with police protection or it may also be related to living in long-familiar surroundings.

In summary, the older respondents in this study may have developed a process to cope with crime stress. The process allows them to maintain their integrity as individuals and their positive feelings about themselves. It also allows them to feel more satisfied with their lives. Feeling good about one's community and perceiving that the community is well protected may serve as important mediators of crime stress.

References

Andrews, F. M., Morgan, J. N., Sonquist, J. A., & Klem, L. (1974). *Multiple classification analysis.* (A report on a computer program for multiple regression using categorical predictors). Ann Arbor: Institute for Survey Research, University of Michigan.

Antunes, G., Cook, F., Cook, T., & Skogan, W. (1977). Patterns of personal crime against the elderly: Findings from a national survey. *The Gerontologist, 17,* 321-327.

Clements, F., & Kleiman, M. B. (1976). Fear of crime among the aged. *The Gerontologist, 16*(3), 207-210.

Cook, F. L., Skogan, T., Cook, D., & Antunes, G. E. (1978). Criminal victimization of the elderly: The physical and economic consequences. *The Gerontologist, 18,* 338-349.

Cunningham, C. (1973). *Crimes against aging Americans, the Kansas City study.* Kansas City, MO: Midwest Research Institute.

Furstenberg, F. N., Jr. (1971). Public reaction to crime in the streets. *American Scholar, 11,* 601-610.

Garofalo, J. (1979). Victimization and the fear of crime. *Journal of Research in Crime & Delinquency, 16*(1), 80-97.

Goldsmith, J., & Tomas, E. (1974). Crimes against the elderly: A continual national crisis. *Aging, 236-237,* 10-13.

Gubrium, J. F. (1973). Victimization in old age: Available evidence and three hypotheses. *Crime and Delinquency, 20*(3), 245-250.

Harris & Associates. (1975). *The myth and reality of aging in America.* Washington, DC: National Council on Aging.

Hindelang, M. J. (1976). *Criminal victimization in eight American cities.* Cambridge: Ballinger.

Hochstedler, E. (1977). *Personal victimization of the elderly in twenty-six cities.* (Monograph). Albany, NY: Criminal Justice Research Center.

Lebowitz, B. D. (1975). Age and fearfulness: Personal and situational factors. *Journal of Gerontology, 30,* 696-700.

Liang, J., & Sengstock, M. (1981). The risk of personal victimization among the aged. *Journal of Gerontology, 36,* 463-471.

McAdoo, J. L. (1979). Well-being and fear of crime among the Black elderly. In D. E. Gelfand & A. Kutzik (Eds.), *Ethnicity and aging: Theory, research, and policy.* (pp. 277-290). New York: Springer.

McAdoo, J. L. (1983). Fear of crime and victimization of Black residents in a high risk urban environment. In R. L. McNeely & J. N. Colen (Eds.), *Aging in minority groups* (pp. 153-161). Beverly Hills, CA: Sage.

McNeely, R. L. (1983). Race, sex, and victimization of the elderly. In R. L. McNeely & J. N. Colen (Eds.), *Aging in minority groups* (pp. 137-152). Beverly Hills, CA: Sage.

Skogan, W. G. (1981). On attitudes and behaviors. In D. A. Lewis (Ed.), *Reactions to crime* (pp. 19-45). Beverly Hills, CA: Sage.

Skogan, W. G., & Maxfield, M. G. (1981). *Coping with crime, victimization, fear, and reactions to crime.* Beverly Hills, CA: Sage.

Sundeen, R. A., & Mathieu, J. T. (1976). The fear of crime and its consequences among the elderly in three urban communities. *The Gerontologist, 16*(3), 211-219.

4

GENDER, MARITAL, FAMILIAL, AND FRIENDSHIP ROLES

Robert Joseph Taylor
Verna M. Keith
M. Belinda Tucker

In the past few years there has been a developing interest in the gender, family, and friendship roles of the elderly in general, and older blacks in particular. During this period, there has been a significant increase in research on older blacks, with the majority of this work addressing issues such as families as a source of informal support (see Taylor, 1988; Taylor & Chatters, 1991; Taylor, Chatters, Tucker, & Lewis, 1990), care giving to frail elderly (e.g., Keith, 1987), and living arrangements (e.g., Mitchell & Register, 1984). Comparatively little work has investigated issues such as gender roles, marital relationships, the division of household labor, and friendship ties among older black adults (some of the earlier works of Jacquelyne Jackson are notable exceptions, e.g., J. J. Jackson, 1972).

This chapter represents an initial attempt to explore gender, marital, familial, and friendship roles among elderly black adults, using data from the National Survey of Black Americans (NSBA). Information and analysis on a broad variety of issues is presented and particular emphasis is placed on examining the univariate distributions and responses from open-ended questions. Bivariate analyses focus on the relationships among three demographic variables that have particular salience for the elderly (i.e., gender, age, and marital status) and several questionnaire items related to role performance.

The chapter is divided into four major substantive sections: (a) gender roles, (b) marital roles, (c) familial and friendship relationships, and (d) friendship networks. Each substantive section begins with a review of relevant literature, followed by analysis of selected variables and a discussion of results. We conclude with a summary and discussion of findings. The array of substantive issues and a reliance on a widely accessible analysis procedure results in a chapter that will be of broad interest and useful to both researchers and practitioners.

Gender Roles

The provision of economic support and the performance of household tasks are two of the most important roles necessary for the maintenance and functioning of the family. Traditionally, the provider and homemaker roles have been divided along gender lines. Men were expected to seek work in the labor market and to provide economic resources for the family; women were expected to contribute their productive time to the care and maintenance of the home and children. Traditional gender distinctions in the family-provider role, however, have lessened as women have increasingly entered the paid labor force. In many families, the wife's wages are necessary for the economic viability of the family (Waite, 1981), and perhaps in recognition of this economic reality, public opinion has become more favorable toward women's labor force participation (Waite, 1980).

In contrast, the blurring of gender differences in the nature of the provider role has not been mirrored in relation to the homemaker role and the allocation of household tasks. Although recent studies indicate that a majority of men and women believe that husbands and wives should share household duties when the wife is employed (Ferber, 1982), these attitudes do not correspond to actual behavior. Studies examining the division of household labor demonstrate that men spend very little time in housework even when their wives are employed outside the home (Berk, 1985; Robinson, 1977; Vanek, 1974). Although husbands tend to devote more time to housework both before the arrival of children and after retirement, gender differences in contributions to household work are significant at all stages of the family life cycle (Rexroat & Shehan, 1987).

Some limited evidence indicates that there are gender differences in the type of work performed in the household. Coleman (1988) notes that men tend to take on jobs that (a) have a clear beginning and ending, such as mowing the lawn; (b) allow greater flexibility, such as home repair; and (c) involve a leisure component, such as playing with the children. Women are still largely responsible for the less appealing and monotonous tasks such as cooking, cleaning, and washing dishes. Husbands' involvement in these tasks tends to be sporadic and appears to be related to the unavailability of the wife (Coleman, 1988).

There is some evidence to suggest that gender distinctions in the provider and homemaker roles are not as rigid among black families (Beckett & Smith, 1981; Ericksen, Yancey, & Ericksen, 1979). Historically, black women have been more likely than white women to work outside the home and therefore to share economic responsibility with their spouse. Maret and Finlay (1984) also reported that black women are less likely to have sole responsibility for household duties. Broman (1988), however, noted that although there may be more sharing in black households, black women still perform most of the traditional chores of cooking and cleaning and are more likely to feel overworked than men.

Little is known about the attitudes and behaviors of older black adults in relation to provider and homemaker roles. Although several studies have examined work and family roles by race and within the general black population, none has focused attention on elderly blacks. In the remainder of this section, we examine provider and homemaker attitudes and behaviors among black adults who are 55 years of age and older. We also assess these attitudes and behaviors by sex and within several age groupings of black elders.

Two questions from the NSBA assess attitudes toward gender equality in housework and labor force participation. Respondents were asked their level of agreement with the following two statements: (a) "Both men and women should share equally in child care and housework" and (b) "Both men and women should have jobs to support the family." Four out of 10 (41.9%) older black adults indicated that they strongly agree that both sexes should share housework, 48.0% agreed with this statement, 8.0% disagreed, 2.1% strongly disagreed. Bivariate analysis revealed a significant gender difference, with women slightly more likely than men to agree with this statement (43.2% of women and 39.6% of men strongly agree). Lower levels of agreement were noted for the statement concerning paid work. Twenty-two percent (21.8%)

of respondents strongly agreed that both men and women should have jobs to support the family, 51.6% agreed, 24.3% disagreed and 2.3% strongly disagreed. Bivariate analysis of this item revealed both significant age and gender differences. Age has a curvilinear relationship, with respondents 75 years old and older being less likely than their younger counterparts to either strongly agree or disagree with the statement. Gender differences indicate that women report higher agreement with the statement that both men and women should be employed (e.g., 24.5% of women strongly agreed as opposed to 17.3% of men).

Respondents were also asked several questions regarding household responsibilities. First, respondents were asked, "Who does most of the cooking, cleaning, and laundry in your household? Is it you, mostly you and someone else helps out, mostly someone else and you help out, or someone else?" Six out of ten (63%) respondents indicated that they do all of the housework, 10.3% indicated that they do most of the housework, 8.7% indicated that they do some of the housework, and 18.0% indicated that they don't do any of the housework. Substantial gender differences indicate that women are twice as likely as men to state that they do all the housework; 79.4% of women indicated that they do all of the housework as compared to 35.2% of the men. Similarly, only 5.8% of the women indicated doing none of the housework as opposed to 38.5% of the men. Respondents were also asked, "How much does housework keep you from doing other things you have to do? Would you say a great deal, a lot, a little, or not at all?" The majority of respondents reported that housework does not interfere with other activities; 7.9% stating that it interferes a great deal, 2.5% indicating a lot, 25.9% a little; and 63.7% reported that it does not interfere at all. Gender differences revealed that 71.4% of men felt that housework did not at all interfere with other activities as compared to 59.2% of women. When asked whether they ever feel overworked because of the things that they have to do, 27% of the respondents stated yes. Significant age and gender differences indicate that younger respondents were more likely than older respondents to indicate that they felt overworked and women (31.3%) were more likely than men (19.8%) to state that they felt overworked.

Respondents were also asked a series of questions exploring the importance of members of the opposite sex across several domains. These questions provide indirect measures of gender and marital roles. Respondents were asked how important was it to have a person of the opposite sex reside with the respondent in relation to: (a) raising

Table 4.1 Univariate Distribution of the Importance of Having a Member of the Opposite Sex Reside With the Respondent Across Several Domains

	Very Important (%)	Fairly Important (%)	Not Too Important (%)	Not Important At All (%)	(N)
Raising Children	63.4	5.7	6.6	24.3	559
Financial Security	53.1	14.2	12.0	20.7	569
Housework	55.1	18.4	10.2	16.3	570
Good Love Life	54.0	14.4	10.3	21.3	564
Companionship	65.7	15.0	4.8	14.5	567

children, (b) financial security, (c) jobs that need to be done around the house, (d) a good love life, and (e) companionship. Univariate distributions for these variables (see Table 4.1) reveal that the majority of respondents feel that across these domains, having a member of the opposite sex reside with them is very important. Bivariate analysis revealed several significant gender, age, and marital status differences. As indicated in Table 4.2, men were more likely than women to endorse the view that it is important to have a member of the opposite sex reside with them for raising children, having a good love life, and companionship. Women were more likely to stress the importance of an opposite-sex partner in relation to financial security. The gender differences were fairly notable across each of the domains except housework.

Significant age differences in the importance of an opposite-sex partner were evident across each of the domains, except raising children. Among this sample of elderly black adults, relatively younger respondents tended to attribute greater importance to having a member of the opposite sex reside with them. Marital status differences indicate that across all domains, married respondents consistently attributed greater importance to the presence of an opposite sex partner, whereas never-married respondents were the least likely of all marital status groups to support this view.

Previous research has demonstrated that gender differences in the provision of economic support to the family have changed markedly over the past four decades. The traditional pattern of the male as the sole breadwinner has increasingly given way to a sharing of economic responsibility between husband and wife. The equitable distribution of household tasks, however, remains elusive. Although in theory Americans

Table 4.2 Gender, Age, and Marital Status Differences in the Importance of Having a Member of the Opposite Sex Reside With the Respondent Across Several Domains (in percentages)

	Raising Children	Financial Security	House-work	Good Love Life	Compan-ionship
Gender					
Male	72.3	42.2	59.2	71.0	79.5
Female	58.1	59.5	52.6	44.1	57.7
Age					
55-64	63.5	60.9	57.9	62.7	73.8
65-74	65.6	53.5	57.5	51.3	63.4
75+	58.1	35.2	44.0	41.1	53.3
Marital Status					
Married	79.3	67.1	69.5	76.2	87.5
Divorced	56.8	53.3	48.9	53.3	65.9
Separated	56.6	35.8	45.3	35.8	50.9
Widowed	53.1	46.1	47.0	38.5	50.2
Never married	21.4	17.6	23.5	29.4	35.3

NOTE: Only responses to the Very Important category in Table 4.1 are presented.

support a shared division of labor within the household, women continue to bear the major responsibility for housework. Although black families appear to have more gender equality in both the provider and homemaker roles than do white families, black women are still disproportionately burdened with household tasks.

The attitudes and behaviors of older black adults in relation to provider and homemaker roles mirror those found in the larger society. Our analysis points to a clear division in the stated beliefs and reported actions of older black adults. Approximately 90% of older blacks in this sample endorse the view that men and women should share housework and child care, and 70% state that the economic role should be shared equally. Moreover, the proportion of males and females who support gender equality in housework is quite similar. Yet, when these attitudes are contrasted with who actually assumes responsibility for cooking and cleaning, women are more than twice as likely to perform these duties. As a consequence, older black women are significantly more likely than older black men to report that housework is associated with time constraints and overwork.

The failure of older black men to assume a fair share of household responsibilities is not inconsistent with patterns found in the general population. Further, this behavior, although unfortunate, is perhaps more comprehensible among older persons than younger groups. Individuals who are 55 years of age and older were socialized in an era when the gender-based division of family roles was much more rigid than it is today. Both men and women came into adulthood during a time when the societal expectation was that the husband would work and the wife would take care of home and children. Although many older black women have a history of working outside the home, their involvement in paid employment may have arisen more out of economic necessity than out of choice. In a sense, older black men and women participated as equals in paid employment activities before the shift in societal expectations and sanctions in support of this practice. Unable to adhere to normative gender distinctions in the economic sphere, black men and women may have endorsed gender differences in role activities within the household and continue to follow these patterns established in early adulthood. Gender differences in the importance of members of the opposite sex reported in this chapter support the notion of traditional sex-role socialization. Men suggested that the presence of women within the household is important for raising children and for companionship, whereas women stated that men were important for financial security.

This cursory exploration of gender equity among older black adults raises more questions than it answers. Future research should assess more fully how older black couples allocate their time and energy in relation to household maintenance and various tasks. Although men may not cook and clean, they may perform other necessary tasks (i.e., repairs and yard work). Other important issues that should be addressed are: (a) the degree to which both men and women perceive inequity and its potential effect on psychological well-being and marital satisfaction, and (b) the role that health disability plays in the sharing of household tasks.

Marital Roles

The marital bond is perhaps the most complex and intimate social tie occurring between two people. In spite of the high probability of failure, the vast majority of Americans do marry at some point in their lives.

Marriage provides companionship, affection, and sexual gratification. Moreover, marital status has been linked to physical and mental health. Married persons report fewer physical health problems and greater psychological well-being than the unmarried (Campbell, Converse, & Rodgers, 1976; Gove, 1973; Pearlin & Johnson, 1977). Indeed, being happily married is predictive of global happiness (Glenn, 1975; Zollar & Williams, 1987).

The advantages associated with marriage—companionship, affection, and sexual gratification—continue into the later years (Hess & Soldo, 1988). Lee (1978) reported that the married elderly tend to have higher morale than the unmarried elderly. Because illness and disability increase as individuals age, spouses become a valuable resource in the provision of long-term care. A number of studies indicate that spouses are more likely than other family members to become the primary care giver (Hess & Soldo, 1988).

Marriage involves a host of complicated patterns of social exchange. According to equity and exchange theories, even intimate ties such as marriage constitute a continuing evaluation process in which inputs are weighed against outcomes (Schafer & Keith, 1981). It is probable that perceptions of equity contribute to the stability of a marriage and to overall marital happiness and satisfaction. Although a number of studies have examined marital satisfaction in later life (e.g., Lee, 1988), less attention has focused on how elderly adults assess their marital roles. Even less is known about the black elderly in relation to these issues. It is important to understand how elders evaluate their marriages because marriage is such a significant social relationship and spouses assume a crucial position in the provision of long-term care. In this section, we take a look at how black adults who are 55 years of age and older evaluate their spousal roles and their assessments of marital equity.

As a consequence of divorce, widowhood, or never having married, large numbers of individuals are unmarried during the later years of their lives. Although most studies indicate that being married as opposed to not married provides certain advantages, it must be kept in mind that these group differences reflect statistical averages. Further, it is important to recognize that the different marital status groups that comprise the unmarried category (i.e., divorced, widowed, and never married) reflect vast differences in the social significance of their current status, as well as lifetime experiences. This diversity suggests that for some portion of unmarried individuals (e.g., never married) being unmarried is not necessarily reflected in lower levels of physical and psychological well-being. But for other persons (e.g., recently widowed) being unmarried represents a significant disruption in an important primary relationship that may impact negatively on physical and psychological health. Consistent with this observation, at least one study has reported that there is little difference in life satisfaction between married and unmarried (as an aggregate group) elderly blacks (J. S. Jackson, Bacon, & Peterson, 1977). Given the apparent complexity of this issue, this section addresses attitudes toward marriage and related issues among married persons, as well as within defined subgroups of unmarried elderly black adults.

Perceptions of Married Life

Married respondents were asked to assess their own performance in the spousal role by the question: "Given the chances that you have had, how well have you done at being a good [husband to your wife/wife to your husband]?" Eighty-four percent (84.8%) of married respondents indicated that they had performed very well in the spousal role. Bivariate analysis revealed no significant gender or age differences. Respondents were also asked the following question: "Many [men/women, same sex as respondent] feel that they are not as good [husbands/wives, same sex as respondent] as they would like to be. Do you sometimes feel this way?" One out of four respondents (27.4%, $n = 61$) answered in the affirmative. Bivariate analysis revealed that younger respondents were significantly more likely to indicate that they were sometimes not as good spouses as they would like to be. Respondents who indicated yes were asked the follow-up question: "What things make you feel you're not as good a [husband/wife] as you'd like to be?" Four out of ten respondents (41.8%) mentioned personal traits or habits (e.g., "I could be more patient," "I'm too submissive," "There are things I could have done and failed to do"), 34.5% stated financial reasons (e.g., "I can't buy the things she would like to have," "Can't give children the things they like"), 10.9% mentioned role overload (e.g., "Have so many things to do," "I get tired"), 9.1% mentioned health or physical problems (e.g., age, impotence), 1.8% noted the spouse's personal traits (e.g., "I would be a better spouse if my husband would straighten up," "My husband is hard to satisfy"), and another 1.8% mentioned role overload of the spouse (e.g., "Spouse has so many things to do").

All married respondents were asked: "Who do you think gets more out of the relationship, you or your [husband/wife]?" A large majority of the respondents (73.3%) indicated that the relationship was equal, 17.9% indicated that their spouse gets more, and 8.8% report that they get more out of their relationship. Respondents who stated that the relationship was not equal were asked the follow-up question: "Why do you feel this way?" One out of ten (10.4%) individuals in this subgroup mentioned that they give more emotional support and assistance (e.g., "I give more of myself"), 6.0% indicated that they provide more services (e.g., "When he comes home all we do is cater to his wants and needs"), 4.5% mentioned that they support their spouse financially, 3% indicated that the spouse gets more from other family members, 11.9% stated that the spouse needed more (e.g., "Because he is more dependent and I am independent"), 6% reported that the spouse had fewer responsibilities, 10.4% mentioned that the spouse had greater personal freedom (e.g., "Because he goes fishing or does what he wants to do"), 6% noted that the spouse gave more emotionally, 4.5% stated that the spouse provided more service, 3% mentioned that the spouse supported them financially, 1.5% indicated that they had fewer responsibilities, and 10.4% indicated that they needed more (e.g., "I'm the aggressor and usually get what I want").

Perceptions of Unmarried Life

Several items in the NSBA data set address issues of concern to nonmarried individuals. Separated and divorced respondents were asked: "Do you think that being [separated/divorced] is better or worse than being married?" Among the 95 older respondents who were separated or divorced, 59.0% indicated that it was better than being married, 18.9% stated that it was worse, and 22.1% expressed mixed feelings. Bivariate analysis revealed significant gender and age differences; women and older respondents were more likely than their male and younger counterparts to indicate that being divorced or separated was better than being married. When asked to elaborate on their response, 28.1% stated that being divorced/separated was better because there was less conflict and disagreement (e.g., "Don't fight anymore," "Could never agree on anything"), 18.0% stated that they generally felt better about not being married (e.g., "Didn't like being married," "Feel relieved"), and 12.4% indicated that they had more freedom. The one out of ten (13.5%) respondents who indicated that being separated or divorced was worse than being married provided responses that revealed their belief in the sanctity of marriage or stated preferences for being married (e.g., "Liked being married better," "Prefer/believe in marriage," "Believe that marriage should last forever").

All unmarried respondents (i.e., divorced, separated, widowed, never married) were asked two questions about their single status. First, respondents were asked: "What is the one thing that you *dislike* most about being single or unattached?" Following that, they were asked the opposite question: "What is the one thing that you *like* most about being single or unattached?" Two out of five respondents (43.9%) indicated what they disliked about being single was the lack of companionship and loneliness (e.g., "Miss companionship"). But one third of respondents (33.9%) indicated that there was nothing that they disliked about being single. Other disadvantages of being single included the lack of a partner to share household duties and family responsibilities (7.8%), financial assistance (2.4%), and general support (e.g., "Nobody there when you need them"). With regard to what they liked most about being single, the majority of respondents indicated being independent (57.4%), 15.1% reported freedom from previous responsibilities, and 7.9% indicated intrapersonal contentment (e.g., being unmarried is more pleasant and peaceful). But 15.4% of the respondents indicated that there was nothing they liked about being single.

Summary of Marital Roles

The marital relationship is perhaps the most significant social bond that links two individuals. Marriage marks the beginning of a new social and economic unit and is, ideally, a public statement of a couple's emotional commitment to one another. In addition to affection, companionship, and physical love, marriage is associated with practical obligations. Spouses are expected to provide instrumental support and to provide care-giving services when the husband or wife is disabled. This latter aspect of marriage is vital for older couples as health status declines.

The complicated patterns of social exchange and negotiation associated with marriage require that marital partners continually engage in an evaluative process in which they weigh the positives and negatives of married life. In this section we attempted to assess how older black adults evaluated their marital roles. On the whole, married respondents were quite positive about married life. Eighty percent felt that they had done well at being a good spouse and three fourths felt that the marriage was an equal partnership. Although a significant 18% of respondents felt that their spouses get more from the marriage, these marriages have remained thus far intact. These findings suggest that although marriage might not be fully equitable, these couples have reached an acceptable compromise.

As noted previously, many older individuals are unmarried owing to divorce or widowhood or because they have never married. In view of the emphasis placed upon marriage, it is reasonable to assess how unmarried older blacks feel about their marital status. The findings revealed a mixed pattern of responses. Among separated and divorced blacks, a majority reported that being unmarried was better than being married, and well over half the respondents reported that they liked the independence associated with being unmarried. But when all unmarried black elders are considered, a significant percentage reported feeling lonely.

This mixed pattern of responses can be interpreted in a number of ways. One possible explanation focuses on divorced and separated persons. Older black adults may have had unpleasant marriages, but still miss the affection, companionship, and other advantages associated with being married. In other words, because of their previous experiences with an unsuccessful marriage, separated and divorced respondents still may desire companionship, but without the formal obligations of marriage. More generally, older black adults (regardless to whether they are widowed, divorced, separated, or never married) may value their personal independence, but still wish to be involved on an emotional level with a member of the opposite sex. Another possible explanation focuses on the sex ratio among older black adults. By age 65, there are approximately 68 black males for every 100 black females. This imbalance may be reflected in the attitudes toward marriage, particularly among older women. With few prospects of finding a partner, elderly black adults (women) may cope with this realization by devaluing the importance of marriage (see Tucker & Taylor, 1989).

The evaluation of marriage and marital roles of older blacks has not received a great deal of emphasis in either the family or gerontological literature. This topic should be examined in more detail. In particular, more information is needed contrasting the experiences and perceptions of divorced or separated and never-married black elderly in relation to attitudes regarding marriage and being single.

Familial and Friendship Roles

Family and Friendship Relations

The social interaction occurring within the context of family and friend relationships is of particular importance to both elderly (J. J. Jackson, 1972) and nonelderly blacks (McAdoo, 1978). Family members are viewed as the most important source of assistance to older persons, and family is distinguished from other groups by the permanence of relationships and the operation of explicit normative expectations for affection and mutual assistance (Branch & Jette, 1983). In contrast to family and kinship ties, friendships are based on individual choice.

Several recent studies have investigated the role of family and friends in the informal social support networks of black Americans. Using data from the 1980 Panel Study of Income Dynamics, Taylor, Chatters, and Mays (1988) examined the utilization of informal helpers during an emergency. Eight out of 10 black respondents (82.8%) indicated that there was a relative or friend who would help them out during a serious emergency. Parents and children were the only kin who were more frequently identified as helpers than were nonkin. Significant age differences in the use of emergency helpers indicated that younger respondents were more likely to rely on parents, whereas older respondents were more likely to utilize children and nonkin. Similarly, using NSBA data, Chatters, Taylor, and Neighbors (1989) found that 85.7% of black respondents with a serious personal problem reported using informal assistance. The most utilized category of informal helper was that of mother, followed by sister, spouse, and female friend.

Two sets of analyses examined the impact of sociodemographic, health, and family factors on the size and composition of the informal helper networks of elderly black adults (Chatters, Taylor, & J. S. Jackson, 1985, 1986). Respondents were asked to choose from a list of twelve informal helpers who would help them if they were sick or disabled. The informal helper list consisted of immediate family members, other relatives, and nonkin. Daughters were nominated to the helper network most often, followed by son, spouse/partner, sister, brother, friend, neighbor, and parents. Analyses indicated that marital status, presence of children, perceived family closeness, and regional differences all reflected the selection of spouse, sister, friend, and neighbor as part of the helper network. Although relatives were nominated to the helper network more often than nonkin, 1 out of 5 respondents nominated friends and 1 out of 10 respondents nominated neighbors.

Taylor and Chatters (1986) examined the patterns of assistance provided to elderly blacks by their family, friends, and church members. Descriptively, 8 out of 10 respondents received support from either a best or close friend, roughly 6 out of 10 received support from church members, and over half received support from extended family members. Only a minority of respondents were "socially isolated" in the sense that they did not have a best or close friend and failed to receive support from either family or church members. Analysis of the type of support received revealed that these three groups may differentially provide particular types of aid. Respondents were more likely to receive either total or instrumental assistance (i.e., goods and services, financial assistance, and transportation) from family members and to receive companionship from their friends. Similarly, there was a greater chance of respondents receiving advice and encouragement, help during sickness, and prayer from church members. In addition, bivariate analyses of the type of assistance demonstrated that individual support sources were distinctive in the assistance they provided to elderly blacks. More information on church members as a source of informal social support is provided in this book in the chapter on religious participation among older black adults (Chapter 7).

Collectively, this body of literature indicates that elderly black adults are embedded in support networks comprised of both family and friends. The analysis reported in this section contributes to this developing body of literature by analyzing two questions that assess the relative importance of family and friends in the support networks of elderly black Americans. Respondents were first asked: "When you visit people, are you more likely to visit friends or to visit relatives?" Almost half of the respondents mentioned friends (46.3%), the other half mentioned relatives (48.4%), and 5.3% reported both. A bivariate age difference indicated that older respondents were more likely to visit friends and less likely to visit relatives than their younger counterparts. Respondents were also asked: "When you think of the people you can count on most in life, are they mostly your relatives or your friends?" Similar to the previous analysis, close to half of the respondents (46.6%) indicated that they count primarily on relatives, 32.3% volunteered that they count on both relatives and friends, and 21.1% reported that they rely mostly on friends. This variable was significantly associated with age, such that relatively older respondents were less likely than younger persons to count primarily on relatives, yet were more likely to count on friends and both relatives and friends.

Consistent with other work, the preliminary analyses presented here reveal that both family and friends are important members of the support networks of elderly blacks. Equal percentages of respondents indicated that they visited family versus friends, but they were somewhat more likely to rely on family members. The finding that friends play an increasingly prominent role in the support networks of older as opposed to younger elderly blacks is intriguing and consistent with other research on this sample. Unpublished analyses of this data among the entire adult age range of 18 to 101 years reveal that older blacks have smaller numbers of proximately residing kin than do their younger counterparts. Given a deficit in kin resources, it is understandable why friends take a more prominent role in the support networks of very old blacks. The present analysis is also consistent with other research indicating that among the elderly, relatively older blacks are more likely than their younger counterparts to have helper networks comprised of distant relatives and nonkin (Chatters et al., 1985). The positive relationship between age and the prominence of friends is also consistent with research from the 1980 Panel Study of Income Dynamics (ages 17-94 years), indicating that older blacks were more likely to rely on friends during an emergency than their younger counterparts (Taylor et al., 1988).

Friendship Networks of Older Blacks

There is a paucity of research on the friendship networks of older black adults. Early examinations of primary group associations among adult urban blacks found that they interacted with their friends on a frequent basis (Feagin, 1968; Martineau, 1977; Meadow, 1962) and a recent analysis found that urban black elders interacted frequently with friends (Wolf, Breslaw, Ford, Ziegler, & Ward, 1983). In addition, J. J. Jackson (1972) reported that older black women interacted frequently with close friends and were satisfied with present levels of contact.

Research on racial differences in level of friendship interaction among elderly adults is mixed. Dowd and Bengtson (1978) found that whites reported higher levels of friendship interaction than did blacks.

But Ortega, Crutchfield, & Rushing (1983) indicated that blacks of all ages had more frequent contact with friends, despite the fact that whites had a greater number of friends. In addition, Ulbrich and Warheit (1989) found that older black adults were significantly more likely than older white adults to ask friends for help with their problems.

The NSBA data contain several measures addressing the nature and quality of friendship relations. Three measures, in particular, provide baseline information on the friendship networks of older black adults: (a) frequency of friendship interaction, (b) reported number of friends with whom respondents can discuss personal problems, and (c) respondents' perceptions of their own adequacy as a friend (i.e., adequacy in the friendship role). Frequency of friendship interaction was measured by the question: "How often do you see, write, or talk on the telephone with your friends? Would you say nearly every day, at least once a week, a few times a month, at least once a month, a few times a year, or hardly ever or never?" One third of the respondents (31.6%) reported that they interact with their friends nearly every day, 34% stated at least once a week, 14.4% stated a few times a month, 6.3% indicated at least once a month, 5.4% a few times a year, and 8.3% reported hardly ever or never. Bivariate analysis revealed significant gender and marital status differences in frequency of friendship interaction. Women interacted with their friends more frequently than men, and widowed respondents interacted with their friends more frequently than any other marital status group, followed by divorced, separated, never-married, and married respondents.

The number of friends with whom respondents can discuss personal problems was assessed by the question: "Think of all the friends, not including relatives, that you feel free to talk with about problems. Would you say that you have many, some, a few, or no friends like that?" Only 9.5% of the respondents indicated that they have many friends like that, 16.5% reported some, 57.9% stated a few, and 16.1% indicated none. This variable was not significantly related to gender, age, or marital status. Perceived adequacy in the friendship role was addressed by the question: "Given the chances that you have had how well have you done at being a good friend—a person your friends can count on?" A large majority of the respondents (80.5%) reported that they have performed very well in the friendship role. Gender and age differences in the adequacy of the friendship role were apparent, with women and older respondents indicating that they have performed better in the friendship role than their counterparts.

The findings presented in this section substantiate the importance of friendship ties among older black adults. The gender differences found here are consistent with work on primary relationships that indicates that among both black and white elderly, women are more likely than men to maintain friendship, kinship, and religious ties. The finding that married respondents interact with friends on a less frequent basis than their unmarried counterparts is consistent with the observation that friends play a more prominent role in the support networks of unmarrieds. For instance, other analyses of these data revealed that separated and widowed older blacks had a higher likelihood than their married counterparts of having helper networks comprised of friends (Chatters et al., 1986).

Summary and Conclusions

In this chapter we have examined various aspects of the social roles and attitudes held by older black Americans. This work, in addressing the gender, marital, family, and friendship roles of this group, represents a significant departure from previous efforts. The acknowledged strengths of a nationally representative sample of older black adults allow the delineation of specific subgroups and the investigation of effects based on social status group membership. Overall, the findings indicate that discrete groups of older black adults (i.e., by age, gender, marital status) are in some areas very similar to one other, yet in other areas significantly diverge in behaviors and attitudes. Older black women and men both strongly endorse gender equality in homemaking and provider role activities. But assessments of actual behavior indicate that older black women are more likely than their male counterparts to perform household tasks and to report that time constraints and burdens are associated with those activities. Relatively younger respondents in the sample indicated a greater sense of burden and overwork from household duties, as well.

Perceptions of the desirability of having a partner in relation to various life domains indicated that whereas men felt that having a partner was crucial for child-rearing and affective domains, women believed that a partner was important for financial security only. Similarly, younger respondents were more likely than relatively older persons to feel that the presence of a partner was important across all domains. Finally, married respondents were more likely to endorse the importance of an opposite-sex partner for all life domains and never-married persons were least likely to concur with this belief.

Focusing on marital roles and attitudes, older black adults (across age and gender) were similar in their perception of having performed well in the spousal role. When asked a slightly different question, younger respondents were more likely to feel that they had not been as good a spouse as they could be. Perceptions of equity in marriage revealed that most respondents felt that their and their spouse's contribution to the marital relationship was about equal.

The section addressing perceptions of unmarried life revealed that separated and divorced older black adults tended to feel that being unmarried was better than being married, and this was particularly true among women and older respondents. Similarly, perceptions of single life among never-married, divorced, separated, and widowed older persons revealed that personal freedom and independence from previous responsibilities were highly valued, although lack of companionship and loneliness were acknowledged disadvantages of being single. These analyses, in particular, alert us to the diversity of individuals who comprise the category of unmarrieds and suggest that the disaggregation of this group would provide important information concerning their perceptions of and satisfactions with single status.

Family and friends were designated as primary social networks for equal numbers of respondents, but relatively older persons were more likely to visit friends. In descending order of importance, respondents indicated that they tended to rely on relatives, both relatives and friends, and friends. Again, relatively older respondents indicated that they were less likely to rely on relatives. Levels of interaction with friends revealed that women and widowed respondents were more likely to maintain contact on a frequent basis. There were no differences across age, gender, and marital status groups in the numbers of friends with whom respondents could share personal problems. The majority of older persons felt that they have performed well as a friend, although women and older respondents were more likely than their counterparts to endorse this view.

The level of diversity in the behaviors and attitudes of older black adults confirms the heterogeneity of this population group. These findings underscore the need for additional studies of social-role perceptions and behaviors, and their relationship to functional aspects of the lives of older black adults. Specifically, it is important to assess how these perceptions and reports on behaviors are related to general issues of support from family and friends, marital functioning and adjustment, and qualitative aspects of unmarried status. In this chapter we employed a descriptive and bivariate analyses approach for examining, in a preliminary manner, the existence of potential differences between major status groups as defined by age, gender, and marital status. Future investigations of these phenomena should employ multivariate approaches to assess the relative and independent contributions of these factors to attitudes and beliefs.

References

Beckett, J., & Smith, A. (1981). Work and family roles: Egalitarian marriage in black and white families. *Social Service Review, 5,* 314-326.

Berk, S. (1985). *The gender factory: The apportionment of work in American households.* New York: Plenum.

Branch, L. G., & Jette, A. M. (1983). Elder's use of informal long term care assistance. *The Gerontologist, 23,* 51-56.

Broman, C. L. (1988). Household work and family life satisfaction of blacks. *Journal of Marriage and the Family, 50,* 743-748.

Campbell, A., Converse, P. E., & Rodgers, W. (1976). *The quality of American life: Perceptions, evaluations, and satisfactions.* New York: Russell Sage.

Chatters, L. M., Taylor, R. J., & Jackson, J. S. (1985). Size and composition of the informal helper networks of elderly blacks. *Journal of Gerontology, 40,* 605-614.

Chatters, L. M., Taylor, R. J., & Jackson, J. S. (1986). Aged blacks' choices for an informal helper network. *Journal of Gerontology, 41,* 94-100.

Chatters, L. M., Taylor, R. J., & Neighbors, H. W. (1989). Size of informal helper network mobilized during a serious personal problem among black Americans. *Journal of Marriage and the Family, 51,* 667-676.

Coleman, M. T. (1988). The division of household labor. *Journal of Family Issues, 9,* 132-148.

Dowd, J. J., & Bengtson, V. (1978). Aging in minority populations: An examination of the double jeopardy hypothesis. *Journal of Gerontology, 33*(3), 427-436.

Ericksen, J., Yancey, W., & Ericksen, E. P. (1979). The division of family roles. *Journal of Marriage and the Family, 41,* 301-313.

Feagin, J. F. (1968). The kinship ties of negro urbanites. *Social Science Quarterly, 69,* 655-665.

Ferber, M. A. (1982). Labor market participation of young married women: Causes and effects. *Journal of Marriage and the Family, 44,* 457-468.

Glenn, N. (1975). The contribution of marriage to the psychological well-being of males and females. *Journal of Marriage and the Family, 37,* 594-600.

Gove, W. (1973). Sex, marital status and mortality. *American Journal of Sociology, 79,* 45-67.

Hess, B., & Soldo, B. (1988). Husband and wife networks. In W. J. Sauer, & R. T. Coward (Eds.), *Social support networks and the care of the elderly* (pp. 67-92). New York: Springer.

Jackson, J. J. (1972). Comparative life styles and family and friend relationships among older black women. *Family Coordinator, 21,* 477-486.

Jackson, J. S., Bacon, J., & Peterson, J. (1977). Life satisfaction among black urban elderly. *International Journal of Aging and Human Development, 8*(2), 169-179.

Keith, V. M. (1987). Long-term care and the black elderly. In W. Jones, Jr., & M. F. Rice (Eds.), *Health care issues in America: Politics, problems, and prospects* (pp. 173-209). New York: Greenwood.

Lee, G. (1978). Marriage and morale in later life. *Journal of M* *40*, 131-139.

Lee, G. (1988). Marital satisfaction in later life: The effects of no *of Marriage and the Family, 50*, 775-783.

Maret, E., & Finlay, B. (1984). The distribution of household 1 dual-earner families. *Journal of Marriage and the Family, 46,*

Martineau, W. (1977). Informal social ties among urban black *A Black Studies, 8*, 83-104.

McAdoo, H. P. (1978). Factors related to stability in upwardly n *Journal of Marriage and the Family, 40*, 762-778.

Meadow, K. I. (1962). Negro-white differences among newcomers area. *Journal of Intergroup Relations, 3*, 320-330.

Mitchell, J. S., & Register, J. C. (1984). An exploration of family i by race, socioeconomic status, and residence. *The Gerontolc*

Ortega, S. T., Crutchfield, R. D., & Rushing, W. A. (1983). I personal well-being: Friendship, family, and church. *Research on Aging, 5*(1), 101-116.

Pearlin, L., & Johnson, J. (1977). Marital status, life strains and depression. *American Sociological Review, 41*, 704-715.

Rexroat, C., & Shehan, C. (1987). The family life cycle and spouses' time in housework. *Journal of Marriage and the Family, 49*, 737-750.

Robinson, J. (1977). *How Americans use time.* New York: Praeger.

Schafer, R., & Keith, P. (1981). Equity in marital roles across the family life cycle. *Journal of Marriage and the Family, 52*, 359-367.

Taylor, R. J. (1988). Aging and supportive relationships among black Americans. In J. S. Jackson (Ed.), *The black American elderly: Research on physical and psychosocial health* (pp. 259-281). New York: Springer.

Taylor, R. J., & Chatters, L. M. (1986). Church-based informal support among elderly blacks. *The Gerontologist, 26*, 637-642.

Taylor, R. J., & Chatters, L. M. (1991). Extended family networks of older black adults. *Journal of Gerontology: Social Sciences, 46*(4), S210-217.

Taylor, R. J., Chatters, L. M., & Mays, V. M. (1988). Parents, children, siblings, in-laws, and non-kin as sources of emergency assistance to black Americans. *Family Relations, 37*, 298-304.

Taylor, R. J., Chatters, L. M., Tucker, M. B., & Lewis, E. (1990). Developments in research on black families: A decade review. *Journal of Marriage and the Family, 52*, 993-1014.

Tucker, M. B., & Taylor, R. J. (1989). Demographic correlates of relationship status among black Americans. *Journal of Marriage and the Family, 51*, 655-666.

Ulbrich, P. M., & Warheit, G. J. (1989). Social support, stress, and psychological distress among older black and white adults. *Journal of Aging and Health, 1*, 286-305.

Vanek, J. (1974). Time spent in housework. *Scientific American, 231*, 116-120.

Waite, L. (1980). Working wives and the family life cycle. *American Journal of Sociology, 86*, 272-294.

Waite, L. (1981). U.S. women at work. *Population Bulletin, 36.*

Wolf, J. H., Breslaw, N., Ford, A. B., Ziegler, H. D., & Ward, A. (1983). Distance and contacts: Interactions of black urban elderly adults and family and friends. *Journal of Gerontology, 38*, 465-471.

Zollar, A. C., & Williams, J. S. (1987). The contribution of marriage to the life satisfaction of black adults. *Journal of Marriage and the Family, 49*, 87-92.

5

INTERGENERATIONAL SUPPORT
The Provision of Assistance
to Parents by Adult Children

Linda M. Chatters
Robert Joseph Taylor

In the past few years there has emerged a growing body of research on the family and informal support networks of black adults in general and elderly blacks in particular (see Taylor, 1988; Taylor, Chatters, Tucker, & Lewis, 1990). Pioneering work by scholars such as Jacquelyne Jackson (1972, 1980), Percil Stanford (1978), and various ethnographers (Aschenbrenner, 1973, 1975; Martin & Martin, 1978; Stack, 1972, 1974) documented the participation of elderly blacks in extensive kin support networks. More recent work has shown that the informal support networks of elderly black adults consist not only of family, but of other groups such as friends and church members (Taylor & Chatters, 1986a, 1986b). Taylor and Chatters (1986b), using data from a national probability sample of black adults, the National Survey of Black Americans (NSBA), found that 8 out of 10 respondents reported receiving assistance from friends, 6 out of 10 received assistance from church members, and over half received support from family. A small minority of respondents were "socially isolated" in the sense that they did not have a best or close friend and did not receive support from either their family or church members. Analysis of the type of support indicated that family, friends, and church members may differentially provide particular types of assistance. Family members were more likely to provide either total or instrumental support (i.e., goods and services, financial assistance, and transportation); companionship came from friends; and assistance in the form of advice and encouragement, help during sickness, and prayer was provided by church members.

Elderly Parent-Adult Children Support Relationships

Research on both elderly blacks and whites underscores the importance of the adult child-elderly parent kinship bond. Children are generally viewed as the preferred source of assistance for the elderly, and the research on the family lives of older adults emphasizes the role of adult children in fulfilling care-giving and support needs (Brody, 1981; Cantor, 1979; Cicirelli, 1981; Shanas, 1979). The importance of this bond is underscored by findings that the greatest amount of interaction in kinship networks takes place between elderly parents and adult children (Adams, 1968). In this vein, Antonucci and Akiyama (1987) found that adult children were most frequently mentioned as members of elderly adults' support networks. Other work indicates that the confidant networks of older adults were found to consist mainly of spouses and adult children (Kendig, Coles, Pittelkow, & Wilson, 1988).

Prior work involving racial comparisons in the support networks of elderly adults suggests that both elderly blacks and whites interact with children and grandchildren on a frequent basis (Cantor, 1979; Mitchell & Register, 1984; Shanas, 1979). Adult children are also primary members of the support networks of older blacks and whites (Cantor, 1979; Mitchell & Register, 1984; Mutran, 1985; Shanas, 1979; Smerglia, Deimling, & Barresi, 1988). Shanas (1979) found that a higher proportion of white elderly reported that they *gave* help to their children and grandchildren, whereas elderly blacks were more likely than whites to *receive* help from children. Although Cantor (1979) failed to find significant racial differences in the amount of support that older adults received from children, both black and Hispanic elderly provided greater amounts of help to children than did white elderly. Mutran (1985) found that black families were more involved than white families in exchanges of help across generations. In comparison to aged whites, elderly black adults provided more assistance to children and grandchildren. Elderly black parents were also more likely to receive support from children, but this effect was attenuated in the presence of controls for socioeconomic status. Subgroup analysis among black respondents revealed several significant differences: Women, older individuals, persons with less formal education, respondents with children under 18 in the household, and those who feel that young individuals deserve more respect received more support from their adult children than their counterparts (Mutran, 1985).

Spitze and Miner (1992) investigated the telephone and visiting patterns of elderly black parents and their adult children using data from the 1984 Supplement on Aging to the National Health Interview Survey. Elderly black women had significantly higher levels of both forms of contact with adult children than elderly black men. Demographic factors such as the number of sons and daughters, proximity to the nearest child, and parental education all significantly influenced the frequency of contact between adult children and elderly parents.

Analysis of data from the Panel Study of Income Dynamics indicated that the parent-child bond was important across the life course and critical in understanding black Americans' use of helpers during an emergency (Taylor, Chatters, & Mays, 1988). Younger blacks were more likely to rely on parents, older blacks were more likely to rely on adult children, and middle-aged parents relied heavily on both children and parents. This work underscores the importance of intergenerational linkages in family support relationships of black Americans.

A group of studies based on the National Survey of Black Americans data reveal that the elderly parent-adult child bond is important for support exchanges among blacks. Elderly blacks with adult children had a greater likelihood of receiving support from extended family members than did their childless counterparts (Taylor, 1985, 1986). Being a parent was also an important determinant of the configuration of the helping networks of elderly blacks (Chatters, Taylor, & J. S. Jackson, 1985, 1986; Chatters, Taylor, & Neighbors, 1989). In comparison to childless elderly, older black adults who had a child had a larger group of individuals to assist them in coping with a serious personal problem (Chatters et al., 1989). Daughters, sons, and spouses were the most frequently mentioned individuals who would assist an elderly person if he or she were sick or disabled (Chatters et al., 1986). Elderly blacks with children were more likely than childless elderly to have larger helper networks and to have networks comprising immediate family members only. The association between being a parent and having large, immediate family networks in part reflects the fact that these older adults had at least one immediate family member (i.e., child) to nominate to their helper networks. In the absence of children, substitutions of other kin and nonkin were made; childless elderly adults were more likely to rely upon brothers, sisters, and friends.

In an analysis of extended family networks of elderly black adults, Taylor and Chatters (1991) found that older blacks with children manifested distinctly positive appraisals of affective dimensions of family life. Additionally, older blacks who were parents tended to reside in closer proximity to relatives than childless elderly. These findings indicate that adult children are particularly important in facilitating integration in family networks.

That the importance of the elderly parent-adult child bond extends beyond family support networks is evident in work examining the role of church members in the informal networks of elderly blacks (Taylor & Chatters, 1986a). For elderly persons with children, advanced age was associated with increases in the frequency of assistance from church members. For childless elderly, however, increases in age were associated with dramatic decreases in the frequency of support. These findings indicate that adult children are instrumental in linking older black adults to church support networks and may function as a bridge between family and church networks.

In summary, current research in the fields of gerontology and family studies indicates that adult children are integral components of the informal support networks of older black adults. As this research typically focuses on older adults' reports of receiving assistance from family and others, we have information on how characteristics of older black adults (e.g., age, gender, and functional status) and their perceptions of family relationships are related to reports of aid from their support networks. Absent from this literature are investigations of intergenerational support relationships among black Americans based on the perspective of the adult child. In this regard, it is important to determine whether characteristics of adult children themselves and their perceptions of family relationships can be used to predict their participation as support providers to parents.

The present investigation attempts to fill this gap by focusing on the provision of support to parents by adult children; the dependent variable is reported frequency of assistance to parents. Two sets of independent variables are utilized: (a) family factors (i.e., family contact, family closeness, satisfaction with family life, and proximity of immediate family) and (b) demographic factors (i.e., age, gender, income, education, marital status, urbanicity, and region).

Methods

Sample

Following completion of the NSBA interview, respondents provided information concerning their family members to determine eligibility for a second investigation—The Three Generation Family Study. Eligible were those families with at least three contiguous generations (i.e., grandparent, parent, and child) of the same lineage. As part of the Three Generation Family Study, these two additional family members were interviewed for information comparable to that available for the original NSBA respondent. Roughly 52% (1,122) of the 2,107 respondents in the NSBA were eligible for the Three Generation Study. Of that group, 865 respondents (567 women and 298 men) were interviewed a second time. These individuals who were interviewed in both the original NSBA and reinterviewed as part of the Three Generation Family Study are the respondents for the present analysis.

Dependent and Independent Variables

The frequency with which adult blacks provided informal support to their parents was assessed by the question "How often do you help your parents out? Would you say very often (4), fairly often (3), not too often (2), or never (1)?" In addition, a few respondents volunteered that their parents never needed help; although reported here, the "never needed" category was excluded from the regression analysis.

Both family and demographic factors were utilized as independent variables. The family variables included: frequency of family contact, perceived family closeness, satisfaction with family life, and proximity of immediate family members. "Family contact" assessed frequency of interaction with family members and relatives who did not reside with the respondent. Response categories were coded: 6 = nearly every day, 5 = at least once a week, 4 = a few times a month, 3 = at least once a month, 2 = a few times a year, and collapsing the last two categories, 1 = hardly ever and never ($\bar{X} = 4.72$, $SD = 1.44$). "Subjective family closeness" asked respondents to assess how close their family members are in their thoughts and feelings toward each other. This variable was coded: 4 = very close, 3 = fairly close, 2 = not too close, and 1 = not close at all ($\bar{X} = 3.52$, $SD = .69$). "Satisfaction with family life" was coded 4 = very satisfied, 3 = somewhat satisfied, 2 = somewhat dissatisfied, and

1 = very dissatisfied ($\overline{X}$ = 2.41, SD = .69). The "proximity of immediate family" measure provided information on where the majority (at least half) of the respondents' immediate family resided: 7 = same household, 6 = same neighborhood, 5 = same city, 4 = same county, 3 = same state, 2 = another state, and 1 = outside the United States ($\overline{X}$ = 5.14, SD = 1.59). The demographic variables investigated were: gender, marital status, age, income, education, urbanicity, and region.

Results

The large majority of respondents indicated that they provide some level of assistance to their parents: 35.4% indicated that they help their parents very often, 36.0% reported fairly often, 20.0% reported not too often, 5.4% reported that they have never helped their parents, and 3.2% volunteered that their parents never needed help. Table 5.1 presents the results of the regression analysis of frequency of aid to parents regressed on the familial and demographic variables. This model explained 11% of the variance in the frequency of assistance (R^2 = .11, df = 16,556, F = 4.39, p<.001).

Among the family factors, degree of family closeness and proximity of immediate family members are significant predictors of aid to parents, and frequency of family interaction borders significance. Each variable is positively associated with the provision of aid. Respondents who are subjectively close to their family members, whose immediate family members are proximate, and who interact frequently with family reported giving assistance to their parents on a more frequent basis.

Among the demographic factors, marital status, education, and urbanicity exhibit significant or near-significant relationships with frequency of support to parents. Among the marital status categories, being separated from one's spouse is significantly related to the frequency of giving help to parents (being divorced approaches significance). Both separated and divorced respondents provide assistance to their parents less frequently than does the comparison group of married respondents. Education and urbanicity also border on significance; respondents who have more years of formal education and persons who reside in rural areas indicated that they provide help to their parents more frequently than do their counterparts.

In the next stage of the analysis we examined the provision of support to parents separately for men and women (Table 5.2). Among men,

Table 5.1 Regression Coefficients for the Influence of Family and Demographic Factors on Frequency of Giving Support to Parents

Predictors	b	β
Intercept	1.35	
Family Factors		
Family contact	.05[a]	.09[a]
Family closeness	.19***	.16***
Family satisfaction	.05	.04
Proximity of immediate family	.08***	.14***
Demographic Factors		
Age	−.003	.03
Gender	.06	.04
Marital status		
Divorced	−.21[a]	−.08[a]
Separated	−.36**	−.13**
Widowed	−.06	−.02
Never married	−.13	−.06
Education	.03[a]	.08[a]
Income	−.05	.02
Urbanicity	−.18[a]	−.08[a]
Region		
Northeast	−.005	−.00
North Central	−.10	−.05
West	−.16	−.04
R^2	.11***	

NOTE: b = unstandardized coefficient; β = standardized coefficient. Several of the predictors in this analysis were represented by dummy variables: Gender—0 = female, 1 = male; Employment status—0 = unemployed, 1 = employed; Marital status—married and common law is the excluded category; Urbanicity—0 = rural, 1 = urban; Region—South is the excluded category.
[a] $.10 > p > .05$; *$p < .05$.; **$p < .01$.; ***$p < .001$.

familial and demographic factors explain 16.5% of the variance in the frequency of giving support to parents ($R^2 = .165$, $df = 15,190$, $F = 2.5$, $p<.01$). Family closeness is significantly related to parental aid, and frequency of family interaction borders on significance. Among the demographic variables, marital status and region are significantly related to the dependent variable. Separated and widowed men give assistance to their parents significantly less frequently than do married men. Men who reside in the North Central region provide assistance to their parents on a less frequent basis than men who reside in the South.

Analysis of the provision of support to parents by women is also presented in Table 5.2 ($R^2 = .11$, $df = 15,351$, $F = 2.94$, $p<.001$).

Table 5.2 Regression Coefficients for the Influence of Family and Demographic Factors on Frequency of Giving Support to Parents by Gender

Predictors	Men		Women	
	b	β	b	β
Intercept	3.97		.18	
Family Factors				
Family contact	.07[a]	.14[a]	.03	.05
Family closeness	.21*	.17*	.20**	.16**
Family satisfaction	.04	.04	.04	.03
Proximity of immediate family	.05	.11	.10**	.17***
Demographic Factors				
Age	−.005	−.08	−.002	−.03
Marital status				
Divorced	−.13	−.05	−.24	−.09
Separated	−.54*	−.15*	−.31*	−.11*
Widowed	−.82*	−.14*	.06	.02
Never married	−.19	−.11	−.11	−.05
Education	.002	.01	.04[a]	.11[a]
Income	.006	.03	−.01	−.05
Urbanicity	−.01	−.01	−.27[a]	−.11[a]
Region				
Northeast	−.23	−.10	.07	.03
North Central	−.31*	−.17*	−.01	−.00
West	−.29	−.09	−.09	−.02
R^2	.16***		.11***	

NOTE: b = unstandardized coefficient; β = standardized coefficient. Several of the predictors in this analysis were represented by dummy variables: Gender—0 = female, 1 = male; Employment status—0 = unemployed, 1 = employed; Marital status—married and common law is the excluded category; Urbanicity—0 = rural, 1 = urban; Region—South is the excluded category.
[a] $.10 > p > .05$; $*p < .05$.; $**p < .01$.; $***p < .001$.

Both subjective family closeness and proximity of immediate family members are positively associated with the frequency of giving help. Women who expressed higher levels of family closeness and whose immediate family members reside nearby indicated helping their parents on a more frequent basis than their counterparts. With regard to demographic factors, separated women provide assistance less frequently than do their married counterparts. In addition, education and urbanicity approach significance; women who have more years of formal education and those who reside in rural areas provide assistance to their parents more frequently than their counterparts.

Discussion

The results of the present analysis indicate that among blacks, adult children are frequent providers of assistance to their parents. Overall, 9 out of 10 respondents reported that they helped their parents and approximately one third stated that they assisted their parents on a frequent basis. These findings are consistent with previous work that indicates that intergenerational support is characteristic of black families. Further, the important and often critical role that adult children assume in providing assistance to the elderly was underscored (Chatters et al., 1985, 1986; Taylor, 1985, 1986).

A select group of family and demographic factors emerged as important determinants of these supportive behaviors. Among both men and women, respondents who reported being subjectively close to their families provided assistance to parents on a frequent basis. This finding is consistent with previous research on blacks demonstrating that affective ties are important in determining the size and composition of helper networks (Chatters et al., 1985), as well as the receipt of support from family (Taylor, 1986). Also consistent with other work (Taylor, 1986) that indicated that degree of family satisfaction was a poor predictor of support from family members, in the present analysis, satisfaction with family was unimportant in predicting the level of assistance that adult children provided to parents.

The significance of marital status for the support recipient has been noted extensively in other work (Chatters et al., 1985, 1986; Johnson & Catalano, 1981; Lopata, 1979; Treas, 1977). Having a spouse is related to an increased likelihood of receiving assistance and the availability of a larger network of informal helpers. In contrast to work that focuses on the support recipient, the present results suggest that marital status has an influence on the supportive behaviors that children display in relation to their parents.

Stoller's (1983) investigation of care giving by adult children found that being married was significantly related to providing *less* assistance to parents. Competing demands for time were viewed as limiting the supportive behaviors of married adult children. In the present analysis, however, married respondents provided assistance to parents on a more frequent basis than separated respondents. One possible explanation for the difference could be that separated persons are in a less advantageous position to provide help to parents than are persons who are married because of potentially greater family and personal responsibilities and stresses. Adult children who are separated are unable to share domestic responsibilities (e.g., child care and household tasks) with another adult (i.e., spouse). As a consequence, adult children who are separated potentially have greater demands on their time and resources that limit their ability to provide support to parents.

Being separated from one's spouse may engender unique ongoing stresses that inhibit the provision of support to parents. Taken together, the burden of family and household responsibilities and heightened levels of stress may render the adult child an ineffective source of support. Further research is needed to reconcile these observed differences and clarify the relationships between marital status, family responsibilities, and aid to parents.

Gender differences in the support networks of blacks suggest that women, and adult daughters in particular, are most frequently the providers of aid to older black adults (Chatters et al., 1985, 1986). Older women are also more inclined than older men to choose daughters as helpers. The present analysis failed to find a significant main effect for gender on the provision of aid to parents. Being a man or a woman had no influence on the reported frequency of aid to parents. Despite the absence of a significant main effect for gender in providing aid to parents, several of the independent variables operated differently for male and female subgroups. Disparities in the sets of predictors suggest that the factors that govern assistance to parents differ for women and men. The comparison of the model for the full sample with separate models for women and men, revealed important differences in the relationships between family contact, proximity of immediate family members, widowhood, education, urbanicity, and region and reports of assistance to parents. The remaining discussion explores the possible mechanisms that create these divergences.

Frequency of family contact failed to emerge as a significant predictor of parental support among women, but bordered significance for men. Men who reported more frequent contact with family members and relatives tended to give assistance to parents more frequently than did their counterparts. This finding is consistent with previous research indicating that frequency of contact is an important determinant of support from family members (Taylor, 1986). Findings for women indicate that proximity of immediate family members is significantly associated with the frequency of aid to parents. Women with proximal immediate family networks tended to give support to parents on a more frequent basis than did women whose networks were distant. This finding contradicts other research that found that proximity of immediate family members was unrelated to receipt of support from family (Taylor, 1986).

A partial explanation for the differential effects of family factors in predicting sons' and daughters' assistance to parents may be found in normative expectations and behaviors for affiliation and support based on gender. Previous research indicates that daughters, and women generally, are more frequently the providers of support to family and elderly adults. Normative expectations and socialization experiences to provide aid to parents and other relatives may be stronger for women than men. Although interaction with family members emerged as an important facilitator of assistance to parents among men, presumably for women the normative expectation to assist parents is so pervasive that it operates independently of any possible salutary effects of interaction levels. But the facilitative effect of proximity of immediate family on the supportive behaviors of women suggests that this factor accentuates the tendency to help. This may occur because the availability of other family resources effectively lessens the burden of domestic responsibilities, thus allowing for a greater contribution to the support of parents. Similarly, Stoller (1983) suggested that family resources within the household (e.g., the presence of older children) may function to reduce domestic demands on care givers.

With reference to demographic factors, dummy variables for widowhood and residency in the North Central region were significantly related to provision of support to parents among men only. Findings for the combined model indicated that widowhood was unrelated to assistance from parents. The gender-specific models revealed that for men a significant negative effect for widowhood emerged, whereas the coefficient for women was insignificant. In essence, widowers gave help to their parents less frequently than did married men, whereas married women and widows were comparable in their level of support to parents.

The finding that widowhood has a differential effect on the frequency of aid to parents may be indicative of several processes. Wives, and women family members generally, constitute an important link and source of cohesion for immediate and extended families alike, and the importance of wives for the integration of men in families and other social networks has been documented. Although widowhood has been associated with a distancing of women from family (Lopata, 1973, 1978, 1979), the death of one's spouse may lead to even greater isolation among men. As a consequence, a widower's ties to family may be more tenuous, affecting his ability to act effectively as support provider. Further, research on adaptation to widowhood suggests that men tend to fare worse than do women (Strobe & Strobe, 1983). If widowhood does represent a special risk to the emotional and physical health of men, we can anticipate that they would be less equipped to function as support providers to others. The absence of an effect for widowhood among women indicates that widows and married women are similar in the reported frequency of support that they provide to parents. This finding suggests that, distinct from their male counterparts, widows are not constrained in their ability to aid parents. Further, the finding may be indicative of the emergence of widowed daughters as major care givers to parents (Brody, 1981).

One limitation of the data is that information on the length of widowed status is not available. Recent work suggests that because remarriage rates are higher for men than women, men tend to be widowed only for the short term whereas women are widowed for longer periods of time. As a consequence, comparisons of widowed women and men frequently involve men who are recently bereaved and women widowed for a longer term. These groups will likely present very different profiles regarding their current physical and mental health, bereavement status, and social functioning with regard to social network obligations.

Men who resided in the North Central region provided help less frequently than men who resided in the South. This finding is consistent with previous research indicating that elderly blacks who reside in the South are generally in a more advantageous position with reference to support relationships involving family and friends (Chatters et al., 1985; Taylor, 1985).

Education and urbanicity bordered on significance as predictors of support to parents among women only. Women with more years of formal education and those who resided in rural areas tended to give help to their parents on a more frequent basis than their counterparts. The finding of a positive education effect is unique. A similar positive effect for a socioeconomic status measure (i.e., income) was found in a study of support among black adults (Taylor, 1986). Other research on the informal support networks of black adults generally has failed to find significant urban-rural differences (Taylor, 1986). Among the elderly, however, rural blacks were more likely than their urban counterparts to report exclusive reliance on immediate family members (Chatters et al., 1985). As these results only border significance, further research is required to confirm whether urbanicity and education have significant relationships with parental support among black women and the specific processes involved.

Summary and Conclusions

In this study we examined the effects of family and demographic factors on the provision of support to parents. The original model indicated that family factors related to affiliation and affection were positive predictors of assistance. A select group of demographic factors had significant influences on the reported frequency of aid to parents. In particular, certain groups (i.e., those separated or divorced from spouse and persons who reported poorer family relations) were less likely to provide support to parents. The absence of a gender difference in the original model indicated that both women and men provided comparable levels of assistance to parents.

The specification of separate models for women and men, however, helped to clarify the operation of family and demographic factors on the provision of assistance to parents. The gender-specific models suggested that the factors that affect aid are different for the two groups. Several of the observed divergences may be related to gender differences in normative expectations for supportive and affiliative behaviors. Other differences in the models for women and men are unique and require further study.

The findings of this study suggest several interesting avenues for further investigation. Future research in this area should examine the impact that domestic responsibilities and time constraints have on the supportive behaviors of adult sons and daughters. Of specific interest is how participation in multiple roles (i.e., spouse, parent, and worker) coincide with providing support to parents, and whether women and men are differentially involved in care giving as a consequence of their other role involvements. Similarly, it is important to assess how specific characteristics of the parent (e.g., health status, age, and marital status) are related to support from adult children, and in what ways the need for support is responded to by adult children (i.e., the enlistment of other informal helpers or use of formal supports). Finally, because support giving is an ongoing process, its study will require longitudinal investigations to determine how changes in need for assistance and support resources are coordinated by adult children and parents. Prospective investigations will also address changes in support levels and patterns that occur in response to life and family events (e.g., onset of major illness).

References

Adams, B. (1968). *Kinship in an urban setting.* Chicago: Markham.

Antonucci, T. C., & Akiyama, H. (1987). Social networks in adult life and a preliminary examination of the convoy model. *Journal of Gerontology, 42,* 519-527.

Aschenbrenner, J. (1973). Extended families among black Americans. *Journal of Comparative Family Studies, 4,* 257-268.

Aschenbrenner, J. (1975). *Lifelines: Black families in Chicago.* New York: Holt, Rinehart & Winston.

Brody, E. (1981). Women in the middle and family help to older people. *Gerontologist, 21,* 471-480.

Cantor, M. H. (1979). The informal support system of New York's inner city elderly: Is ethnicity a factor? In D. E. Gelfand & A. J. Kutzik (Eds.), *Ethnicity and aging: Theory, research and policy* (pp. 153-174). New York: Springer.

Chatters, L. M., Taylor, R. J., & Jackson, J. S. (1985). Size and composition of the informal helper networks of elderly blacks. *Journal of Gerontology, 40,* 605-614.

Chatters, L. M., Taylor, R. J., & Jackson, J. S. (1986). Aged blacks' choice for an informal helper network. *Journal of Gerontology, 41,* 94-100.

Chatters, L. M., Taylor, R. J., & Neighbors, H. W. (1989). Size of informal helper network mobilized during a serious personal problem among black Americans. *Journal of Marriage and the Family, 51,* 667-676.

Cicirelli, V. G. (1981). *Helping elderly parents: The role of adult children.* Boston: Auburn House.

Jackson, J. J. (1972). Black aged: In quest of the phoenix. In *Triple jeopardy: Myth or reality.* Washington, DC: National Council on the Aging.

Jackson, J. J. (1980). *Minorities and aging.* Belmont, CA: Wadsworth.

Johnson, C. L., & Catalano, D. J. (1981). Childless elderly and their family support. *The Gerontologist, 21,* 610-618.

Kendig, H. L., Coles, R., Pittelkow, Y., & Wilson, S. (1988). Confidants and family structure in old age. *Journal of Gerontology: Social Sciences, 43,* S31-S40.

Lopata, H. Z. (1973). *Widowhood in an American city.* Cambridge, MA: Schenkman.

Lopata, H. Z. (1978). Contributions of extended families to the support systems of metropolitan area widows: Limitations of the modified kin network. *Journal of Marriage and the Family, 40,* 355-364.

Lopata, H. Z. (1979). *Women as widows.* New York: Elsevier.

Martin, E. P., & Martin, J. M. (1978). *The black extended family.* Chicago: University of Chicago.

Mitchell, J. S., & Register, J. C. (1984). An exploration of family interaction with the elderly by race, socioeconomic status and residence. *The Gerontologist, 24*(1), 48-54.

Mutran, E. (1985). Intergenerational family support among blacks and whites: Response to culture or to socioeconomic differences. *Journal of Gerontology, 40,* 382-389.

Shanas, E. (1979). *National survey of the elderly.* (Report). Washington, DC: Department of Health and Human Services, Administration on Aging.

Smerglia, V., Deimling, G. T., & Barresi, C. M. (1988). Black/white family comparisons in helping and decision-making networks of impaired elderly. *Family Relations, 37,* 305-309.

Spitze, G., & Miner, S. (1992). Gender differences in adult child contact among black elderly parents. *The Gerontologist, 32,* 213-218.

Stack, C. B. (1972). Black kindreds: Parenthood and personal kindreds among urban blacks. *Journal of Comparative Family Studies, 3,* 194-206.

Stack, C. B. (1974). *All our kin.* New York: Harper & Row.

Stanford, E. P. (1978). *The elder black.* San Diego, CA: Campanile.

Stoller, E. P. (1983). Parental care giving by adult children. *Journal of Marriage and the Family, 45*(4), 851-858.

Strobe, M. S., & Strobe, W. (1983). Who suffers more? Sex differences in health risk of the widowed. *Psychological Bulletin, 93,* 279-301.

Taylor, R. J. (1985). The extended family as a source of support to elderly blacks. *The Gerontologist, 25*(5), 488-495.

Taylor, R. J. (1986). Receipt of support from family among black Americans: Demographic and familial differences. *Journal of Marriage and the Family, 48,* 67-77.

Taylor, R. J. (1988). Aging and supportive relationships among black Americans. In J. S. Jackson (Ed.), *The black American elderly: Research on physical and psychosocial health* (pp. 259-281). New York: Springer.

Taylor, R. J., & Chatters, L. M. (1986a). Church-based informal support among elderly blacks. *The Gerontologist, 26,* 637-642.

Taylor, R. J., & Chatters, L. M. (1986b). Patterns of informal support to elderly black adults: Family, friends, and church members. *Social Work, 31,* 432-438.

Taylor, R. J., & Chatters, L. M. (1991). Extended family networks of older black adults. *Journal of Gerontology: Social Sciences, 46,* S210-S217.

Taylor, R. J., Chatters, L. M., & Mays, V. M. (1988). Parents, children, siblings, in-laws, and non-kin as sources of emergency assistance to elderly blacks. *Family Relations, 37,* 298-304.

Taylor, R. J., Chatters, L. M., Tucker, M. B., & Lewis, E. (1990). Developments in research on black families: A decade in review. *Journal of Marriage and the Family, S2,* 993-1014.

Treas, J. (1977). Family support systems for the aged: Some social and demographic considerations. *The Gerontologist, 17,* 486-491.

6

INTIMATE PARTNERSHIPS

Eleanor Engram
Shirley A. Lockery

Intimate black partnerships have remained unexamined by social science. Historical and contemporary evidence, however, suggests that the intimate partnership is a central organizing feature of African-American life (Blassingame, 1977; Engram, 1982). Intimacy has been noted as a key influence in the lives of black infants (Dougherty, 1978; Lewis, 1975; Young, 1970). Among black adolescents intimacy has been considered only from a deviance perspective and among younger and older black adults, it has been ignored. Yet, intimacy has been related to the well-being of other populations (George et al., 1981; Traupmann, Eckels, & Hatfield, 1982). Marital relationships have been positively related to general well-being and to physical and mental health among older black adults (Chatters, 1988; J. S. Jackson, Chatters, & Neighbors, 1982).

Intimacy or love, whether measured as attraction or attachment, is a central feature of social organization. In this chapter we examine the role of intimate partnerships in the lives of older African Americans through analysis of the National Survey of Black Americans (NSBA) data set. Attempts are made to explore some hypotheses about the nature of intimacy among African Americans and to pose some questions for future research.

Intimacy in African-American Social Life

Social and anthropological researchers contend that intimacy is critical for human development. Studies of black mothers and infants have noted intensely intimate interactions. Dougherty (1978) noted that mothers in her sample interacted extensively with their infants by touching, kissing, and holding their babies' hands. Additionally, Lewis (1975) in her study of black parenting found that black babies are held and fondled by fathers as well as mothers.

The development of the capacity for healthy adulthood is posited by Erikson (1964), Kaplan (1978), and others to be dependent upon the ability of the individual to accomplish "intimacy" as a developmental task. Failure to develop the capacity for intimacy, according to theories of development, leads to isolation and associated pathologies. Despite these theories of its importance to healthy life-styles, primary focus on black intimacy has been from a pathological posture and consequently we know little of the positive role of intimacy in the lives of African Americans. Such a posture is considered by Engram (1982) to be symptomatic of a more serious problem, that is, the failure of the rest of society to incorporate black people as human beings with basic human needs.

Much of the research has focused on black adolescents as a homogeneous group plagued by social problems. These same interactions have been interpreted by using prevailing theoretical orientations based on pathological or deviant perspectives (Anderson, 1989; Taylor, Chatters, Tucker, & Lewis, 1990). As a result, little has been done to understand the black adolescent population in general (Connor, 1988). For example, intimacy in the relationships of black adolescents has for the most part been studied as "premarital sexual permissiveness." Black adolescents have been found to be less optimistic about the significance of marriage, more supportive of sexual freedom, as well as more accepting of children born out of wedlock, than white youth. Conversely, white youth are more likely "to have more sexual partners and engage in more frequent sexual activities," than black adolescents (Connor, 1988, p. 198). Some might interpret the results as an indication of the casual attitudes of blacks toward sexual affairs, that is, that blacks do not need love as a basis for sexual relations. Engram (1982) argued that an equally valid interpretation of the same data is that whites tend to rationalize their sexual behavior by saying they are in love. In any case, it contributes little to our understanding of intimacy to study it from this perspective.

In reality, the development of intimate peer relationships among black adolescents is influenced by structural conditions (limited education, job opportunities, and regular employment) beyond their control (Chapman, 1988; Malveaux, 1988; Voydanoff, 1990).

Although few studies have explained intimacy among black adults, global explanations of adult black sexual behavior exist in the literature. Relationships of black males and females during the post-Civil War Reconstruction era have been labeled pathological, but blamed on the system of slavery that purportedly developed an irresponsible attitude in black men toward women and children. This posture on black America has persisted despite the evidence of heterogeneity in black values (Frazier, 1957; Hare, 1965), in black social and economic status (Blackwell, 1975), and in black culture. The failure to document the heterogeneity in black culture and life-styles is revealed in media portrayals where male-female relationships are depicted as being conflict ridden and children and adolescents are shown as receiving minimal supervision and love (A. W. Jackson, 1982).

Historical evidence shows that despite the experience of slavery, constraint and marital sanctity have prevailed as values in many segments of the black community. At the same time, a high value has been placed on intimacy that often was not possible to consummate sexually. Below, for example, a slave husband writes to his wife from whom he has long been separated by slavery:

> I hope with gods helpe that I may be abble to rejoys with you on the earth and In heaven lets meet when will I am detemnid to nuver stope praying. . . . In glory there weel meet to part no more forever. So my dear wife I hope to meet you In paradase to prase god forever. (Hobbs, in Blassingame, 1977, p. 19)

And a slave wife writes to her husband:

> for their has ben one bright hope to cheer me in all my troubles, that is to be with you, for if I thought I shoul never see you this earth would have no charms for me. (Newby in Blassingame, 1977, p. 118)

The resources that intimate black partners bring to each other can be deduced from biographies, poetry, music, and literature that express the black experience. Social science, however, is behind in observing love in the black experience, as the most salient analytical model used has been one of conflict. Although there *has* been conflict evident between black partners, there has also been the historical and contemporary economic forces that impede the abilities of black partners to maintain long-term commitments. Where black partners have maintained successful relationships, it is frequently attributable to their ability to jointly define gender roles that create their economic and family success. Intimate partnerships should be considered in light of the greater historical forces that have shaped intimate interactions. These include: (a) slavery and its mutilation of families and intimate relations by slave owners and their employees (Frazier, 1930), (b) rural to urban migration and the employment of black women in households external to their own (Frazier, 1950, 1957; Henri, 1976), (c) wars that further separate partners, (d) economic depressions that require family reorganization (Stack, 1974), and (e) sex ratio (Tucker & Taylor, 1989).

Despite the tendency of social scientists to sensationalize the conflict between black men and women, the cohesiveness of the black community is obvious and has been derived from the union of black men and women against the forces of racism with which they are confronted. Music, literature, and biography all suggest that the intimate relationship, although it can be a source of conflict, is a source of psychological and emotional well-being.

Intimacy and Older Adults

The intimate relationship that generates the most vital social support and companionship for the older adult in the later years is a satisfactory marital dyad (Atchley, 1988; Brubaker, 1990). Intimacy, interdependency, and a sense of belonging are all functions that can contribute to marital satisfaction (Atchley, 1988). Marital satisfaction is known to have a positive effect on social relationships and the subjective well-being of older adults (Brubaker, 1990; Chatters, 1988; Dobson, 1988; J. S. Jackson et al., 1982). Marriage has also been differentially related to mortality among older persons (Brubaker, 1990; Gove, Hughes, & Style, 1983).

Gender and black-white differences in marital status are widely recognized. The majority of the population 65 years of age and over are women and most are single (American Association of Retired Persons & the Administration of Aging [AARP & AoA], 1990). In 1989, nearly twice as many elderly men than elderly women were married (AARP &

AoA, 1990). Almost half (49%) of all older women are widows. Although the actual percentage of older divorcees is small (4%), the proportion is growing and is expected to continue to grow at a rapid pace (Atchley, 1988; Brubaker, 1990).

Older African Americans are twice as likely as whites to be divorced and separated, and proportionately more likely to be widowed. Therefore, older African Americans are apt to be living without a spouse (American Association of Retired Persons [AARP], 1986). To some extent, living without a spouse can be attributed to the lower life expectancy of black men, and for many, a poverty-level income. As reported by Tucker, Taylor, and Mitchell-Kernan (in press), among African Americans 65 years of age or older, there are 66.9 men per 100 women. The male-female sex ratio, coupled with the propensity of men to marry younger women and for wives to outlive their husbands, reduces the opportunity for remarriage among older women.

Researchers have documented the relationship between intimacy and well-being, social network and well-being, and the importance of the quality of the social contact (Atchley, 1988; Brubaker, 1990). Still others have noted a difference between "passionate" and "companionate" love. Passionate love, according to Walster and Walster (1978) is intense, emotional, and embodies feelings of sexuality, as opposed to companionate love, which is affection-based attachment. Despite evidence to the contrary, older persons are perceived as more desirous of companionate love and less capable of passionate love. This posture on the sexuality of older persons is probably symptomatic of another problem, that is, the lack of acceptance of sexuality that pervades societies of Victorian heritage. It is only in recent years, as gains have been made in the health and longevity of older persons, that we have expanded our concept of the roles of the elderly to include a sexual role (Atchley, 1988; Thomas, 1982).

Thomas (1982), evaluating the trend in research on sexuality among the aging, noted a developing position ("the old need sex to maintain health, sexuality and vitality"). Thomas suggested that we have yet to discuss with older people the role of sexuality in their lives or the resources that they derive from intimate partnerships. If this is true of the elderly in general, then we know even less as it pertains to African Americans. In the great historical transformation from slaves to free men and women, from the agricultural to the information society, there has been no topic pertaining to black men and women as sensitive as their sexuality. Because so much energy and interest has been given over to sexual myths and stereotypes, we have learned little of the role of intimacy in the lives of black adults.

In sum, the relationships between older black men and women have been virtually ignored. Yet, throughout their life cycles the relationships between black men and women are the subject of much debate. Popular explanations of this phenomena include the following:

1. Black women constitute a "matriarchy," and consequently a pathological constellation of roles prevails in black families.
2. Black men are exploitative and according to exchange theorists the traditional exchange between men and women of expressive for instrumental rewards is reversed.
3. Black men and women have the same needs as do other human beings, including the need for self-esteem, which is often derived from a sense of adequate performance of societally prescribed roles.

Consequently, the relationships between black males and females suffer to the extent that the roles that are required depart from the roles that they value. If a man is "supposed to work," then he develops adequacy and esteem from doing so. If a woman is "supposed to be taken care of," then she develops a sense of adequacy and esteem from so being. When either partner cannot perform adequately, depression, hostility, and inadequacy affect the relationship. Where black couples have codefined and valued roles that support their experience and validate the economic and expressive contributions of both partners, they have had successful relationships.

The characteristics of the intimate relationships between older African-American men and women have not received sufficient consideration in the literature. Traditional research has focused on structural aspects of intimate partnerships, such as marital status. Thus, the purpose of this analysis is to explore attitudinal beliefs about intimate partnerships and the perceived value of intimate relationships among older African Americans.

Methods

The variables used in this analysis of older respondents are from the NSBA; the sample for this analysis is composed of 367 women and 214 men 55 years of age or older.

Table 6.1 Marital Status by Gender (in percentages)

Marital Status	Gender	
	Male	Female
Married	59.8	26.6
Divorced	9.4	6.8
Separated	7.9	9.9
Widowed	19.6	53.4
Never Married	3.3	3.3
Total	100.0	100.0
(N)	(214)	(365)

Results

Marital Status and Romantic Involvement

Marital status was determined by asking each respondent: "Are you married, divorced, separated, widowed or have you ever been married?" Approximately 39% of the total sample were married. A slightly larger percentage (41%) of all respondents were widowed. Other marital characteristics indicate that smaller proportions of the total sample were separated (9%), divorced (8%), or never married (3%).

Table 6.1 shows that nearly 60% of the male respondents, compared with 27% of the female respondents, were married. Conversely, a larger percentage of the female respondents (53.4%) than male respondents (19.6%) were widowed. The percentage of divorced, separated, and never-married respondents were similar for both men and women.

Intimate relationships or romantic involvement was expanded beyond the traditional marital dyad by asking respondents without marital partners: "Do you have a romantic involvement at this time?" For those respondents without marital partners, nearly 16% (57 of 348) acknowledged being in a romantic relationship. Table 6.2 shows that 40% (33 of 82) of the male respondents, compared with 9% (24 of 266) of the female respondents, have a romantic involvement. A chi-square test of significance, using Yates's Correction Factor, shows a statistically significant relationship between gender and romantic involvement ($\chi^2 = 42.4$, $df = 1$, $p < .0001$). Men were more likely to be romantically involved than women.

Table 6.2   Romantic Involvement by Gender (in percentages)

Romantic Involvement	Gender	
	Male	Female
Yes	40.2	9.0
No	59.8	91.0
Total	100.0	100.0
(N)	(82)	(266)

$\chi^2 = 42.4$; $df = 1$; $p < .001$.

Intimate Partnerships

Intimate partnerships were evaluated by a new measure that was created by combining two items, whether a respondent was married or romantically involved. Approximately half ($N = 282$) of the total sample ($N = 581$) was either married ($N = 225$) or romantically involved ($N = 57$). By gender, almost one half (45.4%) of the men were married in contrast to one third (34.4%) of the women. Male respondents were also more likely to be romantically involved (11.7%) than female respondents (8.5%).

Perceived value of intimate partnerships was ascertained by the responses to: "How important is it for you to have a [person of the opposite sex] live in the house with you for . . . financial security? . . . for jobs that need to be done around the house? . . . for a good love life? . . . for companionship?" For each question, is it "very important, fairly important, not too important, or not important at all?"

The first dimension, financial security, was judged to be very important to intimate partnerships by more than half (53.1%) of all respondents. Conversely, only one fifth (20.7%) of the respondents considered financial security unimportant to intimate relationships. The remainder of the respondents rated financial security as fairly important (14.2%) to not too important (12%). A chi-square statistic was used to determine the significance of financial security in intimate partnerships for both men and women. Table 6.3 shows that the majority of the female respondents, both married (85.4%) and romantically involved (62.5%), were more likely than male respondents (married, 53.1% and romantically involved, 30.3%) to rate financial security as very important. A chi-square test of significance shows a statistically significant relationship between

Table 6.3 Importance of Financial Security by Marital Status, Romantic Involvement, and Gender (in percentages)

Financial Security	Marital Status		Romantic Involvement	
	Male	Female	Male	Female
Very Important	53.1	85.4	30.3	62.5
Fairly Important	17.5	7.3	30.3	4.1
Not Too Important	12.7	5.2	21.2	16.7
Not at All Important	16.7	2.1	18.2	16.7
Total	100.0	100.0	100.0	100.0
(N)	(126)	(96)	(33)	(24)

$\chi^2 = 45.7$; $df = 9$; $p < .0001$.

marriage/romantic involvement and the importance of financial security ($\chi^2 = 45.7$, $df = 9$, $p < .0001$).

Findings from a second dimension, assisting with "jobs around the house," indicate that more than half (55.1%) of the total sample (314 of 570) considered this to be a very important role of intimate partnerships. Another 18.4% of the respondents viewed housework as fairly important to intimate partnerships, 10% felt that housework was not too important, and 16.3% considered housework unimportant. No statistically significant relationship was found between intimate partnership and the importance of having a person of the opposite sex for jobs around the house.

The importance of having a person of the opposite sex for a good love life or lovemaking was judged to be very important by more than half (54.1%) of all respondents; 14.4% stated fairly important, 10% considered lovemaking as not very important to intimate relationships, and almost one fifth (21.3%) of all respondents appraised a good love life as not important at all. A chi-square statistic was used to determine the significance of a good love life among both men and women in either type of intimate partnership. As can be seen in Table 6.4, a majority of the married men (80.2%) and the married women (71.1%) rated a good love life as very important. By gender, men, whether married or romantically involved, were more likely than women to consider a good love life as very important. Among each group of women, married and romantically involved, respondents were somewhat more likely than the comparable group of men to rate a good love life as unimportant.

Companionship, the final dimension of intimate partnerships, was very important to nearly two thirds (65.8%) of the total sample (373 of

Table 6.4 Importance of Good Love Life by Marital Status, Romantic Involvement, and Gender (in percentages)

Good Love Life	Marital Status		Romantic Involvement	
	Male	Female	Male	Female
Very Important	80.2	71.1	63.7	43.5
Fairly Important	11.1	12.4	12.1	34.8
Not Too Important	2.4	7.2	12.1	8.7
Not at All Important	6.3	9.3	12.1	13.0
Total	100.0	100.0	100.0	100.0
(N)	(126)	(97)	(33)	(23)

$\chi^2 = 19.7$; $df = 9$; $p<.05$.

569). Another 15% of the respondents considered companionship fairly important to intimate partnerships. Five percent of the respondents rated companionship as not too important, and the remaining 14% of the respondents considered companionship as not important at all to intimate partnerships. Married men (88.2%) and married women (86.6%) generally agreed that companionship was very important. Romantically involved women (65.2%) were least likely to view companionship as very important to intimate partnerships. Although interesting, the cross tabulations were not statistically significant.

Discussion

The relationships between older African-American men and women have virtually been ignored. The purpose of this analysis was to explore the role and nature of intimacy in the lives of older African Americans. Attitudinal beliefs about intimate partnerships and the perceived value of intimate relationships were the primary areas of study.

Gender was found to have a significant relationship to marital status and romantic involvement. The findings suggest that marital status and romantic involvement are more prevalent among older African-American men than women. Black men were more likely to be married and living with spouses than were women, and women were more likely to be widowed. These findings are consistent with the data that confirm the differential mortality rates among older men and women and the tendency of wives to outlive their husbands (Tucker & Taylor, 1989).

Despite stereotypes to the contrary, the portrait painted in these data is one of sanctity of marriage vis-à-vis other possibilities. And as marriage is less possible, women without intimate relationships seem to accept the reality of the unavailable male partner.

All persons in the NSBA who were married or who had a romantic involvement were asked what they believed to be the value of having a member of the opposite sex in the household. This discussion focuses on those respondents, married or romantically involved, and the importance they placed on having their partner there for financial security, for jobs around the house, for lovemaking, and for companionship. These data provide a one-sided view, as both partners from the same dyad were not surveyed, and references to men and women are to individuals from different partnerships. In spite of this, we can determine from a valid sample of older African-American men and women their sex-role values and the benefits that they perceive to be derived from an intimate partnership.

The results of this analysis verify that financial security is very important to intimate partnerships. Overwhelmingly both men and women reflected the value that has been historically placed on dual earners in black partnerships. That is, a majority of men and women in the sample perceived financial security to be a benefit of having a member of the opposite sex in the household. But women with intimate male partners in the home were more likely to believe that financial security was very important to the relationship. The importance attributed to financial security by female respondents is consistent with Anglo-American cultural values, demonstrating the bicultural influences that shape the experience of African Americans.

Older men and women in the sample are equally likely to believe that it is important to have a member of the other sex in the household for housework. This value, too, departs from dominant cultural views, in which housework is believed to be women's work. Egalitarianism among younger black couples has been noted elsewhere (Taylor et al., 1990). But as more women from other cultural groups enter the labor force, egalitarian roles similar to those of black partners are emerging.

Beyond instrumental relationships, the NSBA explored ways by which black Americans described their sexual behavior. The terms *love* and *love life* were used by older blacks. The findings suggest that the value placed on the presence of a member of the other sex in the household for lovemaking is a little higher among married men than married women.

As mentioned earlier, companionship was not found to have a significant relationship to intimate partnerships. But both men and women, whether married or romantically involved, were in relative agreement that having a member of the opposite sex in the household for companionship was very important. Given that more than half of the sample that is in intimate partnerships value the presence in the household of a person of the opposite sex for companionship (65.5%) and lovemaking (54.1%), we can assume that both passionate and compassionate love are integral to the lives of older black couples.

Conclusion

The overwhelming portrait that is painted in looking at these data is one of a high degree of correspondence in sex-role values among older black adults. Whether these values correspond to the realities they must face in their own intimate partners could not be determined in this analysis.

Given that well-being is associated with the availability of others for support in the form of household chores and companionship (see Chapter 4), and the health of older adults is affected in the same way (see Chapter 9), intimate partnerships stand high among the roles and resources of the black elderly. Unfortunately, however, the availability of intimate partners for older black women is limited.

This excursion into the intimate partnerships of the older black person focuses on the importance of love, companionship, and support among the roles and resources of the black elderly. Because this is an area of black life that has been so little explored, at this point it is not clear whether we have the right questions with which to get the answers. This exploration has perhaps raised more questions than answers and opens some directions for future research.

Specifically, we need to explore the role of intimacy, passionate and companionate, at all stages of the life cycle among older black adults. Further, given the increased likelihood of widowhood among older African-American women, research is needed that addresses the nature and tenure of widowhood. Included would be perceived status of widowhood as well as the acceptance of and adjustment to widowhood among older African-American women.

References

American Association of Retired Persons. (1986). *A portrait of older minorities.* Washington, DC: American Association for Retired Persons.

American Association of Retired Persons & the Administration on Aging. (1990). *A profile of older Americans: 1990.* Washington, DC: American Association for Retired Persons.

Anderson, E. (1989). Sex codes and family life among poor inner-city youths. *Annals of the American Academy of Political and Social Science, 501,* 59-78.

Atchley, R. C. (1988). *Social forces and aging: An introduction to social gerontology* (5th ed.). Belmont, CA: Wadsworth.

Blackwell, J. E. (1975). *The black community: Diversity and unity.* New York: Harper & Row.

Blassingame, J. W. (1977). *Slave testimony: Two centuries of letters, speeches, interviews, and autobiographies.* Baton Rouge: Louisiana State University Press.

Brubaker, T. H. (1990). An overview of family relationships in later life. In T. H. Brubaker (Ed.), *Family relationships in later life* (2nd ed., pp. 13-26). Newbury Park, CA: Sage.

Chapman, A. B. (1988). Male-female relations: How the past affects the present. In H. P. McAdoo (Ed.), *Black families* (2nd ed., pp. 190-200). Newbury Park, CA: Sage.

Chatters, L. M. (1988). Subjective well-being evaluations among older black Americans. *Psychology and Aging, 3,* 184-190.

Connor, M. E. (1988). Teenage fatherhood: Issues confronting young black males. In J. T. Gibbs (Ed.), *Young, black, and male in America: An endangered species* (pp. 188-218). Dover, MA: Auburn House.

Dobson, J. (1988). Conceptualizations of black families. In H. P. McAdoo (Ed.), *Black families* (2nd ed., pp. 77-90). Newbury Park, CA: Sage.

Dougherty, M. C. (1978). *Becoming a woman in rural black culture.* Nashville, TN: Vanderbilt University Press.

Engram, E. (1982). *Science, myth, reality: The black family in one-half century of research.* Westport, CT: Greenwood.

Erikson, E. H. (1964). *Childhood and society.* New York: Norton.

Frazier, E. F. (1930). The negro slave family. *Journal of Negro History, 15,* 198-259.

Frazier, E. F. (1950). Problems and needs of negro children and youth resulting from family disorganization. *Journal of Negro Education, 19,* 269-277.

Frazier, E. F. (1957). *Black bourgeoisie.* Glencoe, IL: Free Press.

George, L. K., & Weiler, S. J. (1981). Sexuality in middle and later life. *Archives of General Psychiatry, 38,* 919-923.

Gove, W. L., Hughes, M., & Style, C. (1983). Does marriage have positive effects on the psychological well-being of the individual? *Journal of Health and Social Behavior, 24,* 122-131.

Hare, N. (1965). *Black Anglo-Saxons.* New York: Marzone & Munsell.

Henri, F. (1976). *Black migration: Movement north 1900-1920.* Garden City, NY: Anchor.

Jackson, A. W. (1982). *Black families and the medium of television.* Ann Arbor: Bush Program in Child Development and Social Policy, University of Michigan.

Jackson, J. S., Chatters, L. M., & Neighbors, H. W. (1982). The mental health status of older black Americans: A national study. *Black Scholar, 13*(1), 21-35.

Kaplan, L. J. (1978). *Oneness and separateness: From infant to individual.* New York: Simon & Schuster.

Lewis, D. K. (1975). The Black family: Socialization and sex roles. *Phylon, 36,* 221-237.

Malveaux, J. (1988). The economic statuses of black families. In H. P. McAdoo (Ed.), *Black families* (2nd ed., pp. 133-147). Newbury Park, CA: Sage.

Stack, C. B. (1974). *All our kin: Strategies for survival in a black community.* New York: Harper & Row.

Taylor, R. J., Chatters, L. M., Tucker, B., & Lewis, E. (1990). Developments in research on black families: A decade review. *Journal of Marriage and the Family, 52,* 993-1014.

Thomas, L. E. (1982). Sexuality and aging: Essential vitamin or popcorn? *The Gerontologist, 22*(3), 240-243.

Traupmann, J., Eckels, E., & Hatfield, E. (1982). Intimacy in older women's lives. *The Gerontologist, 2*(6), 493-498.

Tucker, M. B., & Taylor, R. J. (1989). Demographic correlates of relationship status among black Americans. *Journal of Marriage and the Family, 51,* 655-666.

Tucker, M. B., Taylor, R. J., & Mitchell-Kernan, C. (in press). Marriage and romantic involvement among aged African Americans. *Journal of Gerontology: Social Sciences.*

Voydanoff, P. (1990). Economic distress and family relations: A review of the eighties. *Journal of Marriage and the Family, 52,* 1099-1115.

Walster, E., & Walster, E. G. (1978). *A new look at love.* Reading, MA: Addison Wesley.

Young, V. H. (1970). Family and childhood in a southern negro community. *American Anthropologist, 72,* 269-288.

SECTION II

Church and Religion

7

RELIGION AND
RELIGIOUS OBSERVANCES

Robert Joseph Taylor

Although cohort and historical period variation in religious involvement can be demonstrated for the U.S. population (Wingrove & Alston, 1974), religion and religious observance remain important features in the lives of Americans generally. The continuing personal significance of religion and religious involvement is particularly salient among the older black adult population. Several writers have argued that religion assumes a somewhat more prominent place within the aging population due to the onset of chronic health problems and the realization of one's own mortality (Hunter & Maurice, 1953). Given the historical role that the church has played in the lives of blacks, religion and religious activities have been a special focal point for black Americans in general and elderly black adults in particular.

A general profile of religious involvement of elderly black and white adults can be drawn from available research. Generally, older adults express a higher degree of religiosity than their younger counterparts (Greeley, 1989). Findings from various surveys indicate that almost half of elderly adults attend church on a weekly basis, one out of four reads the Bible daily, one out of five is involved in a prayer group, and a comparable percentage of older adults participate in a Bible study group (Princeton Religion Research Center, 1982, 1984). Comparative analyses of religious participation and attitudes of blacks and whites provide some indication of the unique role of religion and the church among

101

black Americans, and especially older black adults. Aged black adults report participating in religious activities more frequently than aged whites and are more likely to attend religious services, pray regularly, listen to religious programs, and read the Bible (Hirsch, Kent, & Silverman, 1972). Similarly, research on racial differences in social participation indicate that elderly black adults are more likely than their white counterparts to participate in religious activities (Clemente, Rexroad, & Hirsch, 1975; Heyman & Jeffers, 1970).

The group of studies of religious involvement based on the National Survey of Black Americans (NSBA) data reinforces the perception of a high degree of religious commitment among elderly black adults (Chatters & Taylor, 1989; Taylor, 1988a). In comparison to their younger counterparts, older black adults have a higher probability of being a religious affiliate (Taylor, 1988a), of having attended religious services as an adult (Taylor, 1988a), and of being a church member (Taylor, 1988b). In addition, older adults attended religious services (Taylor, 1988b) and engaged in nonorganizational religious behaviors on a more frequent basis (i.e., read religious materials, watch/listen to religious broadcasts, engage in prayer, request prayer from others) (Taylor, 1988b) and expressed a higher degree of subjective religious involvement (Chatters & Taylor, 1989) than did younger adults.

This chapter explores the character and role of the church and religion in the lives of older black adults, examining multiple indicators of religious involvement, including measures of religious affiliation, attitudes, and behaviors. The data for this analysis are from the first national probability sample of blacks in the United States, the National Survey of Black Americans (NSBA). NSBA has a sample size of 2,107 and a response rate of 69%. This analysis will be conducted on the subsample of 581 respondents aged 55 and over.

The chapter is divided into seven sections relating to different aspects of religious involvement: (a) religious affiliation, (b) demographic correlates of religious participation (e.g., frequency of attendance, church membership, prayer, reading religious materials), (c) inter-correlations of religious indicators, (d) measurement models of religious involvement, (e) religion and mental health, (f) church members as a source of informal social support, and (g) perceptions of the sociohistorical role of black churches. Each individual section provides a brief summary and discussion of the findings, and the chapter concludes with a general and integrative discussion of the findings.

Table 7.1 Religious Affiliation of Elderly Respondents

Religious Affiliation	(%)	(N)
Congregational	.3	2
Episcopalian	1.2	7
Lutheran	.2	1
Presbyterian	1.6	9
United Church of Christ	.2	1
African Methodist Episcopal	3.1	18
Baptist	54.7	317
Disciples of Christ	.2	1
Methodist	13.6	79
CME (Methodist)	.3	2
Apostolic	.2	1
Church of Christ	1.0	6
Church of God	.5	3
Church of God and Christ	1.0	6
Fundamentalist Baptist	4.0	23
Pentecostal or Assembly of God	.9	5
Sanctified	.9	5
Seventh Day Adventist	.2	1
Christian	.3	2
Protestant—no denomination given	.3	2
Nondenominational Protestant Church	.5	3
Community Church—no denomination given	.2	1
Roman Catholic	5.7	33
Holiness	2.8	16
Jehovah's Witness	1.2	7
Spiritualist	.2	1
Unity	.2	1
Bahai	.2	1
None-no preference	4.0	23
Atheist-agnostic	.2	1
Other	.2	1

Religious Affiliation

Information on religious affiliation was obtained for respondents' current and childhood affiliation, as well as for respondents' parents. Table 7.1 presents a descriptive profile of the current religious affiliation of elderly respondents. In total, 28 different religious affiliations

Table 7.2 Univariate Distribution of the Current and Childhood Religious Affiliation of Respondents and the Religious Affiliations of the Respondents' Parents (in percentages)

	Baptist	Methodist	Other	Total (N)
Current Religious Affiliation	61.6	14.3	24.1	100.0(552)
Respondents' Childhood Religious Affiliation	65.4	19.6	15.0	100.0(565)
Respondents' Mother's Religious Affiliation	66.3	19.5	14.2	100.0(558)
Respondents' Father's Religious Affiliation	65.4	20.2	14.4	100.0(500)

NOTE: The percentages for respondents' current religious affiliation in Tables 7.1 and 7.2 differ slightly; only respondents who expressed a religious preference are included in Table 7.2, and "Baptist" includes both general and Fundamentalist Baptist.

are reported (excluding the groups, "none-no preference," "atheist-agnostic," and "other"), indicating considerable breadth and variety in religious affiliation. Over half of the respondents stated that they are currently Baptist (54.7%), 13.6% reported being Methodist, 5.7% Roman Catholic, and the remaining 21% reporting a religious preference are divided among 25 distinct religious groups. Finally, only 4% of respondents report that they currently have no religious affiliation.

Table 7.2 presents a univariate distribution of the current and childhood religious affiliation of the respondent and the religious affiliation of respondent's parents. For the purposes of this analysis, religious affiliation has been trichotomized into Baptist, Methodist, and Other. The data in Table 7.2 demonstrate general similarity in the current religious affiliation of respondents and that of their parents. Overwhelmingly, the majority of respondents and their parents are either Baptist or Methodist. Comparing respondents' current religious affiliation with their childhood affiliation and their parents' affiliation reveals that respondents are slightly less likely to indicate presently that they are Baptist or Methodist and more likely to indicate that they have another affiliation.

As might be expected from the comparable percentage distributions for these variables, the bivariate relationships (not shown) between the respondents' current religious affiliation and both childhood and parental religious affiliation are very strong. A comparison of the bivariate measures of association (Cramer's V) indicates that mother's religious affiliation may have a stronger impact than does father's affiliation on respondents' current religious choice.

The finding of a strong association between respondents' religious affiliation and that of their parents is consistent with other research. Several researchers have reported at least 70% agreement between the religious affiliation of adult children and that of their parents (e.g., Hill, Nelson, Aldous, Carlson, & MacDonald, 1970). Similarly, the presence of a stronger relationship between the respondents' and their mother's religious affiliation is consistent with other work. A higher level of agreement on religious beliefs and practices is found between mothers and children than between fathers and children (Hill et al., 1970). Collectively, these findings reinforce the importance of parents, the mother in particular, in transmitting religious beliefs, practices, and primary religious affiliation.

There are several other published works that investigate religious affliation and utilize the complete age range of the NSBA data. Taylor and Chatters (1991b) present a similar analysis on the profile of religious affliation over the life course of black Americans. Ellison and Sherkat (1990) and Sherak and Ellison (1991) conducted some of the most extensive sociological analysis of the patterns of religious affiliation among black Americans. Ellison and Sherkat (1990) examined the degree to which black Americans switched their religious preferences between 1972 and 1988 using data from both NSBA and the General Social Survey (1972-1988). They found that overall religious affiliation among black churches is relatively stable. There were small declines in the percent of black respondents who were Baptist, Methodist, Catholic, or affliated with predominatly white organizations. Among those who did switch affiliations, Baptists were more likely to switch to small conservative Protestant groups, Methodists were more likely to become Baptists, and Catholics and those raised without formal religious ties were more likely to affliate with nontraditional religions. Sherkat and Ellison (1991) found that in comparison to respondents who were raised in mainline religous denominations (Baptists, Methodists), religious switchers (blacks who were raised in one demonination but had a different current religious affliation at the time of the survey) were more likely to be married, reside in urban areas, and support political protest to gain equal rights, but they exhibited lower levels of racial group identity. In addition, Ellison (1991) found that members of traditional black religious denominations (i.e., Methodists) express substantially stronger black identity than do blacks who are unaffliated with a denomination.

Demographic Correlates of Religious Participation

This section of the chapter presents a multivariate analysis of demographic differences in religious participation among older black adults. Following recommendations from previous research, diverse indicators of religious involvement, including organizational (e.g., church attendance, church membership), nonorganizational (e.g., prayer, reading religious materials), and attitudinal (e.g., subjective religiosity) measures are examined. The demographic variables that are examined include gender, age, marital status, urbanicity, region, education, and income. In addition, descriptive information on the personal significance of religion and religious service attendance is included. A more in-depth examination of several of these dependent variables is found in Taylor (1986) and Taylor and Chatters (1991a).

Religious Service Attendance

One major indicator of the spiritual and social importance of religion is the frequency of participation in religious services. Only 20 (3.4%) respondents reported that they have not attended religious services since they were 18 years old (other than for weddings and funerals). Five percent of respondents reported that they attend religious services nearly every day, 46.9% at least once a week, 30.2% a few times a month, 9.4% a few times a year, and 7.9% report less than once a year. Regression analysis revealed that gender, marital status, and urbanicity were significantly associated with the frequency of attending religious services. Women attended services on a more frequent basis than did men, and married respondents attended religious services more frequently than widowed and divorced respondents.

Importance of Attending Religious Services

Respondents were also questioned as to how important to them was attending religious services. Nine out of 10 respondents (92.7%) reported that attending religious services is very important to them, 5.4% stated that it is fairly important, and only 2% stated that attendance is not too important or not important at all. Regression analysis revealed that marital status and region were significantly associated with expressed importance of attending religious services, and income and the dummy variable of being widowed bordered significance. Divorced and widowed respondents assign less importance to attending religious services than do married persons; persons residing in the North Central region attribute a greater importance to attending religious services as compared to respondents who reside in the South. In addition, income is negatively associated with the importance of attending religious services.

Respondents who indicated that attending religious services is either very important or fairly important were further asked: "What is the one most important thing it does for you?" Responses to this question were coded into five main categories: general help, emotional well-being, religious/spiritual experience, social well-being, and physical well-being. Over half (52.6%) of the respondents reported that the most important thing that they receive from attending religious services is emotional well-being. Some of the typical responses found in the emotional well-being category are general positive feelings (17.6%) (e.g., makes me proud; makes me feel good; gives me peace, comfort, and security), helps overcome problems and bad feelings (18.0%) (e.g., keeps me from feeling low or depressed, relieves me of problems), and sustains and strengthens me (16.4%) (e.g., helps me get by from day to day, something to look forward to). Religious and spiritual experience was reported by another 39.6%, and the remaining respondents stated that social well-being (3.6%), general help (6.9%), and physical well-being (0.4%) are the benefits that they derive from attendance.

Church Membership

Three out of four (77.6%) respondents indicated that they are official members of a church or other place of worship. Multivariate analysis revealed that women are more likely than men and divorced respondents less likely than married respondents to be church members. In addition, rural respondents have a greater tendency than urban respondents to be church members. Respondents who indicated that they are official members of churches were further asked how often they participated in other church-related activities in addition to religious services. Five percent reported that they participate in additional church-related activities nearly every day, 29% at least once a week, 33% a few times a month, and 16% a few times a year (17% of persons identified as official church members reported that they do not participate in any activities other than religious services). None of the demographic variables have significant bivariate associations with frequency of participation in other church-related activities. When asked about church clubs and organizations, 6 out of 10 persons who are official members and who also are involved in extra activities indicated that they also hold church positions or offices. Bivariate analysis does not reveal any significant demographic differences in whether or not respondents hold church offices or positions.

Private, Nonorganizational Religious Behaviors

In addition to public forms of religious behaviors, private religious activities (e.g., reading, watching or listening to religious programs) are reported by older black adults.

Reading Religious Materials Close to half of the respondents (43.9%) reported reading religious books and materials nearly every day, and another 23.9% read religious books at least weekly. Regression analyses for frequency of reading religious materials indicate that gender, religious denomination, and an interaction term combining educational level and region are significantly related to reading religious materials ($R^2 = .19$). Women reported reading religious materials more frequently than men. Denominational differences reveal that Catholics and persons with no religious preference read religious materials less frequently than do Baptists (the coefficient for other religious affiliations borders significance). The significant interaction indicates that the relationship between educational level and reading religious materials varies in relation to region of the country. Calculations of the dummy variable coefficients indicate that among Southerners there is a positive association between education and reading religious materials, whereas among respondents who resided in other regions there was no relationship between reading religious materials and education.

Watching or Listening to Religious Programs One third of the respondents indicated that they watch or listen to broadcast religious programs nearly every day (33.8%), 50.1% indicated at least once a week, 9.0% stated a few time a week, 4.0% stated a few times a month, and 3.1% indicated never. Region, education, denomination, and health disability factors explain 16% of the variation in the frequency of watching or listening to religious programming. Denominational differences indicate that Methodists, Catholics, and those with no religious preference listen to or view religious programs at significantly lower

levels than do Baptists. Persons residing in the Northeast listen/view at
lower rates than do Southerners (effect for persons in the West borders
significance). Older persons with poor health are more likely to view
or listen to religious programs than their healthier counterparts, whereas
education level (borders significance) is negatively associated with this
activity.

Prayers Respondents reported that they engage in prayer on a frequent basis; 9 out of 10 indicated that they pray nearly every day
(93.6%). Age and gender are significantly related to the frequency of
prayer, such that older respondents pray on a more frequent basis than
their younger counterparts, and women pray more often than men.
Marital status differences bordered significance, with divorced and
widowed respondents praying on a less frequent basis than married
respondents. Denominational differences indicate that persons with no
religious preference make up the only group that significantly departs
from the behavior of Baptists.

Requests for Prayer Eighteen percent (17.9%) of respondents reported that they ask someone to pray for them nearly every day; 24.2%
at least once a week; 20.5% a few times a month; 14.6% a few times a
year; and 22.8% reported that they never request prayer from others.
Gender and marital status are significantly related to requests for
prayer. Women ask someone to pray for them more often than men, and
divorced respondents ask someone to pray for them on a less frequent
basis than married respondents.

Subjective Religiosity

Information on respondents' own individual perceptions of religiosity were elicited by the question: "How religious would you say you
are—very religious, fairly religious, not too religious, or not religious
at all?" Overall, respondents reported that they consider themselves to
be religious, with 59.4% stating that they were very religious, 35.2%
fairly religious, and 5.4% stating either not too religious or not religious
at all. Dummy variable regression revealed that women are significantly
more likely to characterize themselves as being religious than are men,
and both divorced and widowed respondents reported being less religious than their married counterparts. Further, an age effect was found
among this group of respondents who are 55 years and older, whereby

relatively older persons reported being more religious than their younger counterparts.

Respondents who reported being either very religious or fairly religious were asked the follow-up question: "What is the one most important thing religion gives you or does for you?" Over half (50.1%) of the respondents stated that the one most important function of religion was to provide a sense of emotional well-being. This was followed by reports of enhanced religious or spiritual experiences (43.4%), social well-being (1.4%), and physical well-being (1.3%). Two of the most prevalent responses in the spiritual and religious experience category were moral guidance (23.9%) (e.g., learning to do what is right, live in a righteous way, it keeps me from sinning, and do for others) and religious understanding of faith (13.3%) (e.g., helps me believe in God; religion gives me wisdom, knowledge, and understanding).

Discussion of Findings

The findings are consistent with other research revealing a high level of involvement in religious activities among older black adults (Hirsch et al., 1972; M. Jackson & Wood, 1976). The elderly black adults in this sample reported that they attended religious services frequently, felt that attending religious services was very important, had a high probability of being church members, and expressed a high degree of subjective religiosity. Further, information on private religious behaviors revealed that overall, older persons prayed, read religious materials, and watched or listened to religious programming on a frequent basis. Prayer was the most prevalent nonorganizational religious activity, followed by reading religious books, watching or listening to religious services on television or radio, and soliciting prayer from others.

Discussions of the importance of attending church, and more generally, the importance of religion, revealed the nature of older black adults' conception of the role of religion and the church. In particular, respondents noted that religion and religious institutions were instrumental in enhancing emotional well-being and promoting a personal sense of spirituality. Religion may be crucial in enhancing feelings of self-regard, such as self-esteem, and in reducing negative feeling states that arise from stress. With reference to issues of personal spirituality, respondents indicated that religion provides a framework for behavior in the form of moral teachings and guidance, and further, assisted in their understanding and deepening of religious faith. Based on these findings, it is evident that religion and religious services and activities are multidimensional and are an integral part of the lives of older blacks.

Gender produced the most consistent demographic differences for the religious indicators: Women consistently reported being more involved in religion and religious activities than did men. Women were more likely to be church members and to report a higher degree of subjective religiosity than men, and additionally, attended religious services, read religious material, prayed, and requested prayer from others on a more frequent basis. These findings are consistent with previous research on gender differences in religious involvement among elderly adults (Bengtson, Kasschau, & Ragan, 1977; Britton & Britton, 1972; Petrowsky, 1976; Riley & Foner, 1968; see Levin & Taylor, in press, for an analysis of gender differences in religious participation among blacks across the life cycle).

It is important to note that despite the higher level of religious involvement among women, they were no more likely than men to hold a church office or position. One possible explanation for these two findings could be that overall men have higher status in churches than women. So that despite the fact that women outnumber men as church members and frequent attenders, those men who are extensively involved may be more likely than women to hold church offices (e.g., ministers, deacons, board of trustees members).

Marital status was significantly related to several of the religious involvement indicators as well. Divorced and widowed respondents (in comparison to married persons), attended religious services less frequently, reported that attending religious services was less important, prayed on a less frequent basis, and characterized themselves as being less religious. Divorced respondents were also less likely to be church members or to request prayer from others than married respondents. These findings contradict earlier research on marital status and religious involvement that indicated that widows have slightly more contact with religious organizations than do married individuals (Berardo, 1967; Petrowsky, 1976). The present findings indicate that among older black adults, divorced and widowed respondents exhibit lower levels of religious involvement than married respondents.

The findings of positive relationships between age and subjective religiosity and prayer are generally consistent with other research on age differences in religiosity. Moberg (1965) found that religious beliefs and feelings increase and intensify with age. Similarly, several studies have reported positive relationships between age and the frequency of prayer (Johnson, Brekke, Strommen, & Underwager, 1974; Moberg, 1971). In contrast, Markides's (1983) longitudinal study of older Mexican Americans and whites found no significant change in frequency of private prayer across a 4-year period.

The present findings indicate that poor health does not have a negative impact on the frequency of attending religious services among older black adults. This finding is significant in view of the number of serious chronic illnesses and the high amount of bed disability and restricted activity days older black adults suffer as a group (Taylor & Taylor, 1982; U.S. Department of Commerce, 1980). In a similar vein, previous research would also predict a negative relationship between age and frequency of attending religious services. In contrast with other work suggesting that older respondents curtail their involvement (i.e., disengage) in religious and other types of voluntary associations (Barron, 1961), the present findings do not indicate a significant decrease in religious services attendance among older respondents. Neither age nor health status had a significant impact on religious service attendance among this group of older black adults.

Chatters and Taylor's (1989) examination of religiosity utilizing the entire age range of the NSBA sample helps to clarify the relationship between age and church attendance. In that study, rates of church attendance demonstrated a steady increase from the youngest age groups on. Further, the increase in church attendance was particularly conspicuous among respondents 55 to 74 years of age, whereas a slight decrease was noted among respondents who were 75 years of age and older. It is important to note that the decrease in attendance among the oldest respondents was minimal; men 75 years of age and older attended services more frequently than their counterparts aged 18 to 64 and women 75 years of age attended services on a more frequent basis than their counterparts who are 18-44 years of age (Chatters & Taylor, 1989). These findings suggest that when considered as a separate group, age variation in church attendance the older population is minimized. But the overall pattern of increasing levels of attendance among older age groups is much more discernible when the entire adult age range is considered.

It was initially expected that elderly black adults who possessed lower levels of income and education would exhibit a higher degree of religious participation than their counterparts. This hypothesis, consistent with the deprivation-compensation model of religious participation (Glock, Ringer, & Babbie, 1967) predicts that extensive involvement compensates persons of lower socioeconomic status for blocked or restricted access to other social institutions. The model has apparent relevancy for elderly black adults who have suffered a lifetime of racism, coupled with much lower levels of income and education than their white counterparts (Taylor & Taylor, 1982). But the results of the present analysis failed to substantiate this theory. Income and educational status were not consistent indicators of religious participation, particularly as it relates to indicators of formally organized behaviors.

The only significant socioeconomic status effects were found for level of education and two forms of private religious activities. Education was positively associated with the frequency of reading religious materials and negatively related to the frequency of watching or listening to religious programming on television or radio. Because elderly black adults average few years of formal education, the effects of educational level possibly reflect differences in literacy levels. The pattern of findings suggests that persons in this sample with few years of formal education (and who presumably have reading difficulties) used religious radio and television programs as an alternative to reading religious materials. Collectively, these findings indicate that among older black adults, gender and marital status were more consistent indicators of religious participation than socioeconomic status factors.

Urbanicity was significantly associated with both the frequency of attending religious services and church membership. Rural respondents attended religious services more frequently and were more likely to be church members than urban respondents. Collectively, these findings indicate that older blacks who reside in rural areas are more involved with religious organizations than their urban counterparts. In terms of regional differences in religious involvement, respondents who resided in the South read religious materials on a more frequent basis, watched religious programming more frequently, and felt that attending religious services was more important than persons who resided in the Northeast. Respondents who resided in the North Central region, however, attributed a greater importance to attending religious services than did Southerners. Overall, these findings are consistent with other analyses conducted on the full age range of the NSBA data set (Taylor, 1988a, 1988b; Taylor, Thornton, & Chatters, 1987) indicating generally higher levels of religious involvement among blacks who reside in the South and corroborating the general depiction of the South as the "Bible Belt."

Table 7.3 Correlation Matrix of the Indicators of Religious Involvement

	1.	2.	3.	4.	5.	6.	7.	8.
1. Church Attendance								
2. Importance of Attending Religious Services	.21***							
3. Church Membership	.36***	.14***						
4. Frequency of Reading Religious Books	.24***	.06	.20***					
5. Frequency of Watching or Listening to Religious Programs	.08	.02	.06	.21***				
6. Frequency of Prayer	.11*	.10*	.23***	.26***	.23***			
7. Frequency of Having Others Pray for You	.15***	.04	.12**	.29***	.24***	.21***		
8. Degree of Religiosity	.33***	.24***	.17***	.09*	.07	.12**	.13**	
	1.	2.	3.	4.	5.	6.	7.	8.

*$p < .05$; **$p < .01$; ***$p < .001$.

Intercorrelations of Religious Indicators

Table 7.3 presents the correlation matrix of the behavioral and attitudinal indicators of religious involvement examined in this chapter. The correlations are positive (indicating congruence across behaviors and attitudes) and the majority of them are significant. None of the relationships are very strong; the largest correlation of .36 is observed for frequency of attending church and church membership. The lack of very strong relationships indicates that these factors, although related, are not identical with one another, and verifies the assertion that religious involvement is multidimensional and should be appropriately represented by several indicators. Turning to the correlations in Table 7.3:

Elderly black adults who attend religious services frequently are more likely to attribute a greater degree of importance to attending church, to being church members, to reading religious books, and to report being religious. Similarly, respondents who attribute a greater degree of importance to attending religious services are more likely to be church members and report a higher degree of religiosity. Church members tend to read religious books and pray more frequently than do nonmembers.

The four measures of the frequency of participating in nonorganizational religious activities (i.e., reading religious books, watching or listening to religious programs, praying, and having others pray for you) are moderately intercorrelated (each correlation is significant and varies between .20 and .29). Surprisingly, frequency of watching or listening to religious programs is not significantly related to the frequency of attending religious services, the importance of attending religious services, or church membership. It has been suggested that extensive religious radio and television programming might result in less frequent church attendance and lower levels of church membership, but the finding that almost 85% of the black elderly in this sample watch or listen to religious programming at least once a week, coupled with the lack of significant bivariate associations between this variable and the relevant church behaviors (i.e., church membership, belief in the importance of attending religious services, and church attendance), does not substantiate this speculation. The results of this analysis indicate that along with other religious activities, elderly blacks have incorporated religious media presentations into their weekly schedule.

Attitudes concerning the importance of attending religious services are not significantly related to reading religious materials, watching or listening to religious programs, or asking others to pray on one's behalf. The absence of significant associations with these variables may be due more to methodological than substantive reasons. With 92.7% of the respondents indicating that attending religious services is very important, there is very little variance to explain. On a substantive level, frequency of church attendance and degree of subjective religiosity are the strongest predictors of the importance of attending religious services. Further, subjective religiosity is significantly related to frequency of church attendance, attitudes about the importance of attending religious services, and church membership. Although subjective religiosity is significantly related to nonorganizational religious participation, these relationships are generally more modest in comparison. Subjective religiosity, or one's personal sense of religion, seems to be strongly associated with and derived from public church involvement and religious attitudes supporting such activities (i.e., importance of church attendance). In contrast, private, nonorganizational religious involvement (i.e., frequency of prayer, frequency of reading religious books) is less strongly related to subjective religiosity and may have a less central role in defining a personal sense of religiosity.

Measurement Models of Religious Involvement

The precise operationalization of religious involvement is a key psychometric issue. Owing to the diverse nature of religious experience (i.e., attitudinal versus behavioral dimensions, public versus private behaviors, intrinsic versus extrinsic religiosity), antecedent influences such as social-structure factors bear unique and individual relationships with specific dimensions of religious involvement. Considerable work is required in order to delineate the separate and distinct dimensions of religious involvement and to determine their independent relationships with social status indicators and relevant outcome measures. One fundamental way in which these aims can be achieved is through the development and confirmation of multidimensional measurement models of religious involvement. Although the development of multidimensional measurement models is increasingly popular in gerontology, it has been applied to religious involvement on only a few occasions. This section of the chapter discusses the findings of papers utilizing measurement models that have been conducted on NSBA data.

Chatters, Levin, and Taylor (in press) proposed and tested a measurement model of religiosity among older black Americans. The model incorporates three dimensions of religious involvement: formal or organizational religious behavior, informal or nonorganizational religious behavior, and intrinsic or subjective religiosity. Findings for the measurement model indicate that the proposed model provides a good fit to the data, is preferable to other alternative models of these relationships, and is acceptable with regard to convergent validity. Exogenous factors (i.e., age, gender, marital status, income, education, urbanicity, and region) perform largely as expected as predictors of religious involvement. They are, in addition, differentially predictive of the three latent religiosity constructs; greater variance is explained for intrinsic or subjective religiosity as compared to the two behavioral constructs. Interpretations for findings of status group differences in religiosity focus on socialization experiences and social environment factors which may promote a religious worldview.

A related analysis (Levin, Chatters, & Taylor, 1992), tested a structural-equation model linking the three dimensions of religiosity to health status and life satisfaction among black adults. Findings indicated that particular aspects of religious involvement exerted significant effects on life satisfaction net of both health and several key exogenous variables.

Lastly, the Krause and Tran (1989) investigation of the impact of religion on self-esteem also used NSBA data, but only a two-dimensional model of religiosity was examined, with nonorganizational religious behaviors and subjective religious attitudes left undifferentiated. The findings from this group of studies suggest that an oblique, three-factor model is both a conceptually preferable and empirically defensible specification of religiosity. The critical distinction, however, is between organizational/public participation and other forms of religious involvement.

Religion and Mental Health

A small group of studies has examined the relationship between religion and mental health within the NSBA data set. Analyses involving the entire age range of the NSBA data revealed that prayer was an option used by respondents to cope with a serious personal problem (Neighbors, J. S. Jackson, Bowman, & Gurin, 1982). Forty-four percent of respondents with such a problem stated that prayer was the coping strategy that was most beneficial. As the seriousness of problems increased, the likelihood that respondents used prayer as a coping response also increased. In addition, a large proportion of respondents reported that they sought specific assistance from ministers in coping with their serious personal problems.

Chatters and Taylor (1989) explored the use of prayer in connection with personal life problems reported by older black adults. The majority of respondents indicated that they had recently experienced at least one problem and identified problems in the areas of health and finances as being the most significant. One in six respondents with money problems reported using prayer as a coping mechanism; 2.6% of respondents with health problems used prayer to cope. Problem type appeared to have a pervasive influence on determining appropriate resource use (i.e., social services, health professionals) and individual responses to life problems. But the authors suggested that although religion and prayer may not be the primary coping mechanism used for the problems examined, they may serve as additional coping resources that ameliorate the emotional stress associated with health and money problems. Similarly, Krause and Tran (1989) found that among older black adults, perceived stress eroded feelings of self-esteem and personal control, but these negative effects of stress were offset by religious involvement.

Church Members as a Source of Informal Social Support

Historical and present-day evidence suggests that black churches are extensively involved in the provision of support to their members. Although it is generally accepted that church members are important sources of assistance to blacks, this issue has received surprisingly little systematic attention and scrutiny. Recent analysis has examined the role of church members as a source of informal support to elderly black adults (Taylor & Chatters, 1986a, 1986b) and blacks across the life course (Taylor & Chatters, 1988).

Church Members as a Source of Support to Black Adults

Taylor and Chatters (1988) explored both sociodemographic and religious factors as predictors of the receipt of support from church members. Overall, two out of three respondents (64.2%) indicated that church members provided some level of assistance to them. Among the religious variables, church attendance, church membership, subjective religiosity, and religious affiliation were all significantly related to the receipt of support. The salience of these involvement variables as determinants of the receipt of support is congruent with research on informal support networks and suggests that current assistance operates as a reward for one's past record of participation in church activities. Demographic differences indicated that men and younger respondents were more likely, and divorced respondents less likely, to receive aid. Catholics were less likely to receive support from church members than were Baptists. In addition, higher incomes and residency in rural areas were associated with never needing assistance from church members versus simply never receiving aid.

Role of Church Members in the
Support Networks of Aged Black Adults

In another analysis focusing on older black adults, Taylor and Chatters (1986a) examined three indicators of church support: frequency, amount, and type of support received from church members. Frequency of church attendance, as a form of public commitment, was a critical indicator of both the frequency of receiving assistance and the amount of aid provided. Respondents' subjective assessments of the importance of attending religious services was also positively associated with frequency of receiving support. Among the demographic factors, an interaction between age and the presence of adult children indicated that for those elderly persons with children, advanced age was associated with more frequent assistance from church members. But among childless elderly, advanced age was associated with dramatic decreases in the frequency of support from church members. This finding suggests that adult children may function to facilitate linkages to church support networks on behalf of their elderly parents.

Taylor and Chatters (1986b) examined whether elderly black adults received concurrent support from family, friends, and church members, and if so, the type of assistance provided. Descriptively, 8 out of 10 respondents received support from either a best or close friend, roughly 6 out of 10 received support from church members, and over half received support from extended family members. Only a minority of respondents were "socially isolated" in the sense that they did not have a best or close friend and failed to receive support from either family or church members.

Analysis of the type of support received from friends, family, and church members indicated that these groups may provide different types of aid. Respondents were more likely to receive either total or instrumental assistance (i.e., goods and services, financial assistance, and transportation) from family members and to receive companionship from friends. Similarly, respondents were more likely to receive advice and encouragement, help during sickness, and prayer from church members. In addition, bivariate analyses of the type and source of assistance demonstrated that individual support sources were distinctive in the assistance they provided to elderly black adults.

These findings indicate that the type of support received by elderly blacks may not be governed by hierarchical or task-specific constraints. Although these data indicate a general tendency to receive a particular type of assistance from one support group, there was considerable overlap in the type of support provided. In addition, although respondents were more likely to receive total support from family, over 5% of respondents who received assistance from friends and church members reported that they received total support from these sources. For certain groups of elderly blacks, friends and church members may be of greater importance than has been previously thought.

Perceptions of the Sociohistorical Role of the Church

Although there is a general consensus as to the prominent role of churches in black communities, theologians have debated the direction and character of its influence. Unfortunately, most discussions of the nature and role of black churches are limited by overemphasis on a single dimension of church functioning, which consequently obscures the multifaceted roles. This section of the chapter focuses on the multiple roles and functions of black churches by examining older black Americans' perceptions of the sociohistorical role of the church. In particular, respondents were asked to assess whether the church has helped, hurt, or made no difference in the condition of blacks in the United States.

The overwhelming majority of elderly black adults indicated that the church helped the condition of blacks in the United States (92.4%), whereas 2.3% reported that the church has been detrimental, and 5.3% reported that the church has made no difference. Respondents were then asked the follow-up question: "Why do you feel that way?" Persons who indicated that the church has helped the condition of blacks in the United States generally responded in one of two ways: (a) the church's influence has been in a spiritual manner (16%), or (b) the church has helped in the areas of personal and social advancement (52.7%). Respondents who reported that the church has helped spiritually state that it has helped either through increased religious activity (6.1%) or through meeting spiritual and religious goals and needs (9.9%). The responses of elderly blacks who reported that the church has helped personally and socially can be categorized into several distinct groups: (a) general positive feelings (2%), (b) sustains and strengthens (17.8%), (c) provides personal assistance (5.7%), (d) provides guidelines for moral behavior and personal conduct (29%), (e) source of unity/ community gathering place (12.7%), and (f) active in attaining specific goals or achieving social purposes for blacks (5.1%).

This analysis reveals extensive support for the perception that the church has had a beneficial impact on the lives of black Americans. Specific spheres of influence include the secular as well as the religious and occur on both the individual and community level. Analysis using the entire age range of NSBA data revealed significant demographic differences in perceptions of the sociohistorical role of the church, suggesting considerable diversity of opinion (Taylor, Thornton, & Chatters, 1987). Particularly noteworthy was that older respondents were more likely to indicate that the church has helped as opposed to hurt and were more likely to indicate that the church has helped as opposed to made no difference. This finding is consistent with the overall higher level of religious involvement and commitment of older black adults.

Summary

This chapter has presented a summary of recent analysis on religion and religious observance among elderly blacks. Overall, several conclusions can be drawn. First, as evidenced by the range and extent of religious involvement, religion and religious institutions play a prominent role in the lives of older black adults. Second, despite generally high levels of religiosity, older black adults display a considerable amount of heterogeneity in religious participation and attitudes. This is evident in the vast number of religious affiliations found among this group and observed demographic variation in the religious indicators. Related to the religiosity more generally, the moderate correlations among the religious involvement variables suggests that religiosity is best represented as a multidimensional construct that incorporates attitudes and behaviors occurring in both public and private domains. Third, accumulating evidence suggests that religion is important in maintaining positive mental health by helping reduce stress and enhance self-esteem. Last, older black adults view the role of religion and religious institutions as multidimensional and providing both emotional/personal support and well-being as well as spiritual guidance. Further, their conceptions of the role of black churches in a broader sense reinforce the perception that religion and its institutions have had a long and continuing positive influence on the development of black communities and individuals.

References

Barron, M. L. (1961). *The aging Americans: An introduction to social gerontology and geriatrics.* New York: Thomas Y. Crowell.

Bengtson, V. L., Kasschau, P. L., & Ragan, P. K. (1977). The impact of social structure on aging individuals. In J. E. Birren & K. W. Schaie (Eds.), *Handbook of the psychology of aging* (pp. 327-353). New York: Van Nostrand Reinhold.

Berardo, F. M. (1967). *Social adaptation to widowhood among a rural-urban aged population.* (Washington Agricultural Experiment Station Bulletin 689). Pullman, WA: Washington State University, College of Agriculture.

Britton, J. H., & Britton, J. 0. (1972). *Personality changes in aging.* New York: Springer.

Chatters, L. M., Levin, J. S., & Taylor, R. J. (in press). Antecedents and dimensions of religious involvement among older black adults. *Journal of Gerontology: Social Sciences.*

Chatters, L. M., & Taylor, R. J. (1989). Age differences in religious participation among black adults. *Journal of Gerontology: Social Sciences, 44,* S183-S189.

Clemente, F., Rexroad, P. A., & Hirsch, C. (1975). The participation of the black aged in voluntary associations. *Journal of Gerontology, 30,* 469-472.

Ellison, C. G. (1991). Identification and separatism: Religious involvement and racial orientations among black Americans. *Sociological Quarterly, 32,* 477-494.

Ellison, C. G., & Sherkat, D. E. (1990). Patterns of religious mobility among black Americans. *Sociological Quarterly, 31,* 123-147.

Glock, C. Y., Ringer, B. R., & Babbie, E. E. (1967). *To comfort and to challenge.* Berkeley: University of California Press.

Greeley, A. M. (1989). *Religious change in America.* Cambridge, MA: Harvard University Press.

Heyman, D. K., & Jeffers, F. C. (1970). The influence of race and socioeconomic status upon the activities and attitudes of the aged. In E. Palmore (Ed.), *Normal aging: Reports from the Duke longitudinal study, 1955-1969* (pp. 304-310). Durham, NC: Duke University Press.

Hill, R., Nelson, F., Aldous, J., Carlson, R., & MacDonald, R. (1970). *Family development in three generations: A longitudinal study of changing family patterns of planning and achievement.* Cambridge, MA: Schenkman.

Hirsch, C., Kent, D. P., & Silverman, S. L. (1972). Homogeneity and heterogeneity among low-income negro and white aged. In D. P. Kent, R. Kastenbaum, & S. Sherwood (Eds.), *Research planning and action for the elderly: The power and potential of social science* (pp. 400-500). New York: Behavioral Publications.

Hunter, W. W., & Maurice, H. (1953). *Older people tell their story.* Ann Arbor: Institute for Human Adjustment, Division of Gerontology, University of Michigan.

Jackson, M., & Wood, J. L. (1976). *Aging in America: Implications for the black aged.* Washington, DC: National Council of the Aging.

Johnson, A. L., Brekke, M. L., Strommen, M., & Underwager, R. C. (1974). Age differences and dimensions of religious behavior. *Journal of Social Issues, 30,* 43-67.

Krause, N., & Tran, T. V. (1989). Stress and religious involvement among older blacks. *Journal of Gerontology: Social Sciences, 44,* S4-13.

Levin, J. S., Chatters, L. M., & Taylor, R. J. (1992). *A structural model of religiosity, health status, and life satisfaction in black Americans.* Manuscript submitted for publication.

Levin, J. S., & Taylor, R. J. (in press). Gender differences in religious participation across the life span. *The Gerontologist.*

Markides, K. (1983). Aging, religiosity, and adjustment: A longitudinal analysis. *Journal of Gerontology, 36,* 621-625.

Moberg, D. O. (1965). Religiosity in old age. *The Gerontologist, 5(2),* 78-87.

Moberg, D. O. (1971). *Spiritual well-being: Background and issues.* Washington, DC: White House Conference on Aging.

Neighbors, H. W., Jackson, J. S., Bowman, P. J., & Gurin, G. (1982). Stress, coping and black mental health: Preliminary findings from a national study. *Prevention in Human Services, 2,* 5-29.

Petrowsky, M. (1976). Marital status, sex, and the social networks of the elderly. *Journal of Marriage and the Family, 38(3),* 749-756.

Princeton Religion Research Center. (1982). *1982 Religion in America.* Princeton, NJ: Gallup Poll.

Princeton Religion Research Center. (1984). *1984 Religion in America.* Princeton, NJ: Gallup Poll.

Riley, M., & Foner, A. (1968). *Aging and society: Vol. 1. An inventory of research findings.* New York: Russell Sage.

Sherkat, D. E., & Ellison, C. G. (1991). The politics of black religious change: Disaffiliation from black mainline denominations. *Social Forces, 70,* 431-454.

Taylor, R. J. (1986). Religious participation among elderly blacks. *The Gerontologist, 26,* 630-636.

Taylor, R. J. (1988a). Correlates of religious non-involvement among black Americans. *Review of Religious Research, 30,* 126-139.

Taylor, R. J. (1988b). Structural determinants of religious participation among black Americans. *Review of Religious Research, 30,* 114-125.

Taylor, R. J., & Chatters, L. M. (1986a). Church-based informal support among elderly blacks. *The Gerontologist, 26,* 637-642.

Taylor, R. J., & Chatters, L. M. (1986b). Patterns of informal support to elderly black adults: Family, friends, and church members. *Social Work, 31,* 432-438.

Taylor, R. J., & Chatters, L. M. (1988). Church members as a source of informal social support. *Review of Religious Research, 30,* 193-203.

Taylor, R. J., & Chatters, L. M. (1991a). Non-organizational religious participation among elderly blacks. *Journal of Gerontology: Social Sciences, 46,* S102-S111.

Taylor, R. J., & Chatters, L. M. (1991b). Religious life of black Americans. In J. S. Jackson (Ed.), *Life in black America* (pp. 105-123). Newbury Park, CA: Sage.

Taylor, R. J., & Taylor, W. H. (1982). The social and economic status of the black elderly. *Phylon, 43,* 295-306.

Taylor, R. J., Thornton, M. C., & Chatters, L. M. (1987). Black American's perception of the socio-historical role of the church. *Journal of Black Studies, 18,* 123-138.

U.S. Department of Commerce, Bureau of the Census. (1980). Social and economic status of the black population. *Current Population Reports* (Series P-23, No. 85). Washington, DC: Government Printing Office.

Wingrove, C. R., & Alston, J. P. (1974). Cohort analysis of church attendance, 1939-1969. *Social Forces, 53,* 324-331.

8

FUNCTION AND SUPPORTIVE ROLES OF CHURCH AND RELIGION

Jacqueline M. Smith

Writers have long attributed a myriad of functions to the church in the African-American community. Some writers suggest that during slavery the church functioned as an agency of social control (Frazier, 1968) and a refuge for the weary spirits of slaves in a hostile white world. Still others suggest that during the Reconstruction era and the waves of black exodus to urban areas, the church functioned as a source of economic cooperation (Dubois, 1973; Mukenge, 1983; Raboteau, 1980) and a sponsor of education. Frazier (1968) argued that the church has "left its imprint upon practically every aspect of Negro life. The Negro church has provided the pattern for the organization of mutual aid societies and insurance companies. It has provided the pattern of Negro fraternal organizations and Greek letter societies" (p. 85). And during the civil rights era, observers (Marx, 1967; Morris, 1984; Nelsen & Nelsen, 1975) point out that the church was an arena for political functions. The church, then, has functioned as "the tie that binds" the fabric of institutions, organizations, and diverse forms of socially created structures that sustain and vitalize life in the African-American community.

Literature Review

Theories of Church Involvement

What, then, is the function or role of the church in the lives of the black aged? Theories such as family surrogate theory, compensation theory, and so forth that explain church involvement offer possible explanations of the role of the church in the lives of the black aged. These theories view involvement as an indicator of social integration and tend to focus on economic deprivation and psychosocial deprivation as factors that influence involvement in organizations like the church.

Family Surrogate Theory Glock and Stark (1965) argued that the principal source of church involvement is social deprivation. When Glock, Ringer, and Babbie (1967) examined the differences between family structures in a study of the church involvement of Episcopalians, they found that unmarried and married but childless persons were more involved in the church than married persons with children. Labeling the unmarried and the married but childless adults as deviants whose family situations do not reflect the "normal" life cycle, Glock et al. (1967) suggested that the high levels of church involvement of these groups results from the church's functioning as a family surrogate for those who find themselves deprived of family relationships. Thus, family surrogate theory implies that unmarried and married but childless adults are psychologically deprived because they are not integrated into primary groups like the family.

Subsequent studies have not replicated Glock and Stark's (1965) findings, and offer, at best, mixed support for family surrogate theory. Christiano (1986) found that the presence or absence of children had no statistically significant effect on church involvement. In addition, he found that spouseless or unmarried church members were more likely than married respondents to demonstrate low levels of church involvement. Christiano also found that gender and marital status interact in that spouseless women and married men were more likely to report high levels of church involvement.

In a provincewide sample of adults in Alberta, Canada, Hobart (1974) found that only among Nazarenes, Jehovah's Witness, and Pentecostals (as compared with Roman Catholics, Presbyterians, and Lutherans) was church attendance and participation in church organizations higher among the elderly widowed than among those with families. Mueller and Johnson (1975) in a national sample found, for whites, higher average frequency of church participation among the married with children and the unmarried without children than among the married but childless or the unmarried with children. In addition, when the effects of marital status and the presence of children were added to the measured effects of economic deprivation, the explained variance of church involvement increased only 5%.

Deprivation Theory Family surrogate theory can be seen as a variation of deprivation theory, a theoretical approach that attempts to account for the levels of church involvement of blacks, the aged, and low-status groups by focusing on structural isolation or deprivation. Some sociologists argue that the marginal structural position and low level of social integration of low-status groups and persons, like blacks and the aged, have resulted not only in deprivation of material resources, but psychological alienation and deprivation of or separation from social relationships. According to these theorists (Glock & Stark, 1965; Glock et al., 1967; Niebuhr, 1957), the socially deprived escape to the comforts available from the church as a formal organization and use religion as a means of compensation for that deprivation. Thus, some sociologists argue that the relatively high levels of church involvement of blacks, women, and the aged are types of compensatory behavior and attitudes caused by high levels of psychological deprivation and relatively low levels of social integration (Demereath, 1974; Marx, 1967).

Social Participation Theories

Theories that account for church involvement can be seen as a subset of more general theories explaining racial variation in rates of participation in voluntary associations. Generally, this body of theories explains racial differences in social participation as an outcome of the combined effects of attitudes and socioeconomic status (Williams & St. Peter, 1979). Findings from these studies, which sometimes treat church participation as a form of voluntary association participation, are somewhat inconsistent. Writers who have attempted to interpret early findings that blacks participate less frequently in voluntary associations than whites (Hyman & Wright, 1971; Wright & Hyman, 1958) either argue that inappropriate cultural attitudes and social skills of blacks inhibit black social participation or that structural isolation (Lipset, 1960) is the source of black-white differences in rates of participation in voluntary associations. Some writers (Babchuk & Thompson, 1963; Myrdal, 1944; Williams & St. Peter, 1973) who have observed that blacks have higher rates of voluntary association participation than whites argue that blacks, bruised by discriminatory practices in the larger society, seek to bolster low self-esteem (i.e., overcompensate) and obtain social recognition in voluntary associations; others argue that blacks, as a result of heightened ethnic community cohesiveness (Olsen, 1970), participate in groups in order to collectively solve problematic aspects of minority group status.

In an attempt to determine the validity of competing theoretical perspectives accounting for social participation (overcompensation, cultural inhibition, ethnic compensation, and normal participation), Guterbock and London (1983) examined the effects of political efficacy and trust, socioeconomic status, and race on social participation (including participation in religious organizations). They found after controlling for the effects of socioeconomic status, gender, region, urbanism, and denomination that blacks with a high sense of political efficacy and a low sense of trust in the political system demonstrated greater overall social and political participation than any other group. Thus, their work suggests that under some circumstances, a low degree of integration into social structure (i.e., alienation) is associated with low levels of social participation (including participation in religious organizations).

Perspective on both the general theory of deprivation and its special variation—family surrogate theory—can be gained by examination of another important theoretical viewpoint, found in the seminal writings of Emile Durkheim (1956). Durkheim suggested that involvement in organizations like the church and in primary groups like the family enhances involvement in organizations of the larger society. Participating and becoming involved in the patterned activities of social life serves to attach each person occupying a specific position in the social structure to other persons occupying related structural positions. Thus, the more one is involved, the more one gets involved. Isolation also generally diffuses throughout the web of social relationships and weakens individual involvement (i.e., integration) in society. Durkheim's work, then, suggests that the church, as well as other socially created structures, functions to integrate or attach individuals to the social structure.

If, indeed, social integration is associated with physical and psychological well-being, then the integrative function of the church may benefit the well-being of the black aged. Studies have demonstrated that participation in organized religious activities and cognitive commitment to religious beliefs are significantly correlated with morale, adjustment, and subjective coping (Koenig, Kvale, & Ferrel, 1988; Koenig, George, & Siegler, 1988; Markides, 1983; Steinitz, 1980). Indeed, religiosity accounted for approximately 13% of the explained variance in morale. Further, participation in organizational religious activities (attendance at services, Bible study groups, prayer groups, and Sunday school classes) contributed more to the explained variance of subjective well-being than participation in nonorganizational religious activities (private prayer, devotional reading, and religious TV viewing or radio listening). Attendance at church services and church membership are associated with the receipt of church-based informal (Taylor & Chatters, 1986) and formal (Lindsay & Hawkins, 1974) support among aged blacks. Krause and Tran (1989) demonstrated that religiosity is positively associated with self-esteem and mastery. Interestingly, religiosity does not appear to be stress responsive. Thus, religiosity can have beneficial effects on mastery and self-esteem even in the absence of life crises (Krause & Tran, 1989). The church also functions, via ministerial counseling, as a mechanism to assist individuals in coping with stressful life events (Neighbors, Jackson, Bowman, & Gurin, 1982).

Empirical Studies of Church Involvement of Aged Blacks

Empirical studies of the church involvement of aged blacks demonstrate that achieved social statuses (income and education) are not associated with participation in formal church activities (Taylor, 1986). Community studies of the general population, however, have found that socioeconomic status, when operationalized as educational attainment, does have a significant effect on attendance at church services (Adams & Britain, 1987).

The achieved status of marriage also appears to be associated with attendance at church services. Elderly married blacks were more likely, net the effects of gender, region, age, socioeconomic status indicators, and health disability, to frequently attend church services as compared to the divorced and separated (Taylor, 1986). In addition, urbanicity has a significant effect on attendance at church services. Rural elderly blacks are more likely than the urban black elderly to frequently attend church services (Taylor, 1986).

Studies of the religious involvement of the black aged have demonstrated that when church involvement is operationalized as attendance at church services, the socially ascribed status of gender does have a statistically significant effect on church involvement. Taylor (1986) found that when the effects of urbanicity, region, age, education, income, and health disability were controlled, elderly black women attended church services more frequently and were more likely to be church members than elderly black men. Taylor's findings are consistent with other studies (Heisel & Faulkner, 1982) that have demonstrated gender differences in religious behavior in the black aged population.

Methodology

Existing theories explaining church participation, or the more general phenomenon of participation in voluntary associations suggest that: (a) the structural form of primary groups, (b) the structural position (i.e., where an individual or group stands in relation to another individual or group) in more complex social organizational forms (e.g., voluntary associations, social class, economic strata, and reference groups, etc.), and (c) the nature of an individual's attachment to various social structures (i.e., the degree of social integration) affect participation in organizations and associations.

Research Strategy

The existing literature provides a theoretical context for several research questions that will serve as the focus of this study. These are:

1. What is the effect of the family (i.e., structural relationships and perceived closeness) on involvement in the activities of the church?
2. What are the effects of occupying the larger society's structural positions (socioeconomic statuses) on involvement in activities of social institutions like the church?
3. If the effects of an individual's structural location in complex social organizational forms (occupational and economic strata) are controlled, what is the effect of the form or structure of family life on church involvement?

To empirically answer the first question, I will test the hypothesis suggested by family surrogate theory that:

The unmarried (never married with children, once married with children, once married childless, never married childless) and those persons who are married but childless are more involved in church activities than persons who are married and have children (Hypothesis 1).

Durkheim's seminal work *Suicide* suggested that social participation in general is a consequence of the regulative pressures that social structure exerts on individual behavior. The overall configuration of social structures consists of two components—interdependent positions and sentiments that connect or bond persons occupying the positions. Structures vary in the amount of regulative pressure exerted on individual behavior because of differences in these two structural components. It seems reasonable, therefore, to assume that the effects of sentiments such as closeness to primary group members directly affect levels of participation and probably even mediate the effects of family structure on church involvement.

Deprivation theory suggests that persons with low achieved statuses (i.e., low socioeconomic status) have high levels of church involvement because involvement in church activities serves as compensation for low status rewards in the larger society; to address this point, I will test the following hypothesis suggested by deprivation theory:

Persons with relatively low socioeconomic status (low income, low level of education, and low occupational prestige) are more likely to have high levels of involvement in church activities than persons with relatively high socioeconomic status (high income, high level of education, and high occupational prestige) (Hypothesis 2).

Age and gender are ascribed statuses that some researchers have demonstrated to be associated with church involvement (Adams & Britain, 1987; Petrowsky, 1976; Riley & Foner, 1968). Older people and women are generally assumed to have lower or more marginal structural positions than younger persons and men. Deprivation theory, then, suggests the following testable hypothesis:

Women and the "old old" will report high levels of church involvement more frequently than men and "young old" (Hypothesis 3).

Sample Description

Most respondents (47%) attended church services at least once a week, and most (60%) reported that church services were held one to

three times a week. An overwhelming majority (93%) of study participants reported that going to church services was "very important." A
smaller portion of the sample reported high rates of participation in
activities other than services. More specifically, 29% of those sampled
reported that they participated in church activities other than services
one to three times a week. Substantial numbers of aged blacks also
reported that they are involved in nonorganizational religious activities.
Sixty percent of those sampled reported that they read religious books
nearly every day. Forty-four percent of the sample report that they
watch religious TV or listen to religious radio programs one to three
times a week. Fifty-nine percent of the sample report that they are very
religious (see Table 8.1). The majority (67%) of sampled respondents
also appear to feel that they are very close to their family. Fifty-five
percent of the sample also have a best friend to whom they feel close.

Measures

Church involvement was indicated by responses to questions concerning frequency of attendance at church services and activities, and
number of church organizations in which the respondent participated.
Frequency of attendance at church services was measured by response
to the question: "How often do you usually attend religious services?
Would you say nearly every day, at least once a week, a few times a
month, a few times a year, or less than once a year?" Frequency of
participation in church activities other than services was measured by
response to the question: "Beside regular service, how often do you take
part in other activities at your place of worship? Would you say nearly
every day, at least once a week, a few times a month, a few times a year,
or never?" The importance of going to church services was measured
by response to the question: "How important is going to church or a
place of worship to you? Is it very important, fairly important, not too
important, or not important at all?" Level of participation in nonorganizational religious activities was measured by a summary index
score that represented responses to four questions. Respondents were
asked: "How religious would you say you are—very religious, fairly
religious, not too religious, or not religious at all?" Respondents were
also asked "How often do you read religious materials?" "How often
do you watch or listen to religious programs on TV or radio?" "How
often do you pray?" For each of these questions respondents were
asked: "Would you say nearly every day, at least once a week, a few

Table 8.1 Frequency Distributions of Study Variables

Study Variable	(%)	(N)
Occupation		
Professional and managers	12	23
Sales and clericals	6	11
Crafts and operatives	19	37
Farmers, farm laborers	11	20
Service workers	52	99
Family Closeness		
Not close at all	3	20
Not too close	5	29
Fairly close	25	143
Very close	67	381
Do You Have a Best Friend?		
Yes	55	114
No	45	94
Frequency of Attendance at Church Services		
Less than once a year	8	44
A few times a year	9	53
Few times a month	30	169
At least once a week	47	261
Nearly every day	6	31
Frequency of Participation in Activities Other Than Services		
Never	16	71
A few times a year	17	72
1-3 times a month	33	142
1-3 times a week	29	125
Nearly every day	5	20
Frequency Church Services Held		
A few times a year	3	16
1-3 times a month	14	75
1-3 times a week	60	307
Nearly every day	23	116
How Often Read Religious Books		
Never	6	33
A few times a year	9	53
1-3 times a month	17	101
1-3 times a week	24	137
Nearly every day	44	254
How Often See Religious TV/Radio		
Never	3	18
A few times a year	4	23
1-3 times a month	9	52
1-3 times a week	50	290
Nearly every day	34	194

continued

Table 8.1 Continued

Study Variable	(%)	(N)
How Often Pray		
Never	1	6
A few times a year	1	3
1-3 times a month	2	11
1-3 times a week	3	18
Nearly every day	93	541
How Religious Is Respondent?		
Not at all religious	2	8
Not too religious	4	24
Fairly religious	35	203
Very religious	59	34

times a month, a few times a year, never?" Primary group integration was indicated by response to questions concerning subjectively perceived psychological closeness to family and friends. Closeness to family was measured by response to the question: "Would you say your family members are very close in the feeling to each other, fairly close, not too close, or not close at all?" Psychological closeness to friends was measured by response to the question: "Do you have a best friend?" Respondents who were married or had partners were asked to respond yes or no to the question: "Not counting your husband/wife/partner, do you have a best friend?" Family structure was indicated by response to questions concerning marital status and children. Marital status was determined by response to the question: "Are you married, divorced, separated, widowed, or have you never been married?" Presence or absence of children was indicated by response to the question: "Are there any children under 18 years living with you?" Acceptable responses were yes or no. Responses to these two questions were combined and recoded as married with children, once married with children, never married with children, married with no children, once married with no children, never married with no children.

Achieved socioeconomic status was indicated by responses to three separate questions concerning education, occupation, and family income. The use of multiple indicators of socioeconomic status permitted the multiple dimensions, rather than the unidimensional, aspects of status to be utilized in the analysis. Educational status was indicated by response to the question: "How many grades of school did you finish?" Family income was indicated by response to the question: "What was the total income of persons living in your household in 1978, that is, considering all sources such as salaries, profits, wages, interest, and so on, from all family members?" The actual response of study participants was coded as one of 17 categories. Ascribed social status was indicated by gender, and actual age measured in years.

Analysis Strategy

Ordinary least squares regression was used to test inferences about relationships of study variables. The F statistic summarized the goodness of fit of the multivariate distribution of the observed sample data with the estimated or predicted distribution. If the sampling distribution of F demonstrated that the value of F observed in the sample data had an alpha value of .05 or less, the statistical hypothesis (i.e., the study hypotheses restated for statistical testing) was rejected. Using the t statistic, the analysis followed a similar procedure in deriving inferences about the regression coefficients.

Results

The Effects of Family Structure

At the gross or zero order level of effects, the value of the regression coefficients demonstrates that persons who have never married and have children ($b = .70$) or who have never married and do not have children ($b = .53$) attend services more frequently than married persons with children. This pattern of effects, as shown in Table 8.2, holds net the effects of demographic variables (i.e. urbanicity and region), the frequency with which services are held, and the ascribed statuses of age and gender. Moreover, this pattern persists when measures of achieved status are simultaneously controlled with measures of demographic and ascribed status (see Column 3 of Table 8.2). At the gross level of effects, the positive direction and the magnitude of the family structure regression coefficients shown in Table 8.2 demonstrate that both categories of the never married (i.e., those who have nonadult children in the home and those who do not) participate in church activities other than church services with relatively greater frequency than persons who are married and have children and persons who were formerly married (i.e., divorced or separated). The strength of this pattern, as shown in Table 8.2, however, attenuates when the effects of demographic, ascribed, and achieved statuses are statistically controlled. Nor does this pattern of effects ever attain statistical significance. For example, at the gross level the unstandardized coefficient for the never married with children, as shown in Table 8.2, has a value of .70 and has a t statistic with a probability value of .32. Net the effects of measures of demographic and ascribed status, the unstandardized coefficient is reduced to .44 and a t statistic with a probability of .39. Because the F statistic for each of the regression equations containing these coefficients is statistically significant, the t statistics for the regression coefficients representing types of family structure are not statistically significant. It seems likely, therefore, that the observed tendency of the never married to attend church services more frequently than other family types may well be a result of chance factors.

When frequency of participation in church activities other than services, as shown in Table 8.3, is used as a measure of church involvement, the never married with children and the never married who have no children continue to demonstrate a higher level of participation in church activities than that demonstrated by other types of family structures. The positive direction of the effects shown in Table 8.3 remains the same as those effects shown in Table 8.2, but the magnitude of the effects for participation in church clubs and organizations decreases somewhat from the levels shown in Table 8.2 for attendance at church services. For example, the unstandardized coefficient for the never married with children has a value of .47 at the gross effects level. Net the effects of demographic, ascribed and achieved statuses, the unstandardized coefficient for the married with children reduces to .27.

When frequency of participation in nonorganizational religious activities is regressed on study variables, the pattern demonstrated by the effects of family structure on nonorganizational religious involvement almost reverses. As shown in Table 8.4, the never married with children at either the gross ($b = -.31$) or the higher order level of effects ($b = -.37$, $b = .26$) are the least likely family structure type to demonstrate a high rate of participation in nonorganizational religious activities such as praying, watching or listening to religious programs on TV or radio, or reading religious materials. At the gross level of effects, the never married who do not have children ($b = .12$) under 18 in the home depart

Table 8.2 OLS[1] Estimates of Gross and Net Effects of Primary Group Integration (Represented as Family Structure, Family Closeness, and Best Friend Closeness) on Attendance at Church Services

	\multicolumn{6}{c}{*Effects*}					
	Gross		\multicolumn{4}{c}{*Net*}			
Indicator of Primary Group Integration			*Controlling Demographic[2] and Ascribed[3] Status Variables*		*Demographic, Ascribed, and Achieved[4] Status Variables*	
	$b(\beta)$	*s.e.*	$b(\beta)$	*s.e.*	$b(\beta)$	*s.e.*
Family Structure						
Once married with children	.22(.06)	.21	.23(.08)	.16	.14(.05)	.20
Never married with children	.70(.04)	.71	.44(.04)	.50	.47(.03)	.71
Married— no children	.16(.08)	.16	.14(.09)	.12	.09(.06)	.14
Once married— no children	−.01(−.01)	.16	−.04(−.02)	.12	−.13(−.09)	.14
Never married no children	.53(.09)	.29	.51*(.11*)	.22	.42(.09)	.25
Family Closeness						
Not close at all	−.43(−.07)	.24	−.06(−.01)	.20	.08(.02)	.23
Not too close	−.57**(−.13**)	.19	−.33(−.09)	.15	−.33(−.09)	.17
Fairly close	−.14(−.06)	.10	−.14*(−.08*)	.07	−.07(−.04)	.08
Best Friend Closeness						
Feels close to best friend	.13(.05)	.15	.13(.07)	.07	.10(.05)	.09

1. Ordinary least squares estimates of unstandardized (b) and standardized (β) regression coefficients when frequency of attendance at church services is regressed on selected study variables. The approximate standard error of the coefficients is indicated in the column labeled *s.e.*
2. Demographic variables are represented as dummy variables for: urbanicity—rural is the excluded category; region—South is the excluded category. Frequency with which church services is also included in the regression equation as a continuous variable.
3. Ascribed status variables are represented as age, a continuous variable, and gender—0=female and 1=male.
4. Achieved status variables are represented as annual family income in 1978, years of education, and occupation. The excluded category is farmers and farm laborer.
*$p<.05$; **$p<.01$

from this pattern. This pattern, however, reemerges once the effects of demographic, ascribed, and achieved statuses are held constant.

Table 8.3 OLS[1] Estimates of Gross and Net Effects of Primary Group Integration (Represented as Family Structure, Family Closeness, and Best Friend Closeness) on Frequency of Participation in Religious Activities of Church Other Than Services

	Effects					
	Gross		Net			
			Controlling Demographic[2] and Ascribed[3] Status Variables		Demographic, Ascribed, and Achieved[4] Status Variables	
Indicator of Primary Group Integration	b(β)	s.e.	b(β)	s.e.	b(β)	s.e.
Family Structure						
Once married with children	.05(.01)	.27	−.02(−.00)	.28	.05(.01)	.33
Never married with children	.47(.03)	.82	.53(.03)	.86	.27(.01)	1.17
Married—no children	−.05(−.02)	.21	−.06(−.03)	.21	−.01(−.01)	.24
Once married—no children	−.19(−.08)	.20	−.29(−.13)	.21	−.32(−.14)	.25
Never married—no children	.39(.06)	.37	.39(.06)	.37	.18(.03)	.43
Family Closeness						
Not close at all	.02(.00)	.38	−.01(−.00)	.38	.12(.02)	.44
Not too close	−.57(−.09)	.29	−.55(−.09)	.29	−.58(−.09)	.34
Fairly close	−.14(.05)	.13	−.12(−.04)	.13	−.05(−.02)	.14
Best Friend Closeness						
Feels close to best friend	−.01(−.01)	.13	−.01(−.00)	.13	−.06(−.02)	.14

1. Ordinary least squares estimates of unstandardized (b) and standardized (β) regression coefficients when frequency of attendance at church services is regressed on selected study variables. The approximate standard error of the coefficients is indicated in the column labeled s.e.
2. Demographic variables are represented as dummy variables for: urbanicity—rural is the excluded category; region—South is the excluded category. Frequency with which church services is also included in the regression equation as a continuous variable.
3. Ascribed status variables are represented as age, a continuous variable, and gender—0=female and 1=male.
4. Achieved status variables are represented as annual family income in 1978, years of education, and occupation. The excluded category is farmers and farm laborer.

The Effects of Subjectively Perceived Family Closeness

At the gross level of effects, subjectively perceived closeness to family has a statistically significant association with attendance at church services. The negative sign of the regression coefficients, as shown in Table 8.2, for the three categories of family closeness, indicates that persons who reported that they are "very close" to their families are more likely than persons who perceived themselves to be "not close at all," "not too close," or "fairly close" ($b = -.43$, $b = -.57$, $b = -.14$) to attend church services frequently. Only the effects of being "not too close" have a statistically significant effect on attendance at church services. The effect of being "not too close" is reduced to statistical insignificance, however, when the effects of demographic and status variables are held constant.

The direction and magnitude of the effects of subjectively perceived family closeness on participation in religious activities of churches other than services parallels in direction and magnitude the pattern of effects of family closeness on attendance at church services. But neither gross order effects nor higher order effects are statistically significant.

At the gross level of effects, the perception of being "not too close" or "fairly close" to family has statistically significant effects on the frequency of participation in nonorganizational religious activities. More specifically, persons who reported that they are "not too close" ($b = -.41$), or "fairly close" are less likely to participate in nonorganizational religious activities than persons who perceive themselves to be "very close" to their family. This pattern of effects, as shown in Table 8.4, persists even when the effects of demographic and status variables are statistically controlled. Net the effects of demographic and status variables the reduction of the size of the gross order coefficient for "not too close" from $-.41$ to $-.26$ suggests that some of the effects of family closeness on participation in nonorganizational religious activities might be explained by structural factors (i.e., location/position in the family), the larger society's socioeconomic strata, and geographic areas.

Effects of Subjectively Perceived Closeness to Best Friend

The effects of subjectively perceived closeness to a best friend are generally negligible, irrespective of whether religious involvement is indicated by participation in organizational activities such as attendance at church services or by participation in nonorganizational activities. The size of the unstandardized coefficients for this variable range from a low of .01 to a high of .13. None of the coefficients, at either the gross or higher order levels of effects, ever attains statistical significance.

Table 8.4 OLS[1] Estimates of Gross and Net Effects of Primary Group Integration (Represented as Family Structure, Family Closeness, and Best Friend Closeness) on Frequency of Participation in Nonorganizational Religious Activities

		*Effects*				
	Gross		*Net*			
			Controlling Demographic[2] and Ascribed[3] Status Variables		*Demographic, Ascribed, and Achieved[4] Status Variables*	
Indicator of Primary Group Integration	$b(\beta)$	*s.e.*	$b(\beta)$	*s.e.*	$b(\beta)$	*s.e.*
Family Structure						
Once married with children	.19(.09)	.12	.09(.04)	.11	.16(.08)	.13
Never married with children	−.31(−.03)	.40	−.37(−.05)	.33	−.26(−.03)	.46
Married— no children	.03(.02)	.09	−.02(−.02)	.08	.01(.01)	.09
Once married— no children	.11(.10)	.08	−.01(−.01)	.08	.02(.02)	.09
Never married— no children	.12(.03)	.16	−.02(−.01)	.15	−.02(−.01)	.16
Family Closeness						
Not close at all	−.12(−.04)	.13	.18(.06)	.14	.38(.11)	.15
Not too close	−.41***(.16***)	.11	−.28***(−.12***)	.10	−.26*(−.11*)	.11
Fairly close	−.12**(−.09**)	.05	−.11**(−.10**)	.05	−.08(−.08*)	.05
Best Friend Closeness						
Feels close to best friend	.07(.05)	.05	.09(.08)	.05	.04(.04)	.05

1. Ordinary least squares estimates of unstandardized (b) and standardized (β) regression coefficients when frequency of attendance at church services is regressed on selected study variables. The approximate standard error of the coefficients is indicated in the column labeled *s.e.*
2. Demographic variables are represented as dummy variables for: urbanicity—rural is the excluded category; region—South is the excluded category. Frequency with which church services is also included in the regression equation as a continuous variable.
3. Ascribed status variables are represented as age, a continuous variable, and gender—0=female and 1=male.
4. Achieved status variables are represented as annual family income in 1978, years of education, and occupation. The excluded category is farmers and farm laborer.
$*p<.05$; $**p<.01$; $***p<.001$.

The Effects of Status

Ascribed Status Age has no statistically significant effect on attendance at church services (see Table 8.5), participation in activities other than services, or participation in nonorganizational religious activities. In contrast, gender does have a statistically significant effect on selected measures of religious involvement. Gender has a statistically significant effect on attendance at church services and participation in nonorganizational religious activities. Women are more likely than men, net the effects of status and demographic variables, to attend church services and participate in devotional activities like watching religious TV programs. The effects of gender on participation in activities other than services and in nonorganizational religious activities are not statistically significant (see Tables 8.6 and 8.7).

Achieved Socioeconomic Status The effects of income, education, and occupation on church services or participation in activities other than church services are not statistically significant. Occupation, however, does have statistically significant effects on participation in nonorganizational religious activities like reading religious books. Sales and clerical workers ($b = -.35$ in Table 8.7) and skilled workers—crafts and operatives—($b = -.18$) are less likely to participate in these kinds of activities than farm workers and laborers.

Discussion

This study began with the question: What is the function or role of the church in the lives of the black aged? I attempted to answer this question by examining factors that contribute to the religious and church involvement of the black aged. Findings from multivariate statistical analysis demonstrate that family structure, net the effects of status and demographic factors, has no statistically significant effect on either involvement in the organizational activities of the church (attendance at church services, participation in other church activities) or nonorganizational religious activities (watching religious programs on TV, listening to religious programs on the radio). These findings suggest that neither the overall configuration of a family—the interdependent positions—nor the sentiments that connect or bond persons occupying the various positions within the family structure exert any significant regulative pressure for involvement in organizations like the church. This absence of regulative pressure for involvement in the organizational activities of the church may be a response to the increased secularization in today's society. This study's findings, then, offer no

Table 8.5 OLS Estimates of Frequency of Attendance at Church Services Regressed on Demographic Variables, Achieved and Ascribed Statuses, and Primary Group Integration Variables

Predictor	b	β
Constant	+1.55	
Ascribed Social Statuses		
Age	+.01	+.08
Gender		
Men	−.34***	−.21***
Achieved Social Statuses		
Education	+.01	+.06
Family income in 1978	+.01	−.05
Occupation		
Professionals and managers	−.08	−.02
Sales and clericals	−.19	−.03
Crafts and operatives	−.13	−.04
Service workers	+.02	+.01
Primary Group Integration		
Family Structure		
Once married with children under 18 in home	+.14	+.05
Never married with children under 18 in home	.47	.03
Married—no children under 18 in home	.09	.06
Once married—no children under 18 in home	−.13	−.09
Never married—no children under 18 in home	+.35	+.07
Family Closeness		
Not close at all	+.08	.02
Not too close	−.33	−.09
Fairly close	−.07	−.04
Best Friend Closeness		
Yes	.10	.05
Control Variables		
Region	+.00	+.00
Northeast	+.05	+.03
North Central	−.22	−.07
West		
Urbanicity	−.22**	−.13**
Frequency Services Held	+.41***	+.37***

Adjusted R^2 = .16267; F = 4.69995; p = .000.
** $p < .01$
*** $p < .001$

Table 8.6 OLS Estimates of Effects of Achieved and Ascribed Status and Primary Group Integration Variables on Frequency of Participation in Activities Other Than Church Services

Predictor	b	β
Constant	+2.66	
Ascribed Social Statuses		
Age	+.01	+.05
Gender		
Men	−.22	−.10
Achieved Social Statuses		
Education	−.02	−.08
Family income in 1978	−.02	−.08
Occupation		
Professionals and managers	+.41	+.82
Sales and clericals	−.78	−.10
Crafts and operatives	−.00	−.00
Service workers	−.05	−.02
Primary Group Integration		
Family Structure		
Once married with children under 18 in home	.05	.01
Never married with children under 18 in home	+.27	+.01
Married—no children under 18 in home	−.01	−.01
Once married—no children under 18 in home	−.32	−.14
Never married—no children under 18 in home	+.18	+.03
Family Closeness		
Not close at all	+.12	+.02
Not too close	−.58	−.09
Fairly close	−.05	−.02
Best Friend Closeness		
Yes	.06	−.02
Control Variables		
Region	−.29	−.10
Northeast	+.14	+.054
North Central	−.07	−.01
West		
Urbanicity	+.14	+.06

Adjusted R^2 = .00; F = 1.06; p = .39.

Table 8.7 OLS Estimates of Effects of Achieved and Ascribed Statuses and Primary Group Integration Variables on Participation in Nonorganizational Religious Activities

Predictor	b	β
Constant	+3.84	
Ascribed Social Statuses		
Age	+.00	+.05
Gender		
Men	−.21***	−.22***
Achieved Social Statuses		
Education	+.00	+.01
Family income in 1978	+.01	−.06
Occupation		
Professionals and managers	−.16	−.07
Sales and clericals	−.35*	−.10*
Crafts and operatives	−.18	−.09
Service workers	+.02	+.01
Primary Group Integration		
Family Structure		
Once married with children under 18 in home	+.16	+.08
Never married with children under 18 in home	−.26	−.03
Married—no children under 18 in home	+.01	+.01
Once married—no children under 18 in home	+.02	+.02
Never married—no children under 18 in home	−.02	−.01
Family Closeness		
Not close at all	+.38	+.11
Not too close	−.26**	−.11**
Fairly close	−.08**	−.08**
Best Friend Closeness		
Yes	+.04	+.04
Control Variables		
Region	−.23**	−.18**
Northeast	−.04	−.03
North Central	−.05	−.02
West		
Urbanicity	−.00	−.00
Frequency Services Held	+.08*	+.11*

Adjusted R^2 = .13203; F = 3.86; p = .000.
* $p < .05$
** $p < .01$
*** $p < .001$

empirical support for the theory that the church or religion functions as a surrogate family organization in the lives of black aged.

Nor do the findings from this study offer any empirical confirmation of deprivation theories that suggest that marginal structural position in the larger society (i.e., low socioeconomic status) contributes to high levels of church involvement. The findings from this study demonstrate that income, education, and occupation have no statistically significant effects on involvement in the organizational activities of the church.

This set of findings contradicts the findings of many other studies. An overwhelming majority of empirical studies undertaken since 1960 have found a relationship between various indicators of socioeconomic status and church involvement (Estus & Overington, 1970; Lazerwitz, 1961; Roof & Dean, 1980; Sasaki, 1979; Stark, 1964). Although these studies debate the magnitude and direction of the relationship of socioeconomic status with church involvement, they all have demonstrated the presence of a statistically significant association between socioeconomic status and church participation.

Because other empirical studies of the general population (Mueller & Johnson, 1975; Stark, 1964) or studies in which race was held constant (Sasaki, 1979) have demonstrated the effects of socioeconomic status why, then, did the structural positions occupied by aged blacks in this study appear to have no "real" effect on their church involvement? One possible explanation, not examined in this study, is that there may be some organizational features or characteristics of the church in black or African-American communities that suppress the effects of socioeconomic status observed in the general population. It is also possible that the indicators of status used in this study do not have "single" effects, but instead have effects that combine or join together in some fashion. It is conceivable that aged blacks are unlike the elderly of other racial or ethnic groups in the way they attain status, or even in how they interpret or attach meaning to the experience of marginality. If the effects of socioeconomic status combine with ethnicity and race in some manner, the pattern of effects of socioeconomic status may be present in a white population but absent in a black population due to cultural differences in the interpretation and attachment of meaning to social experiences.

Although this study failed to confirm the often demonstrated association of socioeconomic status and participation in the organizational activities of the church, it did replicate the pattern of effects of gender often demonstrated in other empirical studies (Argyle, 1959; Glock &

Stark, 1965; Mueller & Johnson, 1975). Brown and Walters (1979), writing about the black church, pointed out that women "make up the largest proportion of its membership and an even larger proportion of its active participants. The findings demonstrate that, net all the demographic and achieved status factors and age, aged black women are more likely to participate in the organizational activities of the church. Interestingly, gender differences persisted when nonorganizational religious activities were examined.

Even though the overall configuration of the family or occupancy in structural positions in the socioeconomic strata of the larger society did not have a significant effect on involvement in the organizational activities of the church for the black aged, the sentiments that connect or bond persons occupying the various positions in the family did have consequences for religious activities that take place outside any formalized organizational sphere of life. Aged blacks who perceive that they are "very close" to family members are more likely than persons who perceive themselves as "not too close" or "fairly close" to engage in nonorganizational religious activities. Perhaps there must be a relatively high level of sentiments (i.e., subjective perception of closeness to family members) reached before this aspect of family life exerts regulative pressure on the religious activities that take place inside the home (watching religious programs on TV, etc.). For example, in a family in which members perceive themselves as "not too close," if one member watches a religious program on television, other members would not feel pressure to watch or listen to the same program and might because of the relatively "weak" sentiments bonding members together engage in some other activity. In contrast, in a family in which member(s) perceive themselves to be "very close," the relatively stronger sentiments probably exert pressure on other members to join in watching or listening with other members. In this sense, the Durkheimian notion that the more one is involved, the more one gets involved is descriptive of religious activities that take place inside the home, but outside of the organizational setting of the church.

References

Adams, R., & Britain, J. (1987). Functional status and church participation of the elderly: Theoretical and practical implications. *Journal of Religion and Aging, 3,* 35-47.

Argyle, M. (1959). *Religious behavior.* London: Free Press.

Babbie, E. (1973). *Survey research methods*. Belmont, CA: Wadsworth.

Babchuk, N., & Thompson, R. V. (1963). The voluntary associations of negroes. *American Sociological Review, 27,* 647-655.

Brown, D., & Walters, R. (1979). *Exploring the role of the black church in the community*. Washington, DC: Howard University, Institute for Urban Affairs and Research.

Christiano, K. J. (1986). Church as a family surrogate: Another look at family ties, anomie, and church involvement. *Journal for the Scientific Study of Religion, 25,* 339-354.

Demereath, N. J. (1974). Social stratification and church involvement: The church-sect distinction applied to individual participation. *Review of Religious Research, 2,* 146-155.

Dubois, W. E. B. (1973). *The Philadelphia negro*. Millwood, NY: Krauss-Thomson.

Durkheim, E. (1951). *Suicide, a study in sociology*. Glencoe, Il: Free Press.

Durkheim, E. (1956). *The division of labor in society*. New York: Free Press.

Estus, C. W., & Overington, M. (1970). The meaning and end of religiosity. *American Journal of Sociology, 75,* 760-781.

Frazier, E. F. (1968). *The negro church in America*. New York: Schocken.

Glock, C. Y., Ringer, R. B., & Babbie, E. R. (1967). *To comfort and to challenge*. Berkeley: University of California Press.

Glock, C. Y., & Stark, R. (1965). On the study of religious commitment. In C. Y. Glock, & R. Stark (Eds.), *Religion and society in tension* (pp. 18-38). Chicago: Rand McNally.

Guterbock, T. M., & London, B. (1983). Race, political orientation and participation: An empirical test of four competing theories. *American Sociological Review, 48,* 439-453.

Heisel, M., & Faulkner, A. (1982). Religiosity in an older black population. *The Gerontologist, 22,* 354-358.

Hobart, C. W. (1974). Church involvement and the comfort thesis in Alberta. *Journal for the Scientific Study of Religion, 13,* 463-470.

Hyman, H. H., & Wright, C. R. (1971). Trends in voluntary association memberships of American adults: Replication based on secondary analyses of national sample surveys. *American Sociological Review, 36,* 191-206.

Koenig, H. G., George, L. K., & Siegler, I. C. (1988). The use of religion and other emotion regulating coping strategies among adults. *The Gerontologist, 28,* 303-310.

Koenig, H. G., Kvale, J. N., & Ferrel, C. (1988). Religion and well-being in later life. *Gerontologist, 28,* 918-928.

Krause, N., & Tran, V. T. (1989). Stress and religious involvement among older blacks. *Journal of Gerontology: Social Sciences, 44*(1), S4-S13.

Lazerwitz, B. (1961). Some factors associated with variations in church attendance. *Social Forces, 39,* 301-309.

Lindsay, I., & Hawkins, B. (1974). Research issues relating to the black aged. In L. Gary (Ed.), *Social research and the black community: Selected issues and priorities* (pp. 53-65). Washington, DC: Howard University, Institute for Urban Affairs and Research.

Lipset, S. M. (1960). *Political man*. Garden City, NY: Anchor.

Markides, K. S. (1983). Aging, religiosity and adjustment: A longitudinal analysis. *Journal of Gerontology, 38,* 621-625.

Marx, G. T. (1967). Religion: Opiate or inspiration of civil rights militancy among Negroes. *American Sociological Review, 32,* 64-72.

Morris, A. (1984). *The origins of the Civil Rights Movement*. New York: Free Press.

Mueller, C., & Johnson, W. T. (1975). Socioeconomic status and religious participation. *American Sociological Review, 40,* 785-800.

Mukenge, I. R. (1983). *The black church in urban America: A case study in political economy*. Lanham, MD: University Press of America.

Myrdal, G. (1944). *An American dilemma: The negro problem and modern democracy*. New York: Harper & Row.

Neighbors, H. W., Jackson, J. S., Bowman, P. J., & Gurin, G. (1982). Stress, coping and black mental health: Preliminary findings from a national study. *Prevention in Human Services, 2*, 5-29.

Nelsen, H. M., & Nelsen, A. K. (1975). *Black church in the sixties*. Lexington: University of Kentucky Press.

Niebuhr, H. R. (1957). *The social sources of denominationalism*. New York: Meridian.

Olsen, M. E. (1970). Social and political participation of blacks. *American Sociological Review, 35*(4), 682-697.

Petrowsky, M. (1976). Marital status, sex, and the social networks of the elderly. *Journal of Marriage and the Family, 38*, 749-756.

Raboteau, A. J. (1978). *Slave religion: The "invisible institution" in the antebellum South*. New York: Oxford University Press.

Riley, M., & Foner, A. (1968). *Aging and society, Vol. 1, An inventory of research findings*. New York: Russell Sage Foundation.

Roof, W., & Dean, H. R. (1980). Church involvement in America: Social factors affecting memberships and participation. *Review of Religious Research, 21*, 405-426.

Sasaki, M. S. (1979). Status inconsistency and religious commitment. In R. Wuthnow (Ed.), *The Religious Dimension: New Directions in Quantitative Research* (pp. 135-156). New York: Academic Press.

Stark, R. (1964). Class, radicalism and religious involvement in Great Britain. *American Sociological Review, 29*, 698-706.

Steinitz, L. Y. (1980). Religiosity, well-being and weltanschauung among the elderly. *Journal for the Scientific Study of Religion, 19*, 60-67.

Taylor, R. J. (1986). Religious participation among elderly blacks. *The Gerontologist, 26*, 630-636.

Taylor, R. J., & Chatters, L. M. (1986). Church-based informal support among elderly blacks. *The Gerontologist, 26*, 637-642.

Williams, J. A., & St. Peter, L. (1979). Ethnicity and socioeconomic statuses determinants of social participation: A test of the Interaction Hypothesis. *Social Science Quarterly, 57*, 892-898.

Wright, C., & Hyman, H. (1958). Voluntary association memberships of American adults: Evidence from national sample surveys. *American Sociological Review, 23*, 284-294.

SECTION III

Health, Social Functioning, and Well-Being

9

PHYSICAL HEALTH

Mary McKinney Edmonds

Health is a multidimensional concept that is difficult to operationalize, but there is a set of indicators that do give a relative sense of healthiness. Indicators such as self-assessed health status, physician-diagnosed pathology, need for medication, use of sick time, physician visits, ability to perform activities of daily living, hospital days, and use of ambulatory care facilities provide some measure of health. Several of these indicators are used in this analysis to determine the health of older black Americans.

In this chapter I present a descriptive analysis of the data for questions relating to the health of the black aged, 55 years of age and older. For clarity, I begin with a literature review of topics relevant to understanding responses and validating methods. Attention will be given to the roles and resources of older persons as they interact with and are acted upon by the health care delivery system. The sociohistorical context in which these survivors have lived will be addressed. A brief discourse on perceptions is presented as one explanation for the responses that, given the circumstances, may appear to be unrealistically optimistic.

Many myths surround blacks in general and specifically the health of black people in this country. We know blacks do not live as long as their white counterparts. We know blacks have different patterns of gaining access to the health care delivery system and different utilization patterns. It appears that for blacks once in the system, institutional racism often dictates the quality and nature of the services rendered. As

Haynes (1975) documented, blacks enter the health care delivery system later than their white counterparts, are sicker on entry, and stay longer. Blacks consider themselves ill only when illness has progressed to a higher level of severity than in the population as a whole. Reasons given for delay in help seeking are finances, child care problems, fear of hospitals, possibility of becoming a guinea pig, and fear of death (White, 1977). It is important to note that blacks are just as concerned about their health and their ability to maintain their roles in society as others.

A Description of the Older Black American

Overall, the black elderly suffer more illnesses and die earlier. Compared to whites, blacks spend less on health, see a doctor less often, receive less preventive care, and are more dependent on self-diagnosis and self-treatment. They are more likely to have heart disease, strokes, diabetes, and high blood pressure. They also tend to feel more sustained unhappiness, which makes them prone to mental breakdown (*Plight of the Black Elderly,* 1978).

Nonwhite elderly, most of whom are black, are 1.38 times as likely as white elderly to have trouble getting around alone and more than 1.5 times as likely to be confined to their homes. On the average, elderly blacks had to cut down substantially on their daily activities for almost 60 days in 1977, almost one and two thirds as long as elderly whites. Elderly blacks spent an average of almost 25 days disabled in bed during that year, more than twice as many days of bed disability as elderly whites.

For a variety of reasons, elderly blacks more than whites tend to put off seeking medical care and are also less likely to have a regular source of medical care. There are proportionately fewer doctors, clinics, and other health care providers in black neighborhoods, and many inner-city hospitals are either closing or moving to the suburbs.

The patient-to-doctor ratio is two or more times as high in poverty neighborhoods (where many black elderly live) as in nonpoverty areas. Moreover, the doctors who are most readily available to the black elderly tend to be generalists rather than specialists, much older than average, from medical schools that no longer exist, and lacking in board certification. It is not surprising that not only do elderly blacks receive less health care, but also an estimated 4% are said to have unmet health care needs. Indications are that what health care black elderly do receive is less effective (*Plight of the Black Elderly,* 1978).

Sociohistorical Context

To understand the subjects, it is necessary to understand the forces impacting their lives at critical developmental stages. The ages in this sample ranged from 55 to 101 years of age. Using 1980 as the reference point, the oldest respondent was born in 1879 or 1880. The Emancipation Proclamation was signed in 1863, so the parents of the oldest respondent could have been slaves. The youngest respondents, age 55, were born in 1925. These respondents were approximately 29 years of age in 1954, when the first of the civil rights laws came into effect. The majority of the sample, 59.2%, were living in the South in 1980. It is safe to posit that the majority of the respondents were born and received their health care in a segregated health care system for at least three decades of their lives. Their perception of the comprehensiveness and quality of available resources may be limited by that fact.

An interesting discovery, however: Should older blacks reach the age of 75 years, they will most likely outlive their white counterparts. This has been called racial crossover in life expectancy. There is much literature attempting to explain this phenomenon (Manton, 1982; Manton, Poss, & Wing, 1979; Manton & Stallard, 1981). Prevailing theories range from survival of the fittest to the genetic inheritance theory.

Roles

In our lifetime, we occupy many roles and call upon a variety of resources to assist us in playing out these roles. As we age, the role expectations and the resources change. In old age, where society's lack of attention to role expectations prevails, adequate resources may be unavailable to specific subpopulations. Certainly, one's ethnic origins and socioeconomic status may circumscribe one's ability to access specific resources needed to successfully meet role obligations and responsibilities. Blacks, like other Americans in similar situations, assume many roles and use all available resources to fulfill expectations. Unfortunately, ill health becomes an increasing barrier as age increases.

Any discussion of roles and health generally leads to a discourse on sick role theory (Parsons, 1958). Normative expectations have been that the individual is not responsible for the condition, is exempt from normal tasks and social roles, and given a recognition that sickness is undesirable, has a responsibility to get well and a duty to seek out help and comply with remedies to get well (Parsons, 1958). Racial prejudice, lack of education and health knowledge, suspicion of and alienation from bureaucratic organizations, lack of access to facilities, and unrealistic perceptions of health status are all variables that must be considered when analyzing illness behavior (Edmonds, 1982).

Resources

Resources for health care delivery are available on many levels. There are resources available as a result of education, income, and geographic location that place one in a position to take advantage of the health care system. In addition to the traditional resources found in the formal health care delivery system, there are kinship and friendship resources available for assistance. These informal and nontraditional resources may be used alone or as an adjunct to care.

Methods

Self-Rating

Many researchers support the validity of using self-ratings as legitimate indicators of health status. There is a tendency for the self-rating for health to be a better predictor of future physicians' ratings than the reverse (Maddox & Douglass, 1973). Linn, Hunter, and Linn (1980) investigated self-assessed and physician ratings of disability in Anglo, black, and Cuban elderly. They found patients perceived their functioning differently by culture, but physicians' ratings did not discriminate among cultures. Fillenbaum (1979) studied the social context of health self-assessments among the elderly. She confirmed what Maddox and Douglass (1973) and Tissue (1972) had found, that is, among the elderly, self-assessments of health do reflect objective status and are of value in surveys (Fillenbaum, 1979).

To request physician confirmation of disease is considered necessary for one to legitimately claim to be ill. Therefore, a person does not become a true occupant of the sick role until the patient status is made official by the physician (Wolinsky & Wolinsky, 1981). Thus, questions were asked regarding physician-diagnosed conditions.

Table 9.1 Physician-Diagnosed Health Problem by Degree of Problem Severity
($N = 581$) (in percentages)

Health Problem	Diagnosed Incidence	Severity "A Great Deal"
Arthritis	52.8	37.3
Ulcers	9.6	32.7
Cancer	3.1	27.8
Hypertension	54.9	26.5
Diabetes	17.2	26.3
Liver Problems	2.4	7.1
Kidney Problems	12.3	25.4
Stroke	7.2	36.6
Nervous Conditions	32.5	34.9
Circulation Problems	18.2	37.5
Heart Problems	7.5	25.6

Descriptive Data Analysis

Physician-Diagnosed Illness

It is difficult to collect reliable data on health-related matters in the black community because the reactions to health problems and the reporting of health problems appear to be different from those exhibited by other races. Black patients' doctor-seeking behavior is conditioned by customs, culture, and psychosocial factors (Williams, 1975), and the majority of illnesses experienced by the black aged are chronic in nature.

The National Survey of Black Americans (NSBA) respondents were read a list of health problems and requested to tell the interviewer if the doctor had told them they had the problem. If the respondents said yes, they were requested to indicate to what degree the health problem kept them from working or carrying out their daily tasks: a great deal, only a little, or not at all. The percentages of yes responses, indicating a health problem, and the perceived severity of the problem are shown in Table 9.1. Table 9.2 shows physician-diagnosed problems for the three age cohorts.

Arthritis Rheumatoid arthritis is a chronic progressively disabling systemic disease. Of the 52.8% (306) who indicated arthritis, over 37.3% had a great deal of difficulty carrying out their daily tasks. Men

Table 9.2 Physician-Diagnosed Problem by Age ($N = 581$)

Disease	55-64 years	65-74 years	75+ years
Arthritis	41.0	58.7	66.4
Ulcers	13.4	7.5	5.5
Cancer	1.7	4.4	3.7
Hypertension	54.9	57.8	49.1
Diabetes	18.5	17.3	14.5
Liver Problems	2.9	2.6	0.9
Kidney Problems	10.1	12.7	16.4
Stroke	4.6	10.6	5.5
Nervous Conditions	34.5	32.0	29.4
Circulation Problems	16.8	17.3	22.9
Heart Problems	7.1	6.5	10.1

were no more likely to have arthritis than women. The percentage rose in older cohorts.

Ulcers The respondents' definition of ulcers was unclear. Of the 9.6% who had physician-diagnosed ulcers, 32.7% reported a great deal of interference with functional abilities. Respondents 75 years of age and older were less likely to be bothered by ulcers than respondents aged 55-74.

Cancer Only 3.1% of the respondents indicated a physician-diagnosed case of cancer; 27.8% recorded a great deal of difficulty as a result of the disease. By age, the cohort 65-74 years of age had the highest percentage, or 4.4%, as compared to 1.7% for those 55-64 and 3.7% for respondents over the age of 75.

Hypertension In this sample approximately 7.5% of the respondents indicated that a physician had diagnosed heart disease. Yet, over one half of those studied, 54.9%, had been diagnosed as hypertensive, of which 26.5% reported that their hypertension caused them great difficulty. Of those who survived beyond the age of 75, the rate of hypertension declined slightly from 54.9% to 49.1%. At that point, however, heart problems tended to increase.

Diabetes Diabetes is a disorder of metabolism characterized by insulin deficiency. Of the 17.2% who had diabetes, 26.3% were bothered by it a great deal. The percentage across the three age groups was fairly stable: 18.5% in the cohort 55-64 years of age reported physician-diagnosed diabetes as compared to 17.3% in those 65-74 years of age and 14.5% in the oldest age category.

Liver Problems Problems with the liver were not common. Only 2.4% reported a problem and of those, only 7.1% had great difficulty as a result. The numbers decreased with age.

Kidney Problems Kidney disease posed more of a problem, with 12.3% of the sample reporting the diagnostic affirmation. One fourth of them, 25.4%, indicated it bothered them a great deal. Kidney problems may be a pathology exacerbated by hypertension or diabetes. The incidence rose with age.

Stroke Strokes have the capacity to be one of the most catastrophic problems in terms of the survivors' functional abilities. Although only 7.2% of the respondents had had a stroke, one must remember that patients with severe strokes often do not survive. Over one third of those who did, 36.6%, were left with problems severe enough to interfere a great deal with functional capabilities. The cohort aged 65-74 years appeared to survive the stroke more readily than the other cohorts, but the length of time since onset was not ascertained.

Nervous Condition Approximately one third of the respondents, 32.5%, indicated that the physician said they had a "nervous condition." By age, 34.5% of the cohort aged 55-64, 32.0% of the age 65-74 group, and 29.4% of the oldest cohort had a nervous condition. The condition was undefined, but 34.9% of the 32.5% with nervous conditions felt they were quite functionally limited as a result.

Circulation Problems Circulation problems plagued 18.2% of the respondents. This was also a rather vague medical problem. Thirty-seven and one half percent of the 18.2% indicating a problem were greatly affected as a result. Problems with circulation tended to increase with age.

Heart Problems The diagnosis of heart problems was not specifically asked. The calculation of 7.5% with heart problems was based on additional information solicited from the open-ended questions. Of this

7.5%, 25.6% indicated that they were bothered a great deal by the condition. With age, there appeared to be a higher incidence of heart problems, although the overall incidence remained low: 7.1% of those aged 55-64 years, 6.5% aged 65-74 years, and 10.1% aged 75 years and older had heart problems. This may reflect the higher mortality rate at lower ages.

In addition to the 11 conditions listed on Tables 9.1 and 9.2, an open-ended question allowed respondents to name other health problems. These problems fell into the following broad categories: eyes and vision; ears and hearing; muscular, skeletal, and nervous system problems such as phlebitis, anemia, varicose veins; digestive system disorders; respiratory system problems; urogenital system diseases; headaches; heart problems; and a variety of miscellaneous diagnosed disorders.

Further analysis of Table 9.1 shows the diagnosis and percentage of incidence. Of those indicating great difficulty, at least 62% were not limited to a great extent by a specific condition. Those respondents with arthritis, ulcers, strokes, and nervous and circulatory ailments were more likely to rate themselves as functionally inadequate than those in the other categories. A cautionary comment must be made. A single individual might have indicated four or more of the diagnoses and rated the extent of disability as less than another with only one diagnosis. Although the ratings were subjective, they reflect the nature of chronic disease.

Access to Health Care

Resources: Formal

When asked: "Overall how hard has it been for you to get medical treatment or health services you have needed? Would you say it has been very hard, fairly hard, not too hard, or not hard at all?" The majority, 61.2% (350), responded not hard at all, 27.8% (159) felt access was not too hard, 6.1% (35) believed access was fairly hard, and only 4.9% (28) believed that access to medical treatment was very hard. Again the question arises: By what standard of optimal care are these perceptions measured?

Although the data give no sense of the perceived severity of symptoms or external urging that forced the respondents to seek medical attention, the data do suggest that respondents use legitimate health care facilities. These responses are not meant to imply that the respondents

Table 9.3 Patterns of Utilization and Assessment of the Help Received (in percentages)

Source of Assistance	Degree of Satisfaction			
	A Great Deal	A Lot	Only a Little	None at All
Private Physician 84.4% (N = 488)	64.8	19.0	14.8	1.5
Public Health Clinic 36.7% (N = 201)	51.0	20.9	21.9	6.1
Visit Nurse in the Office 5.5% (N = 30)	55.2	24.1	17.2	3.4
Visiting Nurse 6.8% (N = 37)	54.3	20.0	22.9	2.9

were currently active in utilizing health facilities; rather, the responses indicate use of the services at some time in a respondent's life.

The interviewer read a list of places where people go for medical help. The respondents were asked to indicate if they had ever used the service when they needed help. The categories were private doctor, public health clinic, nurse in own office, visiting nurse, hospital emergency room, and hospital outpatient clinic. They were also asked to indicate how much help they were given. The choices were a great deal, a lot, only a little, none at all.

Table 9.3 reveals that 84.4% of respondents used private physicians and 83.8% of them were satisfied with the care given. Of the 36.7% of the respondents using public health clinics, 71.9% were satisfied. Although only 5.5% of the respondents visited private nursing offices, 79.3% reported satisfaction with the help they received. The low number using this service may be function of the present scarcity of such facilities. Surprisingly few respondents, 6.8%, used the services of a visiting nurse, but of those who did, 74.3% felt they received good service.

Consistent with what is known about patterns of emergency room utilization as primary access points for poor people (Neighbors, 1986), it is not surprising 58.1% of the respondents used this service. Also, older people have had a longer time period in their lives to experience emergency situations, such as accidents, so it is not remarkable that almost three fifths have used the emergency room at some point. A high number, 80%, were satisfied with the help received there. Fewer respondents, 33%, used outpatient services, and 80.5% of them were satisfied with the help given (data not shown).

No questions were asked about recent hospitalizations, which would indicate acute episodes. These data, then, describe conditions for which respondents would be able to leave home (except for the few, 6.8%, who used visiting nurse services).

The profile that emerges from the data is one that depicts the health care system, as the respondents perceive it, as satisfactory to the majority. They appear willing to use it. They appear willing to take the sick role and comply to some degree with medical regimes. But what of those who are not satisfied? Additional research is needed to determine the causes of dissatisfaction.

Two additional questions were asked to determine the degree to which the respondents were involved in the health care network. When asked about their medical insurance, 64.9% responded they had medical insurance (the comprehensiveness of the coverage was not ascertained), and 35.1% had no insurance. Considering the high numbers of retired and the depressed economic status of the majority of the respondents, one can posit that Medicare or Medicaid were prime providers of medical insurance for this subsample. Davis (1975) described wide variation in Medicare provisions and use of services according to income, race, and geographic location. For example, she noted that the populations with the poorest health showed less utilization of services than the more affluent. Those with higher incomes received considerably more for physicians' services than those with less than $5,000 in income. Mechanic's work (1978) suggested that both the quality and quantity of medical resources and facilities were disproportionately distributed so as to benefit the more affluent elderly. Further, because medical and health utilization behavior among poverty groups reflect long-standing patterns of use, persons in poverty may continue to be underserved with respect to necessary services, despite the emergence of the Medicare and Medicaid programs.

When asked if they had used any medicine in the past month or so that should be taken at a certain time, 64.9% indicated that they did. There was no presumption of all medicines being prescribed drugs. Thirty-seven and seven tenths percent skipped medicine. Some reasons given for not taking the medicine were informative. Examples of responses were: (a) I get side effects, (b) I can't drive when I take it, (c) I'm afraid I'll become addicted, (d) There is no money to refill the prescription, (e) I feel good without it, and (f) I forget. Seventy-nine and four tenths percent (446) used home remedies, but only 0.7% (10) reported taking other people's medicine.

When asked: "Do you think that you need more medical care or treatment than you are now getting?" over one third (35.2%) answered yes. No probes were made to elicit further responses, but this response represents a disturbing dissatisfaction with the comprehensiveness of medical care presently available.

Resources: Informal

A surprising finding was that at least 92.4% of the respondents indicated that they did not use nontraditional remedies for their health problems. For example, when asked what other people they might go to for health problems, 1.2% (7) went to an astrologer; 5.1% (29) went to faith healers; 1.1% (6) went to an acupuncturist; 3% (17) used the services of a person who heals with roots and herbs; and 1.8% (10) visited one who reads tea leaves, roots, or palms.

This is contrary to what is currently assumed and supported by White (1977), who emphasized the practice of folk medicine as a popular alternative in all social classes. Furthermore, Suchman (1965) indicated that use of nontraditional remedies may be more prevalent in minority populations.

Resources: Kinship and Friendship

Those who sustain and take care of the sick are a tremendous resource. In this study it appears the strongest resources are found within the family. The question asked of respondents was: "Please look at this list of people. Is there anyone on this list who would give you help if you were sick or disabled? Who is that?" Table 9.4 shows the persons mentioned first and second who would give assistance. Only 3.1% (18) indicated they had no one to take care of them when ill. It is important to note that on first mentions, 82.1% were family members; on second mentions, 71.1% were family. Neighbors and friends comprised 7% of the first mentions and 14.7% of second mentions. This supports the literature, which suggests that black families take care of their own (Chatters, Taylor, & Jackson, 1985; Taylor, 1985).

Table 9.5 displays perceived health satisfaction by the three age cohorts. Respondents were asked: "In general, how satisfied are you with your health? Would you say you are very satisfied, somewhat satisfied, somewhat dissatisfied, or very dissatisfied?" Of the 579 who responded, 17.8% (103) were dissatisfied, 36.4% (211) were somewhat satisfied, and 45.8% (265) were very satisfied with their health status. Table 9.5 suggests the longer one lives, the more likely one is to be very satisfied with one's health status. Fifty-three and two tenths percent

Table 9.4 Partial Listing of First- and Second-Mentioned Helping Resource When Sick

Resource	First Mention (N)	%	Second Mention (N)	%
Husband/Wife/Partner	161	28.0	16	3.6
Son/Stepson	122	21.2	80	17.9
Daughter/Stepdaughter	78	13.6	111	24.8
Father	4	.7	1	.2
Mother	13	2.3	8	1.8
Brother	35	6.1	41	9.2
Sister	58	10.1	61	13.6
Friend	31	5.4	39	8.7
Neighbor	9	1.6	26	6.0
Total	511	89.1	383	85.8

Table 9.5 Perceived Health Satisfaction by Age ($N = 579$)

| | | Health Satisfaction | | |
| | | Dissatisfied | Somewhat Satisfied | Very Satisfied |
Age in Years	n	% (N)	% (N)	% (N)
55-64	240	18.3(44)	42.9(103)	38.8(93)
65-74	230	16.1(37)	34.3(79)	49.6(114)
75+	109	20.2(22)	26.6(29)	53.2(58)

$\chi = 11.324$; $df = 4$; Cramer's Phi = .0989.

Table 9.6 Health Status by Number of Health Problems ($N = 577$)

Number of Health Problems	Dissatisfied % (N)	Somewhat Satisfied % (N)	Very Satisfied % (N)
None	6.2(4)	15.4(10)	78.4(51)
1-2	9.5(26)	37.6(103)	52.9(145)
3	24.3(26)	43.9(47)	31.8(34)
4 or more	35.1(46)	38.2(50)	26.7(35)

$\chi = 85.321$; $df = 6$; Cramer's Phi = .2687.

(58) of those 75 years and older were very satisfied with their health as compared to 49.6% (114) of those 65-74 years and 38.8% (93) of those respondents aged 55-64 years. Quite possibly, the fact that they are still alive may be a wonderment to the very old and a source of celebration. Overall, 20.2% of respondents age 75 and older were dissatisfied with their health.

These findings are consistent with prior studies. For example, Henry (1979) conducted a study of the health status of 400 older blacks in Los Angeles County and reported:

> Our findings showed that 44% of the 60-75 year old blacks perceived their health to be good or very good; 4 percent as fair; and 22 percent as poor or very poor. Based on a lifelong history of poverty, inadequate diets, substandard housing and discrimination experienced by older blacks, these findings were rather surprising. (Henry, 1979, p. 72)

Minkler (1978) surveyed a sample of older, middle- and lower-class respondents in San Francisco. She found a tendency for the majority to rate their health status more positively than that of their peers. Edmonds (1982) had similar results in her study of aged black women in Cleveland, Ohio. Other factors operating could be the desire to be positive, look good, and not complain.

To rate one's health as very good in spite of evidence to the contrary, may be a coping strategy: "Denial, passive acceptance, withdrawal, an element of magical thinking, bordering on blind faith, and belief that the avoidance of worry and tension is the same as problem solving" (Pearlin & Schooler, 1978, p. 7).

Looking at perceived health status yet another way yields additional information about the relationship between it and the number of health problems that have been diagnosed by a physician. Sixty-five respondents reported no diagnosed medical problems, 274 had one or two problems, 107 indicated three problems, and 131 reported four or more problems. As Table 9.6 suggests, the more medical problems the respondents had, the less likely they were to be satisfied with their health status. But one must recognize that in the nature of chronic disease, it is possible to have one that is devastating or four that, taken together, do not cause much discomfort or disability. One could question the 21.6% of those with no physician-diagnosed illnesses who were dissatisfied or only somewhat satisfied with their health. Other problems not diagnosed might be present or a hypochondriac respondent could perceive health problems where none exists. Other explanations could be explored for those who reported no health problems, such as subclinical or prediagnostic feelings of illness, lack of health information, or no access to the health care system.

To assess the respondents' perceptions of their power to shape their own destiny or control their own lives, the question was asked: "Some people feel they can run their own lives pretty much the way they want to, others feel the problems of life are sometimes too big for them. Which are you most like?" The possible responses were: (a) can run own life, and (b) problems of life are too big. The responses were almost evenly split, with 53.7% (302) feeling they were in control and 46.3% (260) feeling overwhelmed. There were 17 respondents with missing data.

Summary

This chapter presents a graphic description of the health of the aged black population in the United States. Univariate and bivariate analyses of relevant variables have been presented. Within the context of roles and resources, the sick role has been identified as one that increasing numbers of elderly persons find it necessary to assume. But there are several resources, formal and informal, that are available to the black aged to assist them when ill or disabled. The comprehensiveness or quality of care and services received were not issues in this analysis. Neither were issues of quality of life addressed. The majority of respondents were found to have substantially reduced educational and financial resources and were living in Southern and rural geographic areas, where medical resources have been historically severely limited.

The respondents from each age cohort were survivors of a myriad of experiences over the course of their life span. Despite medical problems and functional inadequacies, the majority of this sample perceived their health to be satisfactory. One third of the sample, however, felt their medical needs were not being met. At least 25% in all physician-diagnosed categories but one said their medical problems bothered them a great deal. Eleven percent believed access to the health care system was a problem.

Further research into factors that influence the perception of health status, such as ethnicity, must be undertaken. Hickey (1980) indicated that understanding how and why people perform in a certain way in the face of aging and the accompanying chronic conditions is critical at the societal and epidemiological levels. He raised a fundamental question: Why do some people function successfully in the presence of significant chronic disabilities and limitations whereas others in the same condition give up? (Hickey, 1980, p. 61).

Additionally, health knowledge and preventive activities, areas not addressed in this investigation, should be studied in this population to see if they influence the timing of attention to the symptoms or onset of illness. Only limited information can be gathered from a cross-sectional study. A longitudinal study identifying health and illness behaviors over time, cultural influences, and sociohistorical events at signal points would be instructive in better understanding the health needs and perceptions of the black elderly.

References

Chatters, L. M., Taylor, R. J., & Jackson, J. S. (1985). Size and composition of the informal helper networks of elderly blacks. *Journal of Gerontology, 40*(5), 605-614.

Davis, K. (1975). Equal treatment and unequal benefits: The Medicare program. *Milbank Memorial Quarterly (Health and Society), 53,* 449-488.

Edmonds, M. M. (1982). *Social class and the functional health status of the aged Black female.* Unpublished doctoral dissertation, Case Western Reserve University, Cleveland, Ohio.

Engram, E. (1982). *Science, myth, reality: The black family in one half century of research.* Westport, CT: Greenwood.

Fillenbaum, G. G. (1979). Social context and self assessment of health among the elderly. *Journal of Health and Social Behavior, 20*(1), 45-51.

Haynes, M. A. (1975). The gap in health status between black and white Americans. In R. A. Williams (Ed.), *Textbook of black related diseases* (pp. 1-30). New York: McGraw-Hill.

Henry, M. (1978). Perceived health status among the elderly in the urban area: Findings of a survey research project. In W. H. Watson (Ed.), *Health and the black aged: Proceedings of a research symposium,* May 27, 1977. Washington, DC: National Center on Black Aged.

Hickey, T. (1980). *Health and aging.* Monterey, CA: Brooks/Cole.

Linn, M., Hunter, K., & Linn, B. X. (1980). Self assessed health, impairment, and disability in Anglo, black and Cuban elderly. *Medical Care, 11*(3), 282-288.

Maddox, G. L., & Douglass, E. (1973). Self assessment of health: A longitudinal study of elderly subjects. *Journal of Health and Social Behavior, 14,* 92.

Manton, K. G. (1982). Temporal and age variation of United States black/white cause specific mortality differentials: A study of the recent changes in the relative health status of the United States black population. *The Gerontologist, 22*(2), 170-179.

Manton, K. G., Poss, S. S., & Wing, S. (1979). The black/white mortality crossover: Investigation from the perspective of the components of aging. *The Gerontologist, 19*(3), 291-300.

Manton, K. G., & Stallard, E. (1981). Methods for evaluating the heterogeneity of aging processes in human populations using vital statistics data: Explaining the black/white mortality crossover by a model of mortality selection. *Human Biology, 51,* 47-67.

Mechanic, D. (1978). *Medical sociology.* New York: Free Press.

Minkler, M. (1978). Health attitudes and beliefs of the urban elderly. *Public Health Reports, 93,* 426-432.

Neighbors, H. W. (1986). Ambulatory medical care among adult Americans: The hospital emergency room. *Journal of the National Medical Association, 78,* 275-282.

Parsons, T. (1958). Definitions of health and illness in the light of American values and social structure. In E. G. Jaco (Ed.), *Patients, physicians and illness* (pp. 165-187). New York: Free Press.

Pearlin, L., & Schooler, C. (1978). The structure of aging. *Journal of Health and Social Behavior, 19*(1), 2-21.

Plight of the black elderly: A briefing paper. (1978). Washington, DC: National Center on Black Aged.

Suchman, E. (1965). Stages of illness and medical care. *Journal of Health and Human Behavior, 6,* 114-128.

Taylor, R. J. (1985). The extended family as a source of support to elderly blacks. *The Gerontologist, 25,* 488-495.

Tissue, T. (1972). Another look at self rated health among the elderly. *Journal of Gerontology, 27*(1), 91-94.

White, E. H. (1979). Giving health care to minority patients. *Nursing Clinics of North America, 12*(1), 27-40.

Williams, R. A. (1975). Cardiovascular disease in the black patient. In R. A. Williams (Ed.), *Textbook of black related diseases* (pp. 331-332). New York: McGraw-Hill.

Wolinsky, F. D., & Wolinsky, S. R. (1981). Expecting sick role legitimation and getting it. *Journal of Health and Social Behavior, 22,* 229-242.

10

HEALTH DISABILITY
AND ITS CONSEQUENCES
FOR SUBJECTIVE STRESS

Linda M. Chatters

Research in social gerontology has consistently documented the importance of health status and health concerns in the lives of older persons. Data from a variety of sources indicate that older people suffer both chronic and acute health conditions and associated limitations on activity resulting from these problems (U.S. Department of Commerce, 1973; U.S. Department of Health, Education and Welfare, 1971). Health status is a critical determinant of social participation and activity, central to age identity and perceptions of self, and important for its contributions to overall subjective well-being. One dimension of health, disability or limitations on activity, has been investigated extensively for its relationship to overall subjective health assessments, as well as subgroup differences (e.g., women vs. men) in reported levels of disability.

Health concerns are particularly crucial among the older black population, and racial group comparisons of health status demonstrate that older black adults are disproportionately affected by poor health. Older blacks are almost twice as likely as older whites to suffer from the major chronic illnesses (Hill, 1981). Mortality rates for the major illnesses are also greater for older blacks than whites (J. S. Jackson, 1988; U.S. Department of Commerce, 1973; U.S. Department of Health, Education and Welfare, 1971). With regard to activity limitations resulting from chronic illness, older blacks are more likely than whites to experience more disability generally and also to experience the restriction in activity in a major life area (i.e., work outside the home or housework) (Manuel & Reid, 1982; National Center for Health Statistics, 1971).

The gerontological literature has traditionally viewed older age as a period of life with important changes and transitions for individuals. Events in the areas of family and social relationships, economic lifestyle, and personal health frequently cause significant and irrevocable changes in the lives of older persons. Further, late maturity is a momentous period of life because of the tendency for events to be clustered together. Several occurrences, such as retirement and widowhood, often coincide with declines in health and income. These events, and the concomitant stress they engender, are of interest to social scientists. Specifically, researchers have been interested in how older individuals respond to these events and whether the physical changes associated with aging constitute important risk factors for impaired coping and adaptation.

These questions are particularly relevant for the elderly black population. Large segments of the older black population encounter significant and indisputable disadvantage with regard to socioeconomic status, health, and housing. Despite this, older black adults are often described as being survivors and possessing effective coping strategies to deal with life's adversities. Research has examined the existence and operation of supportive networks within families, communities, and churches and their role in bolstering the coping capabilities of older black adults. Very little work has examined the nature and extent of life occurrences among this group and their impact for older black adults (Chatters & Taylor, 1990).

The purpose of the present chapter is to examine the interrelationships among sociodemographic, health disability, and stress factors. Of particular interest is the impact of differing levels of so-called personal and social resources and health status on the amount of stress experienced by the individual. The experience of stressful events is presumably modified by the presence or absence of these resources (Palmore, Cleveland, Nowlin, Ramm, & Siegler, 1979). The central question this analysis addresses is: Whether health disability and sociodemographic factors are associated with differences in the level of experienced stress as reported by older respondents.

Stress and Coping

A tradition of research on stress and coping has examined individual responses through the examination of a group of occurrences such as normative life events and nonnormative events and chronic strains (House & Robbins, 1981; Hultsch & Plemmons, 1979). Life events generally refer to experiences such as marriage, childbirth, and divorce, but also include other, nonnormative events such as natural disasters (Fritz & Marks, 1954) and institutionalization (Lieberman, 1975). Among the types of life occurrences that have been examined are normative transitions, role strain, natural disasters, and unexpected events (Brim, 1980; Hultsch & Plemmons, 1979; Lieberman, 1975; Pearlin, 1980; Pearlin & Radabaugh, 1980), chronic (Lazarus, 1980) and anticipatory (Lieberman, Prock, & Tabin, 1968) stress, and stresses surrounding the timing and scheduling of normative life events (Beeson & Lowenthal, 1975; Neugarten & Datan, 1973).

There are a variety of ways to conceptualize events (i.e., normative and nonnormative events, transitions), as well as procedures by which to assess their effects (i.e., item weighting, simple summation, self-assessments), and relevant outcome criteria (e.g., psychiatric symptomatology, physical problems). But the general properties of these life occurrences are that they produce change or a disruption of customary patterns of behavior and are potentially stressful to the individual (Chiriboga & Cutler, 1980; House & Robbins, 1981).

Aging and Stress

Several important and interrelated issues can be identified within the general topic of age and stress. Briefly, these involve: (a) whether the life events of old age are qualitatively different from the events of young adulthood and (b) possible age differences in the frequency of events experienced by older persons, and/or (c) perceptions of stress and the impact of stress events on the individual. Research on the general topic of life events has been criticized with regard to the question of age representativeness of events (Cochrane & Robertson, 1973; Morrison, Hudgens, & Barchha, 1968; Rabin, Gunderson, & Arthur, 1971; Rabkin & Struening, 1976; Reavley, 1974; Wershow & Reinhart, 1974) and the content validity of life events schedules when applied to elderly and minority groups (Chiriboga, 1977; Lazarus, 1980; Lowenthal & Chiriboga, 1973; Saranson, Johnson, & Siegel, 1978;

Vinokur & Selzer, 1973). Initial attempts to incorporate event items relevant to old age (Amster & Krauss, 1974; Guttmann, 1978) have had limited success (Chiriboga & Cutler, 1980).

Writings on the relationship between age and stress suggest that events occurring in older age may be qualitatively different from those of young adulthood due to the high proportion of events emphasizing losses of same kind (George, 1980; Rosow, 1973). Differences in the proportion of positive to negative events across age (i.e., more negative events among older age groups) may reflect the dimension of loss and provide an oblique measure of this qualitative aspect of life events and transitions (Chiriboga & Cutler, 1980; Lowenthal, Thurnher, & Chiriboga, 1975). The significance of qualitative differences in life events presumably lies in the potential impact they have on outcome measures. Reliance on a standard weighting system for events (i.e., life change scores) fails to reflect potential differences in the impact of stress events (House & Robbins, 1981).

The expectation of a greater number of life events and transitions in older adulthood reflects the notion that due to the normative basis of many of these events (i.e., age or life-stage norms), this period of life is associated with comparatively more events and transitions (Bengtson, 1975; House & Robbins, 1981; Neugarten, 1970) and associated stress (Butler & Lewis, 1977). A related notion suggests that the impact of these occurrences should be more adverse for older than younger persons given that older adults have fewer available personal and social resources with which to handle these exigencies (Hultsch & Plemmons, 1979; Pearlin & Radabaugh, 1980). Available evidence, however, suggests that older adults experience fewer stressful events (Chiriboga & Dean, 1978; Hultsch & Plemmons, 1979; Masuda & Holmes, 1978; Pearlin, 1980) and that these events have less impact on them than is the case for younger adults (Bell, 1978; Horowitz, Schaefer, & Cooney, 1974; Huerta & Horton, 1978).

Hypotheses

Variations in health status and disability are observed for identified subgroups of the elderly population. Age differences in health demonstrate that increasing age is associated with poorer health and higher levels of disability (Verbrugge, 1983). In contrast, previous work suggests that older adults are less likely than younger persons to describe life events and transitions as being stressful (House & Robbins, 1981).

Gender differences in health status and disability indicate that women display poorer health and greater levels of disability than do men (Verbrugge, 1983). Research indicates that women possess a heightened sensitivity to health-related concerns and engage in a variety of health behaviors at higher rates than men (i.e., preventive health measures, utilization of resources). Women appear more likely than men to report symptoms and discomfort and to engage in recuperative episodes (Verbrugge, 1985). Similarly, women report higher levels of psychological distress than do men (J. S. Jackson et al., 1982; Kessler, 1979).

Marital status differences in health demonstrate that married respondents evidence better physical (Nathanson, 1975) and mental (Gove, Hughes, & Style, 1983) health than do unmarried persons (i.e., widowed, divorced, separated, and never married). Socioeconomic factors generally bear a positive relationship to physical and mental health among older groups (Cantor & Mayer, 1974; Ferraro, 1980; J. S. Jackson et al., 1982; Kent & Hirsch, 1972; Nagi & King, 1976; Neighbors, 1986; Paringer, Bluck, Feder, & Holohan, 1979). Limitations on activity due to chronic health conditions are inversely related to family income among older people (National Center for Health Statistics, 1971). Similarly, educational differences in health disability indicate that years of education are inversely related to disability. Finally, although it is likely that health and stress affect each other reciprocally, here I explicitly test health disability as an antecedent to subjective stress (Abrahams & Patterson, 1978; Lieberman, 1975) and predict that disability and stress will be positively related.

The principal concerns I address in this chapter are: (a) determining the general distribution of health disability and stress among a national sample of older black adults, (b) specifying the sociodemographic predictors of both stress and disability, and (c) exploring the consequences of health disability for subjective levels of stress. The tested model examines the direct impact of sociodemographic factors and health disability on levels of stress, as well as indirect influences of social status factors through health disability.

Methods

Health Disability

Respondents were asked whether they had been told by a doctor that they had a particular health problem from among a list of 11 health conditions.[1] Respondents were also asked if they had any other health problems that had not been mentioned. If respondents indicated that they had a problem from among the list provided or volunteered a health problem, they were asked a subsequent question as to how much that problem kept them from working or carrying out their daily tasks (a great deal, only a little, or not at all). Responses to these questions formed the basis of the health disability measure. Individual levels of disability resulting from health conditions were assigned a value from 1 to 3 (higher values reflecting greater disability) and were summed across health problems. Resulting disability scores ranged from 1 to 21. Of the 575 respondents who answered this set of questions, 65 indicated that they had not been told by a doctor that they had any of the stimulus health problems nor did they volunteer any other health problems. This group of older persons with no health problems was coded as the first level of the final health disability measure. Subsequent levels of the variable were composed of the summed health disability scores, resulting in a final measure that ranged from 1 (no health problems) to 22.

Stress

Respondents were asked if within the past month or so they had experienced any of 10 problems listed.[2] Additionally, respondents were asked if within the past month or so any other problem had occurred that was not previously mentioned. Respondents who indicated yes to any of the stimulus problems or provided a self-generated problem were asked a subsequent question assessing how much a particular problem upset them. Individual values of degree of upset caused by a problem were assigned values of 1 to 4 (higher values reflecting greater upset) and summed across problems, resulting in a range of scores from 1 to 36. Of the 571 respondents who provided information on the problem grid, a full 230 (40%) indicated that they had none of the stimulus problems and further, they had no self-generated problems. This group of individuals was coded as the first level of the final stress measure, with subsequent levels made up of the summed stress scores. This resulted in a stress measure that ranged from 1 (no problems) to 37.

Analysis Procedures

A causal model was estimated in which the total, direct, and indirect effects of variables were assessed. Two sets of equations—structural and reduced form equations—were specified. The reduced form equations provide the *total effects* of demographic factors on each of the endogenous variables, plus associated error. In terms of the model tested here, the regression coefficients represent the total effects of the demographic factors on health disability and subjective stress. Structural equations, in which the endogenous variable is regressed on the relevant exogenous and endogenous variables, express the proposed theoretical relationships between each endogenous variable and other variables (exogenous and endogenous). The resulting regression coefficients represent the *direct effects* of variables on a particular endogenous factor. Reduced form and structural equation coefficients are used to provide estimates of the *indirect effects* of a variable that are related through other factors. Specifically, the total effect of an exogenous factor on an endogenous variable can be decomposed into a direct effect and an indirect effect.

Results

The distribution of the health disability and stress measures are presented in Tables 10.1 and 10.2. Table 10.3 presents the results of the regression of health disability on the set of demographic variables. Significant regression coefficients are found for gender, family income, and educational level and indicate that older women experience higher levels of health disability than do older men, and family income and educational level are inversely related to health disability. Regression coefficients for age of respondent and the set of marital status dummy variables are not significant. Overall, the regression is not efficient, accounting for less than 10% ($R^2 = .0995$, adjusted $R^2 = .0856$) of the variation in health disability.

Age and the dummy variable representing persons who are separated from their spouses both have significant direct effects on reported levels of stress (Table 10.4). Respondents who are older reported less stress than younger persons, whereas those separated from their spouses indicated they experience more stress than the comparison group (married). In addition, level of health disability exerts a significant direct effect on stress, in which higher levels of health disability are predictive of greater stress. Gender, income, education, and marital status did not evidence significant direct effects on stress. The regression is moderately successful in explaining stress, accounting for 22% of the variation in stress scores (adjusted $R^2 = .2048$).

Table 10.1 Distribution of Level of Health Disability for Respondents ($N = 575$)

Health Disability	(N)	%	Health Disability	(N)	%
None	65	11.3	11	12	2.1
1	66	11.5	12	14	2.4
2	77	13.4	13	10	1.7
3	71	12.4	14	6	1.0
4	63	11.0	15	4	0.7
5	32	5.6	16	3	0.5
6	40	7.0	17	3	0.5
7	28	4.9	18	1	0.2
8	20	3.5	19	2	0.3
9	29	5.0	20	2	0.3
10	24	4.2	21	3	0.5

Along with the direct effects of age and being separated, indirect influences by way of health disability are also present. A negligible indirect effect of age enhances the total effect of that factor on stress (less than 3% of the total effect of age is transmitted indirectly). The indirect effect of being separated reduces the total effect of membership in that marital status group on reported stress. Finally, gender has a significant total effect on stress but not a significant direct effect, indicating that the effect of gender on stress is mediated by health disability (53% of the total effect of gender on stress is mediated by

Table 10.2 Distribution of Stress Levels for Respondents ($N = 571$)

Stress	(N)	%	Stress	(N)	%
None	230	40.3	11	3	0.5
1	29	5.1	12	8	1.4
2	67	11.7	13	3	0.5
3	37	6.5	14	3	0.5
4	75	13.1	15	1	0.2
5	14	2.5	16	4	0.7
6	28	4.9	17	1	0.2
7	19	3.3	18	1	0.2
8	31	5.4	20	2	0.4
9	5	0.9	24	3	0.5
10	6	1.0	36	1	0.2

Table 10.3 Total and Direct Effects for the Explanatory Variables for Health Disability (Standardized Regression Coefficients)

	Age	Gender	Income	Education	Widowed	Divorced	Separated	Never Married
Total Effect	-.0105	.1422**	-.1452*	-.1695***	-.0323	-.0749	-.0397	.0381
Direct Effect	-.0105	.1422**	-.1452*	-.1695***	-.0323	-.0749	-.0397	.0381

R^2 = .0995; adjusted R^2 = .0856; *p<.05; **p<.01; ***p<.001.

Table 10.4 Total, Direct, and Indirect Effects for the Explanatory Variables for Stress (Standardized Regression Coefficients)

	Age	Gender	Income	Education	Widowed	Divorced	Separated	Never Married	Health Disability
Total Effect	-.1536**	.1096*	-.0468	-.0668	-.0325	-.0118	.1391**	-.0023	.4104***
Direct Effect	-.1493**	.0513	.0127	-.0027	-.0193	-.0189	.1554***	-.0179	.4104***
Indirect Effect via:									
Health Disability	-.0043	.0583					-.0163		

R^2 = .2186; adjusted R^2 = .2048; *p<.05; **p<.01; ***p<.001.

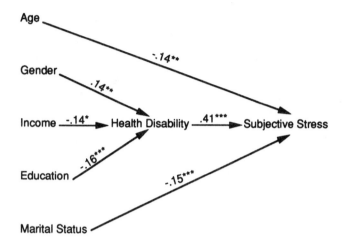

Figure 10.1. Causal Model of Subjective Stress
*p < .05, **p < .01, ***p < .001

health disability). Figure 10.1 presents a model of the direct effects of exogenous and health disability factors on subjective stress.

Discussion

The overall distribution of health disability scores indicated that a sizable portion of the sample experienced relatively low levels of activity restriction as a result of their health problems, but comparable numbers of respondents experienced more extensive disabilities from their health conditions as well. The multivariate findings involving health disability were largely consistent with previous research. Level of disability associated with health problems was negatively related to both family income and educational level. This is in agreement with work demonstrating that among older people, limitations on activity due to health problems are inversely related to family income (National Center for Health Statistics, 1971). More generally, there is confirmation that reduced socioeconomic status is related to lower levels of health among older groups (Ferraro, 1980; Kent & Hirsch, 1972; Nagi & King, 1976; Paringer et al., 1979).

The finding that being female is associated with higher levels of health disability than is being male is consistent with previous work. Several explanatory frameworks have been advanced for the gender differential in health that focus on distinct sources for these disparities (e.g., inherent biological differences, socialization experiences regarding sick role behaviors, role constraints, differences in health reporting). Several hypotheses suggest as a consequence of social roles and obligations centering around paid employment, pressure to ignore symptoms, continue to work when ill, and limit recuperation is compelling. Due in part to greater time flexibility, housewives are more likely to report health concerns, report higher levels of disability, and spend more time in recuperation and recovery. Other work suggests that women are more willing to discuss health conditions, are better able to recall those events, and have a more extensive health vocabulary. Finally, it is suggested that because of differences in the socialization of males and females to personal health concerns, women are more attuned to symptoms and illness, engage in preventive health behaviors at higher rates, and participate in risky behaviors to a lesser extent than do men. Although we are not able to test these various hypotheses here, the observed gender differences are intriguing and deserving of further study.

The failure of age of respondent to emerge as a significant predictor of health disability is puzzling and several explanations are offered for this finding. First, it is possible that age fails to differentiate among level of disability because these older respondents all evidence comparable levels of disability (possibly due to the better health of the oldest of the sample or the comparatively poor health of the youngest respondents).

Studies of survivorship among the older black population note that around 75 years of age older blacks significantly outlive their white counterparts, whereas prior to that age older blacks are less likely than whites to survive (J. J. Jackson, 1982). This crossover in life expectancy could indicate the existence of a group of very old blacks who are particularly suited for survival and longevity (i.e., have better health status). As such, these oldest of the old may have a level of health that is comparable to that of their relatively younger counterparts.

Differential perceptions of health may also account for the absence of an age effect for health disability. Although older age is related to declines in health status and increases in disability, actual perceptions of disability may be conditioned by other factors (Verbrugge, 1987). Age-based normative expectations for health may temper assessments of disability. The oldest respondents, who have lowered health expectations, may as a consequence be more sanguine concerning their health limitations. At the same time, the oldest respondents, because they have relinquished roles and responsibilities (e.g., work outside the home), may perceive that their health problems are not restrictive of what are now their normal activities. Finally, the expectation that married respondents would evidence lower levels of health disability was not borne out.

The distribution of stress scores indicated that for almost half of this older sample, the life problems investigated were not relevant concerns. Forty percent of the sample stated that they had not experienced any of the stimulus life problems within the past month and failed to volunteer additional ones. We do know, however, that women, those who are relatively younger, and persons separated from their spouses reported experiencing more stressful lives than their counterparts.

Focusing on the impact of age on subjective stress, the major portion of the total effect was transmitted directly, whereas only a small part was mediated by health disability. There are several possible explanations for the finding that advanced age was associated with decreased levels of stress. Decreased levels of stress among the oldest respondents may reflect declining levels of involvement in social roles and activities. As a consequence, the opportunity for problems arising from the social or life contexts that make up the life problem scale are reduced. The lower stress scores of the oldest respondents could be related to the fewer number of life problems they report having experienced. Related to this first point, the lower stress scores apparent among the oldest respondents may reflect a lack of age representativeness in the life problem index. The criticism that traditional life event methodologies fail to incorporate items that are particularly relevant for older populations (Chiriboga, 1977; Lazarus, 1980; Lowenthal & Chiriboga, 1973) may be applicable here as well. The lower stress scores among the oldest respondents likely reflect the fact that other areas and situations, which are potentially stressful and more relevant to older groups, are not represented.

An alternative view (not tested here) suggests that the lower stress scores of older groups could be a function of qualitative differences in the perceived impact of events among persons of various ages. Previous research along these lines suggests that older persons experience a flattening of both positive and negative affect (Campbell, 1981) or bring to bear a certain acquired perspective in the experiencing of problems and traumatic events (House & Robbins, 1981). Research on the impact of stressful events on emotional distress highlights the significance of so-called coping resources (Kessler & Cleary, 1980). Specifically, individuals bring to bear a variety of strategies to effectively deal with events (i.e., appraisal processes and personality characteristics). In addition, experience in coping with problems throughout life is seen as actively shaping and refining the elements of one's coping repertoire. The lower stress of older groups may be in part the result of the employment of coping strategies that have proven effectiveness. As a result, their responses to events reflect less distress than do the responses of younger persons. Potentially, these differences in affect, perspective, or coping history could influence problem definition (i.e., threat appraisal) as well, so that the oldest respondents are less inclined to label particular occurrences as "problems." These explanations for the observed effect of age on stress are all certainly plausible. The task of future research will be to determine whether these suggested differences in life stresses/problems and perspective can be identified and isolated, and to assess the relative contribution they make to stress evaluations.

With regard to marital status effects, the higher levels of stress reported by separated persons could result from the larger number of identified problems that are associated with their current status. Specifically, persons who are separated from their spouse would likely indicate that they have had family or marital problems. Other problems associated with being separated could involve financial situation, affectional and sexual expression (i.e., love life), and possible contact with the courts and involvement in litigation (as volunteered life problems). Gender has an influence on subjective stress by virtue of the changes it effects in health disability levels. In essence, older women have higher levels of subjective stress as a consequence of their poorer health.

The absence of significant effects for income and education on subjective stress is somewhat surprising. One hypothesis on the relationship between socioeconomic status and distress suggests that a relatively low position on these status indicators is associated with an increased likelihood of exposure to stressful events or environments (Bengtson, Kasschau, & Ragan, 1977). Alternatively, differential exposure to stressful events may only partially explain the relationship between social class and distress. Due to disadvantages in the areas of social and intrapsychic resources (i.e., coping resources), persons of lower socioeconomic status are additionally more responsive to stressful events (Kessler & Cleary, 1980). The results obtained here are not able to address these issues but do indicate that stress is independent of income and educational levels.

The relationship between health disability and stress provides confirmation of the causal link between these two factors as specified in this particular model. The present research viewed health as a resource that an older person uses to cope with the stresses associated with life problems. Persons with higher levels of disability are less equipped to deal with the various problems that confront them and are therefore more likely to report experiencing high amounts of distress. Conversely, older respondents with lower levels of disability are better able to handle the stresses associated with the problems they encounter. Other views of the health-stress relationship suggest that stress occurs causally prior to health outcomes or that health and stress are part of a reciprocal relationship.

Although the present research examined a recursive model of these relationships, available literature and thinking on the topic increasingly point to a model of reciprocal causation. Further research on this topic should explore the extent and nature of life problems among older groups, potential age differences in the perceived impact of events, and the relationship of life problems to health status.

Notes

1. The list of health problems included arthritis or rheumatism, ulcers, cancer, hypertension or high blood pressure, diabetes or "sugar," a liver problem or "liver trouble," a kidney problem or "kidney trouble," stroke, a nervous condition, a blood circulation problem or "hardening of the arteries," and sickle cell anemia.

2. The list of life problems included difficulties in the areas of health, money, job, family or marriage, problems with people outside of the family, children, crime, police, love life, and racial conflict.

References

Abrahams, R. B., & Patterson, R. D. (1978). Psychological distress among the community elderly: Prevalence, characteristics and implications for service. *International Journal of Aging and Human Development, 2*(1), 1-18.

Amster, L. E., & Krauss, H. H. (1974). The relationship between life crises and mental deterioration in old age. *International Journal of Aging and Human Development, 5,* 51-55.

Beeson, D., & Lowenthal, M. F. (1975). Perceived stress across life course. In M. F. Lowenthal, M. Thurner, D. Chiriboga, & Associates (Eds.), *Four stages of life: A comparative study of women and men facing transitions* (pp. 163-200). San Francisco: Jossey-Bass.

Bell, B. (1978). Disaster impact and response: Overcoming the thousand natural shocks. *Gerontologist, 18,* 531-540.

Bengtson, V. L. (1975). Generation and family effects in value socialization. *American Sociological Review, 40,* 358-371.

Bengtson, V. L., Kasschau, P. L., & Ragan, P. K. (1977). The impact of social structure an aging individuals. In J. E. Birren & K. W. Schaie (Eds.), *Handbook of the psychology of aging* (pp. 327-353). New York: Van Nostrand Reinhold.

Brim, O. G., Jr. (1980). Types of life events. *Journal of Social Issues, 36*(1), 148-157.

Butler, R. N., & Lewis, M. I. (1977). *Aging and mental health: Positive psychosocial approaches.* St. Louis: C. V. Mosby.

Campbell, A. (1981). *The sense of well-being in America: Recent patterns and trends.* New York: McGraw-Hill.

Cantor, M. H., & Mayer, M. (1974). *Health of the inner city elderly.* Paper presented at the 27th annual meeting of the Gerontological Society, Portland, OR.

Chatters, L. M., & Taylor, R. J. (1990). Social integration. In Z. Havel, E. A. McKinney, & M. Williams (Eds.), *Black aged: Understanding diversity and service needs* (pp. 82-99). Newbury Park, CA: Sage.

Chiriboga, D. A. (1977). Life event weighting systems: A comparative analysis. *Journal of Psychosomatic Research, 21,* 415-422.

Chiriboga, D. A., & Cutler, L. (1980). Stress and adaptation: Life span perspectives. In L. W. Poon (Ed.), *Aging in the 1980's: Psychological issues* (pp. 347-362). Washington, DC: American Psychological Association.

Chiriboga, D. A., & Dean, H. (1978). Dimensions of stress: Perspectives from a longitudinal study. *Journal of Psychosomatic Research, 22,* 47-55.

Cochrane, R., & Robertson, A. (1973). The life events inventory: A measure of the relative severity of psycho-social stressors. *Journal of Psychosomatic Research, 17,* 135-139.

Ferraro, K. F. (1980). Self-ratings of health among the old and the old-old. *Journal of Health and Social Behavior, 21,* 377-383.

Fritz, C. E., & Marks, E. S. (1954). The NORC studies of human behavior in disaster. *Journal of Social Issues, 10,* 26-41.

George, L. K. (1980). *Role transitions in later life.* Monterey, CA: Brooks/Cole.

Gove, W. R., Hughes, M., & Style, C. B. (1983). Does marriage have positive effects on the psychological well-being of the individual? *Journal of Health and Social Behavior, 24,* 122-131.

Guttman, D. (1978). Life events and decision making by older adults. *The Gerontologist, 18*(5), 462-467.

Hill, R. B. (1981, April 17). *A profile of the black aged.* Paper presented at a symposium on minority group aged sponsored by the Institute of Gerontology, University of Michigan-Wayne State University, Detroit, MI.

Horowitz, M. J., Schaefer, C., & Cooney, P. (1974). Life event scaling for recency of experience. In E.K.E. Gundersan & R. H. Rahe (Eds.), *Life stress and illness* (pp. 125-133). Springfield, IL: Charles C. Thomas.

House, J., & Robbins, C. (1981). Age, psychosocial stress and health. In B. B. Hess & K. Bond (Eds.), *Leading edges: Recent research on psychosocial aging* (pp. 287-325). (NIH Publication No. 81-2390. Review essays prepared for the White House Conference on Aging, November 1981.)

Huerta, F., & Horton, R. (1978). Coping behavior of elderly flood victims. *The Gerontologist, 18*(6), 541-545.

182 HEALTH, SOCIAL FUNCTIONING, AND WELL-BEING

Hultsch, D. F., & Plemmons, J. K. (1979). Life events and life span development. In P. B. Baltes & O. G. Brim, Jr. (Eds.), *Life-span development and behavior* (Vol. 2, pp. 1-36). New York: Academic Press.

Jackson, J. J. (1982). Death rates of aged blacks and whites: United States, 1964-1978. *Black Scholar, 13,* 21-35.

Jackson, J. S. (1988). Growing old in black America: Research on aging black populations. In J. S. Jackson (Ed.), *The black American elderly: Research on physical and psychosocial health* (pp. 3-16). New York: Springer.

Jackson, J. S., Chatters, L. M., & Neighbors, H. W. (1982). The mental health status of older black Americans: A national study. *Black Scholar, 13*(1), 21-35.

Kent, D. P., & Hirsch, C. (1972). *Needs and use of services among negro and white aged* (Vol. 11). University Park, PA: Pennsylvania State University.

Kessler, R. C. (1979). Stress, social status, and psychological distress. *Journal of Health and Social Behavior, 20,* 259-272.

Kessler, R., & Cleary, P. (1980). Social class and psychological distress. *American Sociological Review, 45,* 463-478.

Lazarus, R. S. (1980). The stress and coping paradigm. In C. Eisdorfer, D. Cohen, A. Fleinman, & P. Maxim (Eds.), *Theoretical bases in psychopathology.* New York: Spectrum.

Lieberman, M. A. (1975). Adaptive processes in later life. In N. Datan & L. H. Ginsberg (Eds.), *Life-span developmental psychology: Normative life crises* (pp. 135-160). New York: Academic Press.

Lieberman, M. A., Prock, V. N., & Tobin, S. S. (1968). Psychological effects of institutionalization. *Journal of Gerontology, 23,* 343-353.

Lowenthal, M. F., & Chiriboga, D. (1973). Social stress and adaptation: Toward a life-course perspective. In C. Eisdorfer & M. P. Lawton (Eds.), *The psychology of adult development and aging* (pp. 281-310). Washington, DC: American Psychological Association.

Lowenthal, M. F., Thurnher, M., Chiriboga, D., & Associates. (1975). *Four stages of life: A comparative study of women and men facing transitions.* San Francisco: Jossey-Bass.

Manuel, R. C., & Reid, J. A. (1982). A comparative demographic profile of the minority and nonminority aged. In R. C. Manuel (Ed.), *Minority aging: Sociological and social psychological issues* (pp. 31-52). Westport, CT: Greenwood.

Masuda, M., & Holmes, T. H. (1978). Life events: Perceptions and frequencies. *Psychosomatic Medicine, 40,* 236-261.

Morrison, J. R., Hudgens, R. W., & Barchha, R. G. (1968). Life events and psychiatric illness: A study of 100 patients and 100 controls. *British Journal of Psychiatry, 114,* 423-432.

Nagi, S., & King, B. (1976). *Aging and the organization of services.* Columbus: Mershom Center, The Ohio State University.

Nathanson, C. A. (1975). Illness and the feminine role: A theoretical review. *Social Science and Medicine, 9,* 57-62.

National Center for Health Statistics. (1971). *Health in the later years of life: Data from the National Center for Health Statistics.* Washington, DC: Government Printing Office.

Neighbors, H. W. (1986). Socioeconomic status and psychologic distress in adult blacks. *American Journal of Epidemiology, 124*(5) 779-793.

Neugarten, B. L. (1970). Adaptation and the life cycle. *Journal of Geriatric Psychology, 4,* 71-87.

Neugarten, B. L., & Datan, N. (1973). Sociological perspectives on the life cycle. In P. Baltes & W. Schaie (Eds.), *Lifespan developmental psychology* (pp. 53-69). New York: Academic Press.

Palmore, E., Cleveland, W. P., Nowlin, J. B., Ramm, D., & Siegler, I. (1979). Stress and adaptation in late life. *Journal of Gerontology, 34,* 841-851.

Paringer, L., Bluck, J., Feder, J., & Holahan, J. (1979). *Health status and the use of Medicaid Services.* Washington, DC: Urban Institute.

Pearlin, L. I. (1980). The life cycle and life strains. In H. M. Blalock, Jr. (Ed.), *Sociological theory and research: A critical approach* (pp. 349-359). New York: Free Press.

Pearlin, L., & Radabaugh, C. (1980). Age and stress: Perspectives and problems. In H. McCubbin (Ed.), *Family, stress, coping and social supports.* New York: Springer.

Rabin, R. T., Gunderson, E. K., & Arthur, R. J. (1971). Life stress and illness patterns in the U.S. Navy IV. Environmental and demographic variables in relation to illness onset in a battleship's crew. *Journal of Psychosomatic Research, 15,* 277-288.

Rabkin, J., & Streuning, E. (1976). Life events, stress and illness. *Science, 194,* 1013-1020.

Reavley, W. (1974). The relationship of life events to several aspects of "anxiety." *Journal of Psychosomatic Research, 18,* 421-424.

Rosow, I. (1973). The social context of the aging self. *Gerontologist, 13,* 82-87.

Saranson, I. G., Johnson, J. H., & Siegel, J. M. (1978). Assessing the impact of life changes: Development of the life experience survey. *Journal of Consulting and Clinical Psychology, 46,* 932-946.

U.S. Department of Commerce. (1973). Social and economic characteristics of the older population: 1973. *Current Population Reports* (Special Studies Series P-23, No. 57). Washington, DC: Government Printing Office.

U.S. Department of Health, Education and Welfare, Social Security Administration, Office of Research and Statistics. (1971, June 23). *Medicare reimbursement for services in 1967 by age, race and sex* (HI-27).

Verbrugge, L. M. (1983). Women and men: Mortality and health of older people. In M. W. Riley, B. B. Bess, & K. Bond (Eds.), *Aging in society: Selected reviews of recent research* (pp. 139-174). Hillsdale, NJ: Lawrence Erlbaum.

Verbrugge, L. M. (1985). Gender and health: An update on hypotheses and evidence. *Journal of Health and Social Behavior, 26*(3), 156-182.

Verbrugge, L. M. (1987). Sex differentials in health and mortality. *Women, health, and medicine, 2*(2), 103-145.

Vinokur, A., & Selzer, M. I. (1973). Life events, stress and mental distress. *Proceedings of the 81st Annual Convention of the American Psychological Association, 8,* 329-330.

Wershow, H. J., & Reinhart, G. (1974). Life change and hospitalization—A heretical view. *Journal of Psychosomatic Research, 18,* 393-401.

11

MENTAL HEALTH
AND HELP-SEEKING BEHAVIOR

Ruth L. Greene
James S. Jackson
Harold W. Neighbors

Today's elderly are a highly diverse population with differences in income, health, and social support significantly affecting their quality of life. Current research suggests that more than 7 million older adults, 65 years of age and over, may suffer from significant mental health stresses and problems (Redick & Taube, 1980; Roybal, 1988; Waxman, Carner, & Kline, 1984), yet very few use professional mental health services. The black elderly, the fastest growing segment of the black population, are more than twice as likely as whites to be poorly educated, divorced, separated, sick, or disabled and generally consider themselves as being in poor health (Edmonds, 1990; Greene & Siegler, 1985).

Following the life span perspective, we conclude that racial, historical, and cohort factors have profound effects on the life chances and personal experiences of black elderly and that these experiences have lasting effects on the psychological aging processes (Jackson, Antonucci, & Gibson, 1990).

Informal Helping Networks

Gerontological literature, recently reviewed by George (1989) on psychological stress and social support, suggests a buffering hypothesis that high levels of social support reduce the negative impact of stress on mental health and that social support mediates the effects of stress in older adults. As a cautionary note, however, she stated that in the absence of good longitudinal data, causal links between stress and support cannot be made. Currently, we know very little about the interaction of race, gender, age, different types of stress, and dimensions of social support. George concluded that the three typical classes of stress, (a) daily hassles of everyday life, (b) chronic conditions, and (c) life events, may have differential effects on the frequency and patterns of formal and informal social support used by older adults. Race and socioeconomic status also impact on vulnerability to life stress and on the use of informal and formal support systems (Barresi & Menon, 1990; Greene, Taylor, & Waite, 1991; Kessler & Neighbors, 1986; Mindel, Wright, & Starrett, 1986), but the research on the basic differences in black and white care giving and support are inconclusive.

Current research on the black elderly document the life Help Seeking Behavior problems, coping strategies, and social networks of older black adults (Aschenbrenner, 1975; Chatters & Taylor, 1989, 1990; Chatters, Taylor, & Jackson, 1986). Family networks, particularly for women with lower incomes and high levels of distress, have been helpful in providing assistance to women with personal problems and worries. Black women have more informal social group networks and use them more often. Other research further underscores the importance of adult children in the support networks of elderly blacks (Taylor, 1986).

There is a large body of literature that documents the strengths and diversity of family ties in the older population and the use of family support systems in times of crises (Antonucci, Fuhrer, & Jackson, 1990; Chappell & Havens, 1985; Gatz, Bengtson, & Blum, 1990; Shanas, 1979). Antonucci's (1990) recent review of the literature in the field suggests that although social support systems may differ in style, number, and composition, a high proportion of families support older adults. The literature also suggests that although women have more family and friend relationships than men, these associations may place heavy demands on women and include conflict as well as helpful support (Antonucci, 1990). This could be particularly burdensome for many black elderly widows with limited income and resources and large intimate networks. There is a small but growing body of literature on help-seeking behavior in aging blacks and the effect of friendships, neighboring, and church relationships (e.g., Cantor, 1979; Taylor & Chatters, 1986a, 1986b). In fact, estimates for the U.S. population as a whole suggest that 80% of interpersonal support and care provided to older adults comes from informal sources that include family and friends, with about 20% coming from formal support systems (Chappell, 1990).

Formal Helping Networks

Currently, there is little research on older adults' seeking either formal or informal help or the possible relationships and linkages between the two (Chappell & Guse, 1989). For example, little is known about the role of family and friends in influencing older adults to use formal services. Chappell and Guse (1989) suggested that older adults need help in dealing with the bureaucracy of formal networks, but that informal groups often help older adults cope with their situation, rather than assist them in the complex help-seeking processes needed in formal support systems. In some cases informal networks may even hinder formal service networks (Bass & Noelker, 1989; Chappell, 1985). When confronted with a stressful personal episode and psychological stress, older adults often do not receive professional knowledge. When one examines the patterns of utilization of formal mental health services, which include mental health centers, community mental health centers, general psychiatric outpatient units, and outpatient psychological services, it becomes clear that only a small percentage of the elderly with mental health problems are using professional services (Gatz & Pearson, 1988; Knight, 1986; Waxman et al., 1984). Several reasons have been given for the low rates of professional mental health involvement with older adults (Smyer, Zarit, & Qualls, 1990). These reasons include: (a) the lack of referrals from health care providers, community agencies, and physicians; (b) the difficulty of obtaining funding for mental health services; and (c) organizational variables, including accessibility and assignment of staff to the program. Waxman et al. (1984) suggested that "ageism," or bias toward the elderly, on the part of mental health professionals is less of a obstacle to program utilization than the elderly's bias toward mental health services and professionals.

Help-Seeking Among the Black Elderly

In this chapter we explore the help-seeking behavior of the black elderly. This issue will be addressed by analyzing data from the National Survey of Black Americans (NSBA) (Jackson, Tucker, & Gurin,

1987). Specifically, this analysis is concerned with the use of informal and professional help in response to personal problems among a national sample of blacks 55 years old and older.

It is important to note that in exploring issues of help-seeking behaviors and the utilization and underutilization of services, this chapter is not limited to an inquiry into the seeking of professional help. Unlike most help-seeking studies, the NSBA collected information in such a manner that the use of both informal and professional help during the same problem episode could be explored. This is important because studies that focus only on the use of professional help neglect to address the fact that there are blacks with serious problems who do not seek professional help. The implication is that people with problems who do not seek formal help go unaided. Given the importance of informal networks for blacks, this is probably not the case. For example, we expect to find substantial numbers of elderly blacks who use informal social networks as an alternative to professional help as well as a supplement to formal assistance. If, however, we find that there are blacks who do not have access to any helping resources (either formal or informal), then we may have uncovered a true group of network underutilizers.

Much of the research on help seeking in the black elderly reviewed in this chapter was conducted with small sample sizes, which limits the complexity of analyses that can be conducted. For example, the majority of the findings are descriptive, with very few multivariate analyses. Similarly, many of these samples are geographically limited. Thus, findings cannot be generalized to the entire black population. Several studies from the NSBA provide a foundation for an analyses of help-seeking behavior of black older adults.

Taylor (1986) performed a multivariate analysis regressing a number of demographic and family variables on the frequency of help received by the black elderly from the extended family. Taylor found that the closer one lives to relatives and the more contact one has with family, the more help one receives. Income and education were also significantly related to the frequency of help. The fewer the years of education the more frequent the support. Paradoxically, income showed a positive relationship to support frequency. It may be that income provides the tangible resources that education does not provide in facilitating support receipt. It is beyond the scope of this chapter to enter into a lengthy discussion of these counterintuitive findings. The point is that socioeconomic status indicators such as income and education should be important factors in any study of informal help seeking among the black elderly.

Cantor (1979) also looked at the independent contributions of socio-economic status to the frequency of interaction and the amount of help given to and received by parents. In her research, the higher the social class, the greater the distance between kinship networks and the less day-to-day interaction between elderly parents and their children. Interestingly, in her early research, Cantor (1979) characterized this sharing of limited economic and social resources between generations in the black community as a positive adaption to meet the pressures of unemployment and poverty, and suggested that it was a further indication of the mutual interdependence between generations of blacks. In her later research she argued that cultural differences may be less important when class and age are controlled (Cantor & Little, 1985; Mutran, 1985).

Taylor and Chatters (1986), in an analysis of frequency of assistance and type of support received from family, church, and friends, found that 80% of the respondents received support from a best or close friend, 80% from church, and 56% from extended family. These findings suggest that formal support systems, like the church, can be effectively linked with support systems that include family and friends.

In an earlier paper on the frequency of help received from family members, Taylor, Jackson, and Quick (1982) reported that 34% of the black elderly received help very or fairly often, 49% not too often or never, and 16% felt they never needed help. When age was taken into account, between 58% and 60% of the elderly fell into the not too often or never category (percentages exclude those respondents who said they never needed help). Categorized by gender, 64% of the men and 56% of the women reported getting help not too often or never receiving it. Taking income into account did not lower the percentages below 53% of elderly falling into these two categories.

Because our focus here is on help-seeking behavior among the black elderly, the fact that almost half of this sample said that they either get help "not too often" or that they "never get help" may be important. What is more important is that neither age, gender, nor family income substantially change the fairly large proportion of elderly in the NSBA sample who do not receive very little help from family. Taylor's data support the theory that black informal networks may not be as extensive as once suspected. The stimulus item that elicited this information on help did not specifically mention the seeking of help in response to a particular problem. Nevertheless, on the basis of these data, it may not be unreasonable to conclude that a pocket of unmet needs may exist among the black elderly, even when informal help (in addition to professional help) is taken into account.

Taylor's analyses focused on informal social support as it takes place under more or less normal social circumstances. In this chapter in contrast we explore seeking informal (and professional) help during personal crises. More relevant to this orientation is the work by Chatters, Taylor, and Jackson (1985) on health factors and informal network size among the black elderly. Because Chatters et al. (1985) examined informal support within the context of serious health problems, it more closely approximates the perspective of the present chapter.

Chatters et al. (1985) indicated that the vast majority of black elderly feel they would have no problem gaining access to some type of informal assistance during a health crisis. Ninety-seven percent could identify at least one person they felt would help them if they were sick or disabled. Contrary to the implications of Taylor's analyses, Chatters et al.'s (1985) results suggest that any pocket of unmet need created by the underuse of professional help by the black elderly will be more than compensated for by members of the informal network.

The results are more complicated than this, however. First of all, Chatters et al. (1985) reported that increasing age was associated with decreases in the size of the informal network. This focuses attention on the oldest old (aged 75 and older) as a potential target group of concern (Gibson & Jackson, 1991). More important, respondents with a high level of health disability were more likely to say that they had no helper network at all. The implication here is that the seriousness of a personal crisis might play an important role in the potential availability of informal support. Thus, in the analyses of help seeking during a serious crisis to be presented below, one might expect that the informal network will not totally compensate for the lack of use of professional help among the black elderly.

It also has to be pointed out that the information on informal help use in the Chatters et al. (1985) analysis was generated in response to a hypothetical situation. Respondents were asked to indicate who on a list of 32 people *would* help them *if* they were sick or disabled. To what extent these respondents' expectations of their family and friends behavior would correspond to actual help giving cannot be ascertained. This is an inherent problem with interpreting hypothetical responses with respect to help seeking (Gurin, Veroff, & Feld, 1960). The analyses in this chapter do not suffer from this problem, however, because they are based on what *actually* happened while the respondent was trying to cope with a stressful personal problem. In a later research study on health, stress, psychological resources, and subjective well-being using the same sample, Tran, Wright, and Chatters (1991) concluded that stressful life events had significant effects on subjective health, levels of self-esteem, as well as the subjective well-being of older black adults.

The above review leads to the following conclusions. It is expected that the elderly will not make extensive use of professional resources. There is a strong assumption that this nonuse will be adequately compensated for by the use of informal help, although data from the NSBA suggest that there may be a number of black elderly who do not have access to all of the informal help they need. The oldest old (75 years and above) may be the most isolated from both informal and professional help. Gender and socioeconomic status should also play important roles in clarifying the manner in which age is related to help seeking, although the exact nature of their relationship to age and help seeking is unclear.

Instrument and Analysis Plan

The section of the questionnaire designed to study help-seeking behavior was problem focused. Respondents were asked if they had ever experienced a personal problem that had caused them a significant amount of distress. If they had experienced such a problem, they were asked what it was about and what they had done to get help for that problem. To measure the use of informal aid, respondents were presented with a list of lay helpers (spouse, son, daughter, father, mother, brother, sister, relative, friend, neighbor, and co-worker) and asked if they had talked to any of these people about their problem. The use of professional help was measured in similar manner. Respondents were presented with a list of formal helping facilities and asked if they had gone to any of the places listed (hospital emergency room, medical clinic, doctor's office, social service agency, mental health center, private therapist, minister, lawyer, police, school, employment agency) for help with their stressful personal problem.

The results of this analysis of help seeking among the black elderly will be presented in three sections. The first section reports on the use of professional help in general. The second section reports on the use of informal help. Finally, the third section looks at the use of informal

Table 11.1 The Use of Informal and Professional Help

	%	(N)
Professional Help		
Used	51	143
Did not use	49	138
Sources of Professional Help		
Hospital	18	51
Physician	17	49
Minister	7	19
Social services	4	11
Other	5	13
No help	49	138
Informal Help		
Used	79	220
Did not use	21	59
Number of Informal Helpers		
None	21	59
1	21	58
2	24	66
3	17	48
4	9	24
5	9	24

and professional help in combination with each other. Within each section, univariate tables on help seeking are highlighted. Next, the bivariate relationships between age cohorts (55-64 years, 65-74 years, 75 years and above) and help seeking are presented. Finally, the relationship between age and help seeking is explored, taking gender and then income into account.

The Use of Professional Help

Focusing on how the black elderly use professional help, Table 11.1 shows that a little more than half (51%) of those with a serious problem seek some form of professional help. Most go either to the hospital (18%) or to the doctor (17%). Approximately 7% contact a minister, whereas only 4% seek help from a social service agency.

Table 11.2 shows the relationship between age and the use of professional help (broadly defined). Although about half of the groups aged

Table 11.2 Age and Help Seeking

Age in Years	% Using Professional Help[a]	(N)	% Using Informal Help[b]	(N)
55-64	53	136	85	134
65-74	56	100	79	100
75+	33	45	53	45

a. $\chi^2(2) = 19.7$; $p<.001$.
b. $\chi^2(2) = 6.8$; $p<.05$.

55-64 and 65-74 seek professional help, only one third (33%) of those aged 75 years and above do so. Taking the gender of the respondent into account, Table 11.3 reveals that age is related to use of professional help among men, but not among women. Among elderly black males, the 75+ age group is again the least likely to seek professional help for their problems, with only 21% doing so. This is in contrast to 49% of those aged 55-64 years, and 59% of those aged 65-74 years. The percentages of users of professional help among the women are 55%, 54%, and 42%, respectively. We also examined age and seeking professional help controlling for income (Table 11.4). Although age is not significantly related to help use at either income level, the percentages do indicate a low proportion of users among those aged 75 years and above.

Table 11.3 Age, Help Seeking, and Gender

Age	% Using Professional Help	(N)	% Using Informal Help	(N)
Males				
55-64	49[a]	37	84[b]	37
65-74	59	32	78	32
75+	21	19	47	19
Females				
55-64	55[c]	99	86[d]	97
65-74	54	68	79	68
75+	42	26	58	26

a. $\chi^2(2) = 7.1$, $p<.05$.   c. $\chi^2(2) = 1.3$, $p>.10$.
b. $\chi^2(2) = 9.1$, $p<.01$.   d. $\chi^2(2) = 9.8$, $p<.01$.

Table 11.4 Age, Help Seeking, and Income

Age in Years	% Using Professional Help	(N)	% Using Informal Help	(N)
Low Income				
55-64	56	70	85[a]	67
65-74	57	70	78	71
75+	37	32	56	32
High Income				
55-64	60	42	95[b]	43
65-74	33	12	92	12
75+	20	5	40	5

a. $\chi^2(2) = 10.1$; $p<.01$.
b. $\chi^2(2) = 15.3$; $p<.001$.

The Use of Informal Help

Professional help is not the only means of coping with personal adversity. In this section we focus on age differences in the use of informal help (family, friends, and neighbors) among the black elderly.

It is obvious from Table 11.1 that many more black elderly utilize informal help than seek professional help. Almost 8 out of every 10 respondents (79%) sought the help of at least one informal helper during their time of crisis. Table 11.1 also reveals that most people use either one, two, or three informal helpers.

When the relationship of age to the use of informal help is explored, the findings are very similar to those uncovered for the use of professional help. Age is significantly related to informal help use (Table 11.2), and again, the lowest amount of use occurs in the oldest age group. A little more than half of those 75 and older seek help from family and friends, compared to 85% in the groups aged 55-64 and 79% of those aged 65-74 years.

Table 11.3 reveals that controlling for gender does not eliminate the association between age and informal help use. The oldest age group (75 years and older) shows the least amount of help use among both males and females. Furthermore, when level of family income is taken into account, age is still related to the use of informal help (Table 11.4). Again, those 75 years and older are less likely than the two younger age groups to seek informal help.

In summary, there is consistent evidence that blacks 75 years old and above are the least likely to seek professional help in times of crisis. This is especially true among males. Despite the fact that overall more black elderly seek informal help than seek professional help, there is even stronger evidence that those 75 years old and older are the least likely to seek informal help. These findings are cause for concern for a number of reasons.

First, analyses of these data have already shown that in comparison to blacks between the ages of 18 and 54 years, respondents aged 55 years and above are the least likely to seek help during times of crises (Neighbors & Jackson, 1984). The present set of analyses shows that this relative underutilization of outside help becomes even more dramatic among older age groups.

Second, the literature shows that older blacks underutilize professional services. The research on informal help among the black elderly implies, however, that such support systems provide an alternative source of help for elderly blacks. In one sense the data presented here show that this is true: More respondents use informal help than use professional help (79% as compared to 51%). But the older a person is, the less likely that person is to get informal help. This points to an apparent pocket of unmet need among the oldest of elderly blacks. Simply put, when compared to younger blacks, this group is less likely to receive formal or informal help—and this is largely true regardless of gender or level of family income.

A "True" Group of Nonusers

The analyses thus far have yielded strong support for the notion that elderly blacks are underusers of both informal and professional helpers, but it may be premature to arrive at such a conclusion. When the use of professional help is examined in isolation, the implication is that people with problems who do not seek formal assistance go unaided. It has already been shown that this is not necessarily the case with respect to this sample of black elderly. Similarly, when the use of informal help is studied in isolation, help-seeking behavior can be viewed as an either-or proposition. That is, one either seeks informal help or no help at all.

One advantage of studying help-seeking behavior within the context of a single stressful episode is the ability to investigate the use of

Table 11.5 Age and Four Patterns of Help Seeking

| | Patterns of Help Seeking (%) | | | | |
	Informal and Formal	Informal Only	Formal Only	No Help	(N)
Univariate					
Distribution	43	35	8	14	277
Age[a]					
55-64	47	38	5	10	133
65-74	46	34	10	10	99
75+	22	31	11	36	45

a. $\chi^2(6) = 25.6$, $p < .001$.

informal and professional help in combination with each other. When informal and professional help seeking are combined, four specific response patterns are possible: (a) the use of informal help only, (b) the use of professional help only, (c) the use of both informal and professional help, and (d) the decision not to seek any outside help at all. This last category is particularly relevant to the present investigation. Despite the fact that most people under stress do seek some form of aid (informal, formal, or both), there may be those who choose not to use any external sources of help. No matter how small this group may be, they are an important risk group. That is, they represent those older blacks who are in distress but neither willing nor able to obtain informal or professional help. If the use of informal and professional help is not studied in combination, this group of true nonusers can not be identified.

Table 11.5 shows that the majority of black elderly either use only informal help (35%) or they use a combination of informal and professional help (42%). Eight percent seek only professional help, and 14% seek no help at all. The results presented in Table 11.5 are striking. Age is significantly related to the four patterns of help seeking, with the oldest age group being distinctive in two ways. First, these persons are the least likely to use both informal and professional help together (22%), and second, they are most likely not to seek any help at all (36%). This last number is three times the percentage of nonusers for the two younger groups. These findings present clear evidence of a large pocket of nonusers among the black elderly and support Gratton and Wilson's (1988) conclusion that the minority family system's ability to support older adults may be overstated. Recent research (Bengtson, Rosenthal, & Burton, 1990) suggests that family structures, roles, and relationships are changing and becoming more diverse. This could alter the traditional black family structure and support system.

Conclusions

In a previous analysis of help-seeking behavior it was demonstrated that those age 55 and above differed from younger age groups in their use of both professional and informal help (Neighbors & Jackson, 1984). Specifically it was shown that older blacks were more likely than the younger age group not to seek any help, either formal or informal, in response to a serious personal problem. This was interpreted as a cause for concern about the black elderly because it indicated that a substantial proportion of older blacks can be classified as true nonusers of help. That is, when faced with a serious crisis, they have no access whatsoever to outside sources of assistance. The present findings yield evidence that there is even more cause for alarm about the possibility of unmet need for help among older blacks. Not only are all blacks above the age of 55 less likely than their younger counterparts to seek help during times of crisis, but the oldest of the old (those 75 years and above) appear to be the most likely to be isolated from outside sources of assistance. Furthermore, there is evidence that this is the case for males as well as females, rich as well as poor.

The findings presented in this chapter raise a number of important issues about coping with stress among the black elderly that need to be addressed. For example, what are the barriers older blacks may face in trying to obtain help for their problems? Is the lack of transportation or money a significant factor in the black elderly's attempts to get professional help? Are older blacks more socially isolated from informal help because of the shrinking size of their informal networks over their life course? More important, what other means besides the seeking of help do the older blacks have at their disposal to cope with the problems they face? These are some of the questions we hope to answer as we continue to explore issues of stress, mental health, and adaptation among the black elderly.

References

Antonucci, T. C. (1990). Social supports and social relationships. In R. H. Binstock & L. K. George (Eds.), *Handbook of aging and the social sciences* (pp. 205-226). New York: Academic Press.

Antonucci, T. C., Fuhrer, R., & Jackson, J. S. (1990). Social support and reciprocity: A cross-ethnic and cross-national perspective. *Journal of Social and Personal Relationships, 7*(4), 519-530.

Aschenbrenner, J. (1975). *Lifelines: Black families in Chicago.* New York: Holt, Rinehart & Winston.

Barresi, C. M., & Menon, G. (1990). Diversity in black family caregiving. In Z. Harel, E. A. McKinney, & M. Williams (Eds.), *Black aged: Understanding diversity and service needs* (pp. 221-235). Newbury Park, CA: Sage.

Bass, D. M., & Noelker, L. S. (1989). Home care for elderly persons: Linkages between formal and informal caregivers. *Journal of Gerontology, 44,* 63-70.

Bengtson, V., Rosenthal, C., & Burton, L. (1990). Families and aging: Diversity and heterogeneity. In R. H. Binstock & L. K. George (Eds.), *Handbook of aging and the social sciences* (pp. 263-287). San Diego, CA: Academic Press.

Cantor, M. H. (1979). Neighbors and friends: An overlooked resource in the formal support system. *Research in Aging 1,* 434-463.

Cantor, M. H., & Little, V. (1985). Aging and social care. In R. H. Binstock & E. Shanas (Eds.), *Handbook of aging and the social sciences* (pp. 745-781). New York: Van Nostrand Reinhold.

Chappell, N. L. (1985). Social support and the receipt of home care service. *The Gerontologist, 25,* 47-54.

Chappell, N. L. (1990). Aging and social care. In R. H. Binstock, & L. K. George (Eds.), *Handbook of aging and the social sciences* (pp. 438-454). San Diego, CA: Academic Press.

Chappell, N. L., & Guse, L. W. (1989). Linkages between informal and formal support. In K. S. Markides & C. L. Cooper (Eds.), *Aging, stress, and health* (pp. 219-237). New York: John Wiley.

Chappell, N. L., & Havens, B. (1985). Who helps the elderly person: A discussion of informal and formal care. In W. A. Peterson & J. Quadagno (Eds.), *Social bonds in later life: Aging and interdependence* (pp. 211-228). Beverly Hills, CA: Sage.

Chatters, L. M., & Taylor, R. J. (1989). Life problems and coping strategies of older black adults. *Journal of Social Work, 34,* 313-319.

Chatters, L. M., & Taylor, R. J. (1990). Social integration. In Z. Harel, E. A. McKinney, & M. Williams (Eds.), *Black aged: Understanding diversity and service needs* (pp. 82-99). Newbury Park, CA: Sage.

Chatters, L. M., Taylor, R. J., & Jackson, J. S. (1985). Size and composition of the informal helper networks of elderly blacks. *Journal of Gerontology, 40,* 605-614.

Chatters, L. M., Taylor, R. J., & Jackson, J. S. (1986). Aged blacks' choices for an informal helper network. *Journal of Gerontology, 41,* 94-100.

Edmonds, M. M. (1990). The health of the black aged female. In Z. Harel, E. A. McKinney, & M. Williams (Eds.), *Black aged: Understanding diversity and service needs* (pp. 205-220). Newbury Park, CA: Sage.

Gatz, M., Bengtson, V. L., & Blum, M. J. (1990). Caregiving families. In J. E. Birren & K. W. Schaie (Eds.), *Handbook of the psychology of aging* (pp. 404-426). San Diego, CA: Academic Press.

Gatz, M., & Pearson C. G. (1988). Ageism revised and the provision of psychological services. *American Psychologist, 43,* 184-188.

George, L. K. (1989). Stress, social support, and depression over the life-course. In K. S. Markides & C. L. Cooper (Eds.), *Aging, stress, and health* (pp. 241-267). New York: John Wiley.

Gibson, R. C., & Jackson, J. S. (1992). The black oldest old: Health, physical functioning, and informal support of the black elderly. In R. M. Suzman, D. P. Willis, & K. G. Manton (Eds.), *The oldest old.* New York: Oxford University Press.

Gratton, B., & Wilson, V. (1988). Family support systems and the minority elderly: A cautionary analysis. *Journal of Gerontological Social Work, 13*(1-2), 81-93.

Greene, R. L., & Siegler, I. (1985) Blacks. In E. Palmore (Ed.), *Handbook of aging in the United States* (pp. 219-235). New York: Greenwood.

Greene, R. L., Taylor, P., & Waite, J. (1991, November). Paper presented at the 44th Annual Scientific Meeting of the Gerontological Society of America, San Francisco.

Gurin, G., Veroff, J., & Feld, S. (1960). *Americans view their mental health.* New York: Basic Books.

Jackson, J. S., Antonucci, T. C., & Gibson, R. C. (1990). Cultural, racial, and ethnic minority influences on aging. In J. E. Birren & K. W. Schaie (Eds.), *Handbook of the psychology of aging* (pp. 103-123). San Diego, CA: Academic Press.

Jackson, J. S., Tucker, M. B., & Gurin, G. (1987). *National Survey of Black Americans, 1979-80.* Ann Arbor: Inter-University Consortium for Political and Social Research, Institute for Social Research, University of Michigan.

Kessler, R. C., & Neighbors, H. W. (1986). A new perspective on the relationships among race, social, class, and psychological distress. *Journal of Health and Social Behavior, 27,* 107-115.

Knight, B. (1986). Management variables as predictors of service utilization by the elderly in mental health. *International Journal of Mental Health, 23*(2), 141-147.

Mindel, C. H., Wright, R., & Starrett, R. A. (1986). Informal and formal health and social support systems of black and white elderly. *The Gerontologist, 26*(3), 279-285.

Mutran, E. (1985). Intergenerational family support among blacks and whites: Response to culture or to socioeconomic differences. *The Gerontologist, 26*(3), 382-389.

Neighbors, H. W., & Jackson, J. S. (1984). The use of informal and professional help: Four patterns of illness behavior in the black community. *American Journal of Community Psychology, 12*(6), 629-644.

Redick, R. W., & Taube, C. A., (1980). Demography and mental health care of the aged. In J. Birren & R. B. Sloane (Eds.), *Handbook of mental health and aging* (pp. 57-69). Englewood Cliffs, NJ: Prentice-Hall.

Roybal, E. (1988). Mental health and aging: The need for an expanded federal response. *American Psychologist, 43*(3), 189-194.

Shanas, E. (1979). Social myth and hypothesis: The case of the family relations of old people. *The Gerontologist, 19*(1), 3-9.

Smyer, M. A., Zarit, S. H., & Qualls, S. H. (1990). Psychological intervention with the aging individual. In J. E. Birren & K. W. Schaie (Eds.), *Handbook of the psychology of aging* (pp. 375-396). San Diego, CA: Academic Press.

Taylor, R. J. (1986). Receipt of support from family among black Americans: Demographic and familial differences. *Journal of Marriage and the Family, 48,* 67-77.

Taylor, R. J., & Chatters, L. M. (1986a). Patterns of informal support to elderly black adults: Family, friends, and church members. *Social Work, 31,* 432-438.

Taylor, R. J., & Chatters, L. M. (1986b). Church-based informal support among elderly blacks. *The Gerontologist, 26*(6), 637-642.

Taylor, R. J., Jackson, J. S., & Quick, A. D. (1982). The frequency of social support among black Americans: Preliminary findings from the National Survey of Black Americans. *Urban Research Review, 8,* 1-4.

Tran, T. V., Wright, R., & Chatters, L. M. (1991). Health, stress, psychological resources, and subjective well-being among older blacks. *Psychology and Aging, 6,* 100-108.

Waxman, H. M, Carner, E. A., & Klein, M. (1984). Underutilization of mental health professionals by community elderly. *The Gerontologist, 24*(1), 23-30.

SECTION IV

Group Identity
and Political Participation

12

IDENTITY AND CONSCIOUSNESS
Group Solidarity

Robert J. Smith
Michael C. Thornton

Emerging evidence points to a consistent relationship between age and various aspects of racial attitudes among black adults. Age has been found to be positively related to racial identification (Broman, Neighbors, & Jackson, 1988), socialization practices of black parents (Thornton, Chatters, Taylor, & Allen, 1990), and to feelings of closeness to other racial minorities (Thornton & Taylor, 1988a, 1988b). The association between age and stronger bonds with other blacks found among older adults is perhaps not surprising, for these persons spent their formative years during a period of pronounced activism and social change, many participating in the struggle for racial equality (Caplan, 1970; Morris, 1984). Nevertheless, few works have explored issues of group identity among older blacks. In the present study we explore the relationship in this group between group solidarity (identification and collective orientations) and a select group of sociodemographic variables.

Historical Context

The current cohort of black elders is an aggregate of individuals who reached maturity during a unique period in U.S. history. As suggested by Mannheim (1972), members within generations share a sense of commonality (Delli Carprini, 1989), which in some cases can motivate them to become politically active and aware. For older blacks there are a number of factors that highlight their common plight. The history of black life in the United States is replete with examples of discrimination and restricted access to political and economic resources. Those born before World War II experienced overt and systemic racism designed to impede, if not fully circumvent, social and economic progress of black Americans. The postwar period was characterized by a reduction of overt and systematic racism and some expansion of political and economic power. Indeed, although much progress has occurred, present data illustrate that black elderly face continued subjugation and economic difficulties. Recent evidence documents the continued importance of race in contemporary U.S. society (Demo & Hughes, 1990; Denton & Massey, 1989; Hughes & Hertel, 1990). The current cohort of older black Americans came of age in an era of political, social, and economic repression and experienced a lifetime of racial discrimination, missed opportunities, and often deferred if not broken dreams.

Although much of the life of elderly blacks was framed by repression, the era following World War II also bore witness to large portions of black communities actively fighting oppression and striving for collective goals of social, economic, and political justice (Morris, 1984). Coalitions of church, civic, and community groups and students led boycotts, sit-ins, and demonstrations to remove earlier racial barriers. Some of the best known black Americans gained notoriety from activism during this period. Martin Luther King, Wyatt Walker, Fred Shuttlesworth, and Ralph Abernathy are just some of the names associated with the civil rights movement. Moreover, although the sit-in movement of the 1960s is often associated with the participation of college students, Morris (1981) provided many examples of the roles played by older adults during this period, primarily through local churches. That many of these political activities were initiated, monitored, and financed by local religious, civic, and political leaders reflects their racial and political consciousness.

This experiential context has provided blacks with a unique set of societal proscriptions. Denied traditional avenues of achieving the American dream and self-esteem, blacks have been forced to turn inward and develop indigenous resources as an alternative means for securing both individual and group interests. Facing an environment frequently incompatible with attaining positive mental health, blacks often must develop self-esteem through alternative frames of reference and by separating one's sense of self from the negative perceptions attached to racial group membership. This was particularly true during the era in which present black elders reached maturity—an era when race was paramount and omnipotent in determining one's life course. Relating to one's group as a foundation of strength, support, and common history is an important resource for coping with a hostile environment (Carter & Helms, 1988; Jackson, McCullough, & Gurin, 1988).

Group Solidarity

This experience with a common deprivation forced many blacks of the postwar era to feel a common bond with one another based on race. To change this common racial fate would require a group effort. Recognizing a bond based on a shared experience and extending that relationship to include a concern for the group as well as the individual provided a motivation to participate in a collective activism. Identification with the group and a collective focus together are what is called group solidarity (Gurin, Hatchett, & Jackson, 1989, p. 75).

Reflecting the importance of these concepts in black lives, over the last several decades researchers have given extensive attention to the relationship blacks have with the racial group (Gurin et al., 1989). In fact, much of the social-psychological literature on black Americans has dealt with issues of group identity and consciousness. These efforts have ranged from focusing on the development of a positive group identity (Cross, 1985) to the creation of a collective commitment to address social inequalities (Gurin & Epps, 1975; Gurin, Miller, & Gurin, 1980). After some debate, emerging evidence points to an independent relationship between personal and group identities (Cross, 1985; Jackson, McCullough, & Gurin, 1988; Rosenberg, 1989). Although there have been several social, economic, and political gains made over the last few decades, black America remains in a subordinate status, reflected by a consistent and unchanging set of beliefs among all groups and age cohorts (e.g., Allen, Dawson, & Brown, 1989; Broman et al., 1988).

Group Identity

Despite this attention, and with few exceptions, research that documents group identification among blacks remains relatively limited in scope (Cross, 1985; Jackson et al., 1988). Research examining group identity among older blacks is rarer still. Traditionally, researchers have focused on social class as the primary determinant of racial group identity. Class position is associated with changes in worldviews and life chances that flow from market position and social prestige (Landry, 1987; Weber, 1946; Wilson, 1979). Class position incorporates a particular set of subjective experiences that are believed to transcend racial boundaries. Nevertheless, the evidence is mixed. When related at all, social class success is generally negatively associated with closeness to black masses (Allen et al., 1989; Allen & Hatchett, 1986; Frazier, 1968; Wilson, 1979). For example, Broman, Neighbors, and Jackson (1988) found those with lower levels of education to be more strongly identified with blacks than their better-educated counterparts. Allen et al. (1989) described those of upper socioeconomic status as feeling less close to black masses and elites. Gurin et al. (1989) utilized two measures of identity: common fate and whether respondents felt more black than American. They described those of upper socioeconomic status and men as having stronger identities based on the first measure. Youth and those not employed full-time were found to hold a stronger black identity based on the second measure. Other work suggests that blacks of the upper social class are the most militant and most strongly identified (Kronus, 1971; Marx, 1969).

Ethnic identity is to a large degree defined by context. The particular context seems to be an essential factor to consider, yet relatively few researchers have examined it in any detail. Socialization in black areas increases group identity, especially being brought up in a black context in grammar, junior, and senior high school, and in black neighborhoods (Broman, Jackson, & Neighbors, 1989). It seems to do so in transitional areas as well, where black parents are more likely to incorporate racial messages into socialization practices (Thornton et al., 1990). Region is also related to identification. Broman et al. (1988) found that race identity is associated with living outside the West.

Although a number of factors such as sex, income, education, and the racial makeup of the neighborhood one is socialized into have been shown to be intermittently related to group identity among blacks, the emerging work in this area has found that age is the most consistent factor in predicting black feelings toward the group. Older blacks are more likely to feel closer and to consider race more important than their younger counterparts (Broman et al., 1988; Thornton et al., 1990). The age effect has also been found for black attitudes toward other racial minorities, such as black Africans and Asian Americans (Thornton & Taylor, 1988a, 1988b).

Group Consciousness

Group consciousness occurs when group identification transforms the social category into a collectivity and deprivation is seen as a common as opposed to an individual condition. Group consciousness involves an ideology about the group's position in society. In contrast to identity, researchers who have investigated this concept have extended it to represent more than thoughts and feelings of association. Rather, it represents a set of political beliefs and action orientations of the individual to work on behalf of group interests. The political hue often given to group consciousness developed out of interest group theories that proposed that group consciousness develops along lines consistent with the prevailing stratification of political and socioeconomic power within groups in the United States (Morris, Hatchett, & Brown, 1987). For example, the long history of racial and economic discrimination against blacks has made race a rallying focus for the development of both group identity and group consciousness. That this has indeed been the case is evidenced by such collective expressions as: (a) the separatist movement by Marcus Garvey, (b) Black Nationalism, and (c) the civil rights activism of the 1960s and 1970s. All of these movements represent collective attempts to act on behalf of the welfare of black Americans.

Empirical studies that have specifically focused on the relationship of age and race to group consciousness have been rare. McCullough (1982) investigated the impact of a number of sociodemographic variables on group consciousness from a national probability sample of black Americans. The results indicated that older individuals were more likely to endorse attitude statements representative of group consciousness than young people. In addition, blacks raised in mostly black neighborhoods were more likely to have group consciousness than any of their sociodemographic counterparts.

Hatchett (1982) investigated the sociodemographic correlates of change in black racial attitudes from 1968 to 1976 in a sample of Detroit residents. Included in this investigation were indices of group consciousness over time. For example, in 1976, blacks were less willing to agree that blacks should shop only in black-owned stores than in 1968. At the same time, there was a rather large increase in the percentage of blacks who endorsed the belief that black children should learn an African language, from 32.8% in 1968 to 54.6% in 1976. When selected sociodemographic variables were examined, the results indicated that sex and age were generally correlated with group consciousness for both 1968 and 1976. Education and income, however, were significantly related to behavioral aspects of group consciousness (e.g., shopping in black-owned stores). Greater support was found for shopping in black-owned stores among those with high school education and above and high income than those with less education or income. In addition, income was found to be related to endorsing support for children learning an African language. In general, individuals of higher socioeconomic status showed greater endorsement than those of lower socioeconomic status. Gurin et al. (1989) included a number of factors in a group consciousness measure. Those with higher educations and income who were older and did not live in the South were both more likely to be discontent with the level of power blacks wielded and more likely to advocate nationalistic policies, such as shopping in black-owned stores or teaching children African languages. The authors of this study concluded that increased education and economic resources were related to increased levels of racial solidarity.

The present study was designed to examine the relationship of a number of theoretically relevant variables to group identity and consciousness in older black Americans. Previous research has indicated that certain sociodemographic variables are related to group consciousness. Among blacks in general, it has been found that such variables as sex, age, education, income, and region of early socialization are likely to have an effect on group identification and consciousness, either singly or interactively (McCullough, 1982; Robinson, 1987).

The Measures

The section of the questionnaire in the National Survey of Black Americans (NSBA) designed to study issues related to group consciousness and group identity was organized around 35 questions related to blacks' perceptions of their racial group and cultural heritage and racial discrimination in the United States. For the present analyses, questions were selected from two major categories: group identity and cultural and collectivist action orientation.

Group Identity The group identity measure consisted of the responses to two questions. Respondents were asked to indicate which group they felt closer to, blacks in Africa, whites in America, neither, or both. For this analysis we were interested in attitudes toward whites versus Africans. The second dimension of group identity was determined by the responses to the question of how close they were to black Africans.

Group Consciousness To assess cultural consciousness and collectivist political action orientation, respondents were queried regarding the extent to which they agreed or disagreed with the following statements: (a) black children should study an African language, (b) black parents should give their children African names, (c) blacks should always vote for black candidates when they run, and (d) black people should shop in black-owned stores whenever possible. The range of responses was from strongly agree (1) to strongly disagree (4) with optional categories of "don't care" and "don't know." The third question is a measure of the political dimension of consciousness, the remainder are aspects of nationalistic thought. These were used to bridge identity and consciousness by referring to both group bonds and action structures.

Results

Table 12.1 reveals the regression results of the relationship between the demographic variables and group identity. As is clear, only sex is significantly related to identity. Black men, more than women, feel closer to black Africans than they do to white Americans. Traditional determinants of importance, such as education and income, are not important influences on older black adults' identification. There were no significant differences based on whether respondents felt closer to blacks in Africa or white Americans.

Table 12.2 illustrates the relationship between the selected sociodemographic variables and two measures of group consciousness (black nationalism and action orientations). In contrast to identity, social class position was an important determinant of consciousness. Education was significantly related to feelings about both always voting for a black candidate and black parents giving their children African names. Similarly, income affected views toward advocating that children learn African languages. The present results reflect an influence of social class that has the opposite effect found in other works. Older blacks

Table 12.1 Regression Coefficients (Model 1) and Logit Coefficients (Model 2) for the Effects of Demographic Variables on Indicators of Group Identity

Predictors[a]	Close to Blacks in Africa (Model 1) b	β	Close to Blacks in Africa vs. Whites in U.S. (Model 2) b
Constant	3.71	—	2.90
Gender	.26**	.12**	.43
Region			
Northeast	−.01	−.00	−.11
North Central	−.09	−.04	
West	−.10	−.02	
Age	−.00	−.04	−.01
Education	−.00	−.09	−.00
Income	−.02	−.07	−.05
Racial Composition of			
Neighborhood of Socialization	.06	.06	.15
R^2	.03		
F	2.18		
N	511		344
χ^2			7.71
df			6

a. Region is represented by a dummy variable; South is the excluded category.
*$p<.05$; **$p<.01$; ***$p<.001$.

who are less educated and with lower incomes are more likely to hold affirmative views on these questions. Other researchers have found a positive relationship between these attitudes and income and education.

Discussion

Black Americans who are 55 years of age or older represent a unique experience within the political, social, and economic spheres of life in the United States. This experience helped formulate particular perspectives regarding attitudes about and behaviors involving their racial group. Much of who and what they are today, as well as their beliefs regarding group solidarity, is deeply embedded in and colored by a host

Table 12.2 Regression Coefficients for the Effects of Demographic Variables on Indicators of Group Consciousness

Predictors[a]	African Language		Vote Black Candidates		Black Owned Stores		Black Children African Language	
	b	β	b	β	b	β	b	β
Constant	.25	—	3.29	—	3.41	—	2.87	—
Gender	.04	.02	.05	.03	.08	.06	.03	.02
Region								
Northeast	.05	.02	-.16	-.07	-.17	-.09	.04	.02
North Central	-.07	-.03	-.11	-.05	-.14	-.08	.00	.00
West	-.18	-.05	-.21	-.06	-.09	.03	.08	-.02
Age	-.00	-.02	.00	-.01	-.00	-.03	-.01	-.07
Education	-.00	-.06	-.01***	-.21**	-.00	-.07	-.01***	-.21***
Income	-.02*	-.12*	-.02	-.10	-.01	.03	-.01	-.08
Racial Composition and Neighborhood of Socialization	-.02	-.02	-.01	-.01	-.04	-.06	.02	.03
R^2	.03		.10***		.03		.06**	
F	1.61		6.54		1.89		3.38	
N	438		501		502		428	

a. Region is represented by a dummy variable; South is the excluded category.
*$p<.05$; **$p<.01$; ***$p<.001$.

of historical circumstances to which they had to respond and adapt. The seasoning of these years impacted on such diverse areas of their lives as their self-esteem, group identity, racial attitudes, and perhaps most important, group consciousness. This unique background perhaps explains why emerging works find consistent differences in racial attitudes between older and younger black Americans.

The results of the present investigation provide one of the first efforts to examine empirically the association between sociodemographic variables and multiple indices of group consciousness and identification among older black Americans. Moreover, because these findings were based upon a national probability sample, they are the most comprehensive and representative to date, redressing the paucity of previous studies on group consciousness and group identity, focused on younger blacks and only including small samples of older blacks or historical or archival evidence. Together, the findings in this chapter strongly support the notion that rather than representing a homogenous group, older blacks represent a rather heterogeneous cohort of individuals. By employing several different measures of the same construct, in the present study we were able to examine the multidimensional nature of many of these measures of group consciousness and race identification.

One of the major concerns of this chapter was to investigate the relationship between the previously discussed sociodemographic variables and group identity among older black Americans. Asking respondents to indicate which group they felt closer to, black people in Africa, or white people in the United States, revealed that men were more likely to identify with blacks in Africa than whites in the United States. The relationship between identity and sex is congruent with other research on black Americans and at least one study on feelings of closeness toward Africans (Thornton & Taylor, 1988a).

Collectively, the finding that only sex among older black Americans differentiated blacks on feelings of group identification suggests that this group is unique in that its common experience and heritage transcend typically powerful determinants such as education. Spending formative years in an environment rife with overt discrimination and few life chances perhaps gave race an omnipotence missing for many of the younger generation. If identity is determined by the extent to which one perceives shared values and beliefs (Gurin et al., 1980), then these results would indicate that black men are more closely tied to blacks in Africa than they are to other U.S. citizens (race being the key). This might be related to a greater alienation from U.S. society among black men, in accord with research on poverty and the underclass suggesting a sizable and growing segment of black men are only marginally attached to the labor force and alienated from society (Wilson & Aponte, 1985). Ultimately, identification may be so strong among this age group that few factors differentiate them except the unique experience of black men in white America.

Group consciousness is a multifaceted concept and sociodemographic variables have a differential impact on its varied dimensions. In the present investigation, group consciousness was divided into two major dimensions: nationalism and political action consciousness. Nationalism was defined as the willingness to engage in behaviors that solidify and advance blacks' cultural heritage, and political consciousness represented as the willingness to engage in political behaviors on behalf of the group. Among older blacks, there were two factors related to nationalistic attitudes: giving children African names and teaching them African languages. Those with less education were most likely to advocate the former, and those with less income the latter. These patterns are in contrast to other works (Gurin et al., 1989). Thus, older blacks of lower education and lower income status were more likely to endorse attitudinal statements representing cultural consciousness. Perhaps elderly blacks who are poorly educated possess memories of African ancestors either from personal experiences or from countless stories recounted by relatives (the youngest in the subsample examined would have been born in 1925). Those more educated possibly attempted to sever their ties with Africa, striving instead to identify with the United States. Naming children African names may have been an attempt to retain connections with their ancestors' homeland or a means to protest their treatment in the United States, as one of the precursors to the "black" movement, controlling what they would be called.

With respect to political consciousness, as education levels declined a similar pattern of greater endorsement was found. Those from the lower strata were more likely to endorse voting for black political candidates than those with greater levels of education. At first, one might conclude that older, poor, uneducated blacks are more culturally and politically conscious than those who are relatively more affluent and educated. The data certainly seem to suggest such an interpretation. But it is equally plausible that blacks who are more educated and affluent may be more closely identified with white cultural values and beliefs than blacks who are less well off. It should be remembered that these are blacks who may have been relatively middle class in the late 1940s and early 1950s. Because of the stress on upward mobility and integration into white middle-class society, as well as racial oppression, it is possible that these middle-class blacks were not only *not* identifying with African culture and political consciousness, but were defining these concepts quite differently. Both reference and interest group theories propose that individuals' social identity derives through a process of social perception, comparison, and evaluation of their places and group membership within the social structure. The extent to which they identify with the dominant group in seeking to advance themselves through the traditional system may affect stratum identification and consciousness along socioeconomic lines. In the present case, the cohort of more affluent and better educated blacks of the 1950s may be expressing cultural and political consciousness in a manner that is consistent with the aspired-to values of full social and economic integration into the broader structure of white middle-class society.

The present results must be treated with caution. The sociodemographic variables utilized in the models in only two cases explain a significant level of the variance. Several other factors of potential importance should be included in future analysis. One factor deserving further consideration is the influence of the church on attitudes of racial solidarity.

How persons identify with their racial group, their perceptions of racial and cultural consciousness, and their views regarding racial discrimination are not only affected by a select group of sociodemographic variables, but these perceptions themselves are imbued with many different dimensions of meaning. The results suggest that racial solidarity (and particularly identity) is strong among older black Americans. But racial solidarity among this group is affected by different factors than has been found for the general population, both black and white. Surprisingly, age was not significantly related to most of the dependent measures. This suggests the life experiences of this group of elderly is not sufficiently different in a variety of attitudes related to race. This is consistent with previous research indicating that age and some sociodemographic variables are often not strong predictors of racial attitudes and perceptions. This study, however, represents one of the first that has been conducted on group consciousness and identity among older black Americans. Given the relationships found in this study, future research needs to focus on more multivariate and causal models underlying the present pattern of findings.

References

Allen, R. L., Dawson, M. C., & Brown, R. E. (1989). A schema-based approach to modeling an African American racial belief system. *American Political Science Review 83*(2), 421-441.

Allen, R. L., & Hatchett, S. J. (1986). The media and social reality effects: Self and system orientations of blacks. *Communication Research, 13,* 97-123.

Broman, C. L., Jackson, J. S., & Neighbors, H. W. (1989). Sociocultural context and racial group identification among black adults. *Revue Internationale de Psychologie Sociale 2*(3), 367-378.

Broman, C. L., Neighbors, H. W., & Jackson, J. S. (1988). Racial group identification among black adults. *Social Forces 67*(1), 146-158.

Caplan, N. (1970). The new ghetto man: A review of recent empirical studies. *Social Issues, 26*(1), 59-73.

Carter, R., & Helms, J. (1988). The relationships between racial identity attitudes and social class. *Journal of Negro Education, 57,* 22-30.

Cross, W. (1985). Black identity: Rediscovering the distinction between personal identity and reference group orientation. In M. Spencer, G. Brookins, & W. Allen (Eds.),

Beginnings: The social and affective development of black children (pp. 152-172). Hillsdale, NJ: Lawrence Erlbaum.

Delli Carprini, M. X. (1989). Age and history: Generations and sociopolitical change. In R. Sigel (Ed.), *Political learning in adulthood* (pp. 1-10). Chicago: University of Chicago Press.

Demo, D. H., & Hughes, M. (1990). Socialization and racial identity among black Americans. *Social Psychology Quarterly, 53,* 364-374.

Denton, N. A., & Massey, D. S. (1989). Racial identity among Caribbean Hispanics: The effect of double minority status on residential segregation. *American Sociological Review, 54,* 790-808.

Frazier, E. F. (1974). *The negro church in America.* New York: Schocken.

Gurin, P., & Epps, E. (1975). *Black consciousness, identity and achievement: A study of students in historically black colleges.* New York: John Wiley.

Gurin, P., Hatchett, S. J., & Jackson, J. S. (1989). *Hope and independence: Blacks' response to electoral and party politics.* New York: Russell Sage.

Gurin, P., Miller, A., & Gurin, G. (1980). Stratum identification and consciousness. *Social Psychology Quarterly, 43*(1), 30-47.

Hatchett, S. J. (1982). Black racial attitude change in Detroit: 1968-1976. Unpublished doctoral dissertation, University of Michigan, Ann Arbor.

Hughes, M., & Hertel, B. (1990). The significance of color remains: A study of life chances, mate selection, and ethnic consciousness among black Americans. *Social Forces, 68,* 1105-1120.

Jackson, J. S., McCullough, W., & Gurin, G. (1988). Family, socialization environment, and identity development in black Americans. In H. P. McAdoo (Ed.), *Black families* (pp. 242-256). Newbury Park, CA: Sage.

Jackson, J. S., McCullough, W., Gurin, G., & Broman, C. L. (1991). Race identity. In J. S. Jackson (Ed.), *Life in Black America* (pp. 238-253). Newbury Park, CA: Sage.

Kronus, S. (1971). *The black middle class.* Columbus, OH: Merrill.

Landry, B. (1987). *The new black middle class.* Berkeley: University of California Press.

Mannheim, K. (1972). The problem of generations. In P. G. Altbach & R. S. Laufer (Eds.), *The new pilgrims* (pp. 101-138). New York: David McKay.

Marx, G. (1969). *Protest and prejudice.* New York: Harper & Row.

McCullough, W. (1982). Factors in the development of a positive black identity: Family socialization, racial environment, and cohort effects. *The role of racial identity and consciousness in the ascendency of black people: Issues, research directions and implications.* Cincinnati, OH: Association of Black Psychologists.

Morris, A. D. (1981). Black southern student sit-in movement: An analysis of internal organization. *American Sociological Review, 46,* 755-767.

Morris, A. D. (1984). *The origins of the civil rights movement: Black communities organizing for change.* New York: Free Press.

Morris, A. D., Hatchett, S. J., & Brown, R. E. (1989). The civil rights movement and black political socialization. In R. S. Roberts (Ed.), *Political learning in adulthood: Constancy and change* (pp. 272-305). Chicago: University of Chicago Press.

Robinson, D. M. (1987). The effect of multiple group identity among black women on race consciousness. Unpublished doctoral dissertation, University of Michigan, Ann Arbor.

Rosenberg, M. (1989). Old myths die hard: The case of black self-esteem. *Revue Internationale de Psychologie Sociale, 2*(3), 355-365.

Thornton, M. C., Chatters, L. M., Taylor, R. J., & Allen, W. (1990). Sociodemographic and environmental correlates of racial socialization by black parents. *Child Development, 61*, 401-409.

Thornton, M. C., & Taylor, R. J. (1988a). Intergroup perceptions: Black American feelings of closeness to black Africans. *Ethnic and Racial Studies, 11*, 139-150.

Thornton, M. C., & Taylor, R. J. (1988b). Intergroup attitudes: Black American perceptions of Asian Americans. *Ethnic and Racial Studies, 11*, 474-488.

Weber, M. (1946). Class, status and party. In H. Gerth and C. Wright Mills (Eds.), *From Max Weber: Essays in Sociology* (pp. 180-195). New York: Oxford University Press.

Wilson, W. J. (1980). *The declining significance of race: Blacks and changing American institutions* (2nd ed.). Chicago: University of Chicago Press.

Wilson, W. J., & Aponte, R. (1985). Urban poverty. *Annual Review of Sociology, 11*, 231-258.

13

GROUP CONSCIOUSNESS
AND POLITICAL BEHAVIOR

Ronald E. Brown
Rupert W. Barnes-Nacoste

Much of the recent research on the political participation of black Americans shows that they are more active than one would predict in view of their long history of second-class citizenship and powerlessness. The reason for this level of participation seems to be racial identification (Campbell, Converse, Miller, & Stokes, 1960; Miller, Gurin, Gurin, & Malanchuk, 1981; Verba & Nie, 1972). That literature suggests that an awareness of racial subordination serves as a motivator of political behavior. Indeed, racial identification may in part explain why it is that among black Americans, the highest level of voter turnout is found for elderly blacks (J. J. Jackson, 1980; Sears & McConahay, 1973), the group with the fewest resources. In this chapter, we argue that what accounts for the higher level of voter participation of elderly blacks relative to younger blacks is the racial environment in which elderly blacks were reared and the level of racial identification they hold as a consequence.

Severity of Conditions

An important developmental antecedent of racial identification is differential treatment on the basis of racial group membership (Simpson & Yinger, 1972). Yet, much of the work prior to the modern-day civil rights movement virtually ignored this important linkage. On the whole, the focus has been on how restrictions imposed by the superordinate group on the subordinate group influenced the development of personality traits or psychological attributes that were pathological (see Jackson, McCullough, & Gurin, 1981; Walton, 1985). Consequently, blacks were largely described as cynical, alienated, and lacking self-esteem and racial pride. Though much of the recent work has examined correlates of racial identification (see Gurin, Miller, & Gurin, 1980; Sears & McConahay, 1973), very little consideration has been given to whether the domination relation existing between groups may have social-psychological consequences that are important in understanding the political behavior of members of a subordinate group.

Domination relations have been defined as "a confrontation between two fundamentally *heterogeneous* opponents, the inequality lying in differential access to the decision-making concerning values and rules that control the future" (Apfelbaum, 1979). Generally speaking, this type of intergroup relationship will differ for various pairs of groups, so that for configurations of different groups, certain qualities of the domination relation (e.g., scope and intensity) will vary. Of course, over time there may be changes in the quality of a domination relation between particular groups (Simpson & Yinger, 1972, pp. 36-38).

Changes in the nature of a domination relation will involve positive or negative shifts in the severity of conditions affecting the subordinated group. An important outgrowth of change in the severity of conditions is that individual members of the subordinate group reared in different periods in the history of the domination relation will be exposed to dissimilar social, political, and economic environments. The contingencies operative during the particular period in which an individual is socialized will influence group members' perception of overall conditions. Thus, group members socialized during periods in the relationship that differ in scope and intensity will have divergent perceptions of present-day conditions. Likewise, group members reared in geographic areas where the domination relation is taken less seriously by the superordinate group or in areas that provide some insulation from the harsh consequences of the group's status will differ in their perceptions and behaviors.

Variations in the severity of conditions experienced should influence the individual's level of psychological identification with the group. When the domination relation requires that members of the subordinated group receive continual treatment on the basis of the group category (e.g., race or ethnicity), there is likely to develop a heightened level of shared identification among members of the categorized group (Lewin, 1948; Simpson & Yinger, 1972, pp. 198-200). Consistent categorical treatment is likely to influence members to infer high degrees of similarity among group members on other dimensions, hence increasing feelings of attachment to the group (Tajfel & Turner, 1979). In the main, severity of conditions should directly influence group members' sense of common or group identity such that these feelings are strongest for individuals reared when conditions are most severe. Those reared when conditions are not as severe will display less intense group orientations. As Simpson and Yinger (1972) speculated, "The reduction of prejudice and discrimination may weaken group solidarity" (p. 198).

Even when conditions were generally severe, however, other factors influenced the extent to which members of the subordinated group were exposed to the same level of intensity in the domination relation. To fully investigate the possible long-term social-psychological effects of conditions between a superordinate and subordinate group, we must take into account the fact that the intensity and scope of experienced categorical treatment would have depended on the area of the country in which the individual was reared. Although it is true that before the 1950s black Americans were the subject of widespread prejudice and discrimination, it is also true that in certain areas of the country, the social norms regarding the treatment of blacks were not uniform or as openly visible (Danigelis, 1977, 1982; Key, 1949; Matthews & Prothro, 1966). Generally speaking, the most negative conditions have been attributed to the South. But deep South states should be distinguished from border South states because the norms of the border states were qualitatively different from those in the deep South (Corzine, Creech, & Corzine, 1983). Overall, those reared in the deep South would have been subjected to the most severe conditions, the border South states having less severe conditions, and areas outside of the South being characterized by the least severe conditions. For the most part, elderly blacks should be more likely to have been reared in the deep South and show objective indications of severe conditions (e.g., low levels of education). All in all, if our idea about the impact of severity of racial conditions is accurate, then elderly blacks should show a higher sense of racial identification.

No matter how you look at it, that hypothesis conflicts with empirical evidence showing younger blacks born and socialized in the North as more likely to exhibit stronger positive attitudes toward their racial group (Aberbach, 1977; Aberbach & Walker, 1970; Caplan, 1970; Sears & McConahay, 1973). That work has, however, suffered from a serious theoretical limitation, being for the most part focused on the extent to which members of the group hold attitudes that indicate disaffection from the societal mainstream, such as racial militancy, black nationalism, or power discontent. Very few studies have focused on identification with the feelings of mainstream segments of the black population. No studies have examined how this mainstream identification is simultaneously influenced by age and differences in experienced socialization conditions.

Our premise is that black senior citizens came to identify closely with their racial group in an era of oppression that was not experienced by younger blacks. That idea is guided by the persistence hypothesis described in political socialization research (Dawson, Prewitt, & Dawson, 1977; Miller & Sears, 1986; Sears, 1983; Sears & McConahay, 1973), which suggests that political attitudes that have high ego involvement, including attitudes about race, religion, or gender, are more likely to remain stable throughout the life cycle. Attitude centrality and continued social reinforcement are said to maintain key political orientations (Miller & Sears, 1986; Sears, 1983). In the context of the black elderly, we postulate that they are what Mannheim (1972) referred to as a "generational unit" that experienced a form of racial oppression much more severe in nature than that experienced by younger cohorts. As a result, older blacks developed a much stronger sense of racial identification, which has remained with them.

The severity of conditions notion suggests that the relationship between age and voting behavior is best explained by considering the socialization conditions of the black elderly. Elderly blacks as well as blacks reared in the deep South can be expected to have consistently higher levels of racial identification given the extent of categorical treatment to which they have been subjected. Consequently, elderly blacks can be expected to be more likely to vote, because they were reared under conditions that fostered this high level of racial identification. It is assumed here that this identification motivates their voting behavior because denial of voting rights was one of the symbols of the lower status of blacks. Thus, we expected to find that the established relationship between age and voting would be qualified by interactions with racial identification and region of socialization. This hypothesis was explored through use of data from the National Survey of Black Americans (NSBA).

Methodology

The measures used in these analyses were derived from questions included in a large general questionnaire that covered many aspects of black American life—neighborhood, family, friends, work and unemployment, mental and physical health, coping and help seeking, racial identity, and political orientations and behavior.

The only information obtained by the national survey on presidential voting relates to the 1976 presidential election. As will be noted below, this necessitated a reduction of the sample as certain individuals in the total sample were not eligible to vote in 1976.

Age, Education, and Region of Socialization

Respondent age was determined through birth dates provided during the interview. In the present analysis only individuals born before or during 1958 are included. Individuals born after 1958 would not have been eligible to vote in 1976. This restriction required dropping of 6.2% ($n = 143$) of the total sample. The remaining subsample ($n = 1958$) was categorized into three age groups. In terms of age at the time of the interview, 23.2% of the sample were classified as elderly (ages 59-101), 30.2% as middle aged (ages 40-58), and 46.6% as young (ages 21-39).

As education has been shown to be a consistent correlate of voting turnout, it is taken into account in the analyses conducted (see Verba, Nie, & Kim, 1978; Wolfinger & Rosenstone, 1980). Respondents provided information on the level of education attained. This information was used to create a two-level variable. Forty-five percent of the sample had attained from 0 to 11 years of education and 55.5% a high school education or more. Region of socialization was derived from responses to a question regarding where the individual had mostly lived while growing up. Region was coded from these responses and collapsed into deep South, border South, and non-South.[1] Among those eligible to vote in 1976, 41.8% reported having been reared in the deep South, 19.8% in the border South, and 38.3% outside of the South.

Racial Identification

Racial identification was based on responses to a set of items regarding how closely respondents felt in their "ideas and feelings about things" to 11 categories of black people. The four available responses ranged from very close to not too close at all. A varimax factor analysis of the correlates among the 11 racial identification items produced two dimensions of racial identification. The first factor accounted for 33% of the total variance. Responses to eight of the categories (black people who are poor; religious church-going black people; young black people; middle-class black people; working-class people; older black people; black elected officials; and black doctors, lawyers, and other professional black people) were used to form a racial identification variable.[2] Responses to these items were summed for each respondent and dichotomized into high and low identifiers on the basis of the median. Fifty-one percent of the eligible voting sample fell into the high identification category and 49.0% in the low identification category.

Voting

To measure voting behavior respondents were asked whether they voted in the "last presidential election." Of those eligible to vote in 1976, 58.6% reported voting in the presidential election and 41.4% reported not voting.

Analysis Approach

The variables outlined were analyzed in two steps. In the first step a set of bivariate analyses was conducted to ascertain the distribution of the age groupings on education, region of socialization, measures of racial identification, and voting turnout. These analyses were undertaken in order to provide preliminary evidence regarding the plausibility of the hypotheses involving severity and its outcomes.

The second step involved multivariate analyses. The analytic technique used was hierarchical log-linear analysis (Knoke & Burke, 1980). This was done in order to determine whether any bivariate relationships obtained persist when other variables are taken into account as well as to obtain a proper test of the basic hypothesis. In this analysis age (A), education (E), racial identification (I) and region of socialization (R) were included as predictors of voting turnout (V).

A best-fitting model was identified through an elimination procedure that involved estimation of the extent of difference between models on the basis of each models likelihood ratio chi-square. This best-fitting model and other models are presented along with the appropriate likelihood ratio chi-square and degrees of freedom. The specific within-model effects that make up the best-fitting model are displayed by way of standardized lambda coefficients. These lambda coefficients indicate within-model effects and are statistically significant ($p<.05$) when the value is greater than or equal to $+1.96$ or less than or equal to -1.96.

Results

The percentages from the bivariate analyses are presented in Table 13.1. As expected the elderly are more likely to have been reared in the deep South ($\chi^2 = 78.75$, $p<.001$, tau-b = .18) and to have a low level of attained education ($\chi^2 = 364.69$, $p<.001$, tau-b = .41). In the case of region of socialization the difference appears to be between the two older groups and the young group ($\chi^2 = 78.75$, $p<.001$, tau-b = .18). This finding reflects the migration patterns of blacks from the rural South to the urban North. Essentially, older blacks were more likely than younger blacks to have been socialized in the South.[3]

In terms of the covariation pattern between age and racial identification, the data show a linear relationship ($\chi^2 = 149.69$, $p<.001$, tau-b = .26). The relationship between age and identification is such that elderly and middle-aged blacks are more likely to have a high level of racial identification than younger blacks. This finding lends support to our hypothesis, but is counter to arguments that the events of the late 1950s and 1960s caused the reemergence of racial identification and consciousness. Again, prior studies may not have accurately examined the interaction between region of socialization and racial identification. For the most part, as cited earlier, the concern was with racial militancy and protest behavior rather than with tapping racial identification and consciousness.

The relationship between age and presidential voting is similar to those between age and region and age and identification. Both groups of older blacks are more likely to vote than the young group ($\chi^2 = 101.65$, $p<.001$, tau-b = .36).

It should be noted that life cycle forces could help to explain this covariation pattern. Older blacks have had more opportunities to be voters, and we cannot rule out at this level the possibility of age having a residual effect on turnout.

Aside from the relationship between age and certain variables, the severity framework suggests that region of socialization should influence racial identification (Table 13.2). There is a moderately strong relationship with racial identity ($\chi^2 = 144.02$, $p<.001$, tau-b = .24) such that those

Table 13.1 Relationships Between Age and Indicators of Socialization Conditions, Racial Identification, and Voting Behavior (in percentages)

	Age		
	Elderly (N = 454) (23.2%)	*Middle-Aged* (N = 592) (30.2%)	*Young* (N = 912) (46.6%)
Region of Socialization[a]			
Deep South	53.8	45.2	33.8
Border South	22.4	19.8	18.6
Non-South	23.8	35.0	47.6
Attained Education[b]			
0-11 years	76.2	53.4	23.3
High school and above	23.8	46.6	76.7
Racial Identification[c]			
High	69.2	60.2	36.4
Low	30.8	39.8	63.6
Voting Behavior[d]			
Yes	69.2	69.2	46.6
No	30.8	30.8	53.4

a. χ^2_2 = 78.75; p>.001; tau-b = .18.
b. χ^2_2 = 364.69; p>.001; tau-b = .41.
c. χ^2_2 = 149.69; p>.001; tau-b = .26.
d. χ^2_2 = 101.65; p>.001; tau-b = .36.

reared in the deep South and border South are more likely to be highly identified with the group than those reared outside of the South.

Overall, these analyses provide very good preliminary evidence for the severity of conditions framework. Among this sample of eligible voters, older blacks in general did show a higher propensity to vote. This is true though they have lower levels of attained education relative to the young. In terms of the framework, however, older blacks are more likely to have been reared in the South. Moreover, both elderly and middle-aged blacks and those reared in the South show a high level of racial identification. This suggests the potential importance of region of socialization and racial identification for understanding the relationship between age and voting.

Multivariate Analysis

Because the hypothesis implied interactions between a number of variables, the log-linear procedure was used to allow a complete test of

Table 13.2 The Relationship Between Region of Socialization and Racial
Identification (in percentages)

	Region of Socialization		
	Deep South (N = 800) (41.8%)	Border South (N = 379) (19.8%)	Non-South (N = 733) (38.3%)
Group Identification[a]			
High	62.4	61.9	33.3
Low	37.6	38.1	66.7

a. $\chi^2 = 144.02$; $p > .001$; tau-b = .24.

our framework. Table 13.3 shows a number of the models we tested
using the log-linear analysis procedure. The best-fitting model is made
up of a number of interactions that are relevant to our ideas about the
relationship between age and voting behavior for blacks. Those interactions are between education and voting; age and voting; and finally,
region of socialization, racial identification, and voting.

By looking at the standardized lambda coefficients underlying the
interactions in the best-fitting model (see Table 13.4), the nature of the
relationships within the interactions can be seen. The interaction between education and voting turnout is such that blacks with more
education are more likely to vote than those with less education. The
pattern of the age × voting interaction shows that elderly blacks (aged
more than 59 years old) are more likely to vote than both middle-aged
blacks (aged 40-58 years) and younger blacks (aged 21-39 years). The
findings for both interactions replicate the typical findings in the research on voting behavior (Campbell et al., 1960; Verba & Nie, 1972;
Wolfinger & Rosenstone, 1980).

The pattern for the interaction between region, racial identification,
and voting sheds some light on why it is that older blacks, who surely
are the least educated, are more likely to vote than other age groups of
blacks. The lambda coefficients show us (see Table 13.4) that blacks
reared in the deep South who are high racial identifiers are more likely
to vote than: (a) blacks reared in border South states who are high
identifiers and (b) blacks reared in the deep South who are low group
identifiers. At this point, keep in mind the bivariate relationships between age and region of socialization and age and racial identification.
What we saw earlier (Table 13.1) was that elderly blacks were more

Table 13.3 Models for Voting Behavior as a Function of Education (E), Racial Identification (I), Region of Socialization (R), and Age (A)

Model*	DF	$LR \times 2^2$	p
M V	35	232.37	.00
M2 AV	33	126.29	.00
M3 RV	33	224.44	.00
M4 IV	34	227.26	.00
M5 EV	34	223.10	.00
M6 AV,RV	31	122.99	.00
M7 AV,RV	32	125.97	.00
M8 AV,EV	32	51.95	.01
M9 RV,EV	32	221.11	.00
M10 RV,IV	32	221.27	.00
M11 IV,EV	33	213.44	.00
M12 AV,RV,EV	30	122.67	.02
M13 AV,RV,EV	30	46.77	.02
M14 AV,IV,EV	31	51.59	.01
M15 RV,IV,EV	31	204.71	.00
M16 ARV,IV,EV	25	39.29	.03
M17 AIV,RV,EV	27	46.43	.01
M18 AEV,RV,IV	28	45.85	.01
M19 RIV,AV,EV	27	35.35	.1303
M20 REV,AV,IV	27	37.83	.08
M25 ARV,REV	24	33.16	.1007
M28 AIV,REV	25	37.13	.0561
M29 AEV,RIV	25	34.53	.0971

* Arie Implicit in each model.

likely both to have been reared in the deep South and to be high racial-group identifiers. Thus, the interaction between region, identification, and voting supports the severity of conditions idea by showing why elderly blacks are more likely to vote than other age groups of black Americans.

The lambda coefficients also show us that, surprisingly, blacks reared in border South states who are low racial identifiers are more likely to vote than: (a) low identifiers reared in the deep South or (b) high identifiers reared in border states.

Table 13.4 Standardized Lambda Coefficients for Variable Interactions Involving Voting Behavior (V), Education (E), Region of Socialization (R), Group Identification (I), and Age (A)

Education × Vote	
High School above × Yes	8.254
11 yrs. × Yes	−8.254
Age × Vote	
Elderly × Yes	7.058
Middle × Yes	−4.342
Young × Yes	−11.922
Region × Identification × Vote	
Deep South × High × Yes	2.480
Border South × High × Yes	−2.895
Non-South × High × Yes	.957
Deep South × Low × Yes	-2.480
Border South × Low × Yes	2.895
Non-South × Low × Yes	.957

Discussion

The results of this investigation suggest that the severity of conditions framework is useful for furthering our understanding of the voting participation of older black Americans. Taking other important variables into account, the multivariate analysis confirmed the higher likelihood of voting for those with the most education and for elderly black Americans. These findings replicate the results of research by others on the political participation of blacks. It is the apparent inconsistency in these findings that we set out to explain by considering the implications of the severity of the experienced racial environment for the development of racial identification. In support of the severity idea, the interaction between region of socialization, racial identification, and voting indicates that racial identification has a motivational impact on voting that is mediated by region of socialization. What that interaction shows specifically is a positive influence of high racial-group identification on voter turnout exclusive to those reared in the deep South. This pattern was predicted on the basis of the severity of conditions framework.

Although quite supportive of the severity of conditions framework, the evidence is not always clearly interpretable. For example, a very surprising finding was that being reared in a border state made those with a high level of racial identification less likely to turn out. It seems that mixed messages in the sociopolitical environment may have depoliticized these respondents. On the one hand, border states historically were not as repressive as deep Southern states. For example, in 1948 border Southern states gave the Democratic candidate for president far less support than received from the deep Southern states (Matthews & Prothro, 1966, pp. 170-171). Moreover, in 1964 when the deep Southern states aligned with the Goldwater camp, border states (like the rest of the nation outside of Arizona) supported Johnson for the presidency. On the other hand, some counties in border states like Virginia have been found to restrict the right of blacks to cast the ballot (Goldenstein, 1982). Being socialized in communities where race-relevant messages were not overtly or consistently discriminatory may have led to a black electorate that is not as strongly mobilized by group attachments. For those reared in these areas the social antecedents of racial identification would be based in part on a less intense experience of categorical treatment. Given this varying experience of categorical treatment, racial identification may not have the same bases as in the deep South nor straightforwardly predictable motivational effects.

Conclusion

The findings do make it clear that the nature of the domination relation existing between blacks and whites during socialization influences the extent of psychological group identification black Americans develop. These findings support a number of theoretical frameworks in social psychology (e.g., Thibaut, 1950) that would make that prediction. Although certain relationships have been presumed, there are no empirical demonstrations of the relationship between the racial environment one knows early on and the persistence of racial identification for subordinate groups. Nor do we have an ample amount of research on how changes in the racial climate affect the intensity of racial identification and its role in political mobilization. The present research suggests the need for more research on long-term social-psychological effects of intergroup relations and the development of theoretical frameworks that account for the behaviors that these long-term outcomes should influence. In our opinion, an integration of social-psychological frameworks with a field-theoretic orientation (e.g., Lewin, 1939; Thibaut & Kelley, 1959) and theories that deal specifically with political psychology (e.g., Miller & Sears, 1986; Sears, 1983; Sears & McConahay,

1973) will be the most helpful in guiding that type of research and theory development.

We have demonstrated that the psychological tie to their racial group developed by black Americans might be a result of the harsh racial climate in which they were socialized. Moreover, because of racial identification and region of socialization elderly blacks are voting activists.

Our findings reinforce the thesis that because of their experience in harsh racial conditions, older blacks may place more symbolic importance on the ballot than younger cohorts. As a result, older blacks may be using the ballot to erase the old symbolism of second-class citizenship. Moreover, elderly blacks may perceive the ballot as a means to maximize their political influence inasmuch as the vote can be used in exchange for goods and services (see Hamilton, 1979; Morris, 1984). Older blacks more than younger blacks may also believe that patterns of dominant/subordinate relationships can be altered fundamentally if the vote is used to gain influence within the existing institutional bases of political power.

But what of other cohorts of blacks: What will motivate them to vote? Given that the most visible forms of economic, political, and social racial subordination have been removed, will this make the linkages between political climate, racial identification, and turnout less important? If that is the case what factors will affect black voter turnout in the future? When we turn our attention to poor urban blacks who suffer high unemployment rates, we can see that these are critical questions For poor urban blacks, overt racial discrimination may not be apparent. Yet governmental and corporate policymaking that does not adequately address joblessness in black communities may result in severe economic conditions resulting in a lower quality of life in black than in white communities.

Work by Hamilton (1979) would indicate that being socialized in a high unemployment environment may not lead to mobilization if there is (heavy) dependency on social welfare agencies. His case study of voting patterns among New York City blacks (1961-1977) led him to conclude that governmental antipoverty programs may have depoliticized the constituencies they were designed to serve. Hamilton argued that the low black voter turnout can be attributed to blacks not being required to use votes to obtain rewards from the political system. Instead as recipients of services, their only requirement was to be eligible. Without the development of the ballot as an instrument to gain access to political decisionmaking, poor blacks in New York became passive actors in the system. As a result, racial identification would not be a principal resource for political mobilization insofar as the environment does not socialize blacks to see the importance of traditional political participation.

A more recent case study of the successful electoral victory of the late Harold Washington, Chicago's first black mayor, implies that mobilization may occur even where a heavy social welfare dependency exists. Preston's (1983) analysis reveals that Washington's campaign organizers were able to register and get poor blacks to the polls in significant numbers to vote for Washington. For many of these low-income blacks, Washington's candidacy and victory may have symbolized the possibility that "one of their own" could change the harsh economic conditions that exist in their communities. In the main, future research should focus on how less severe as well as changing types of racial conditions impinge upon socialization, identity, and the political behavior of present and future age groups.

Notes

1. The region of socialization variable is based on coding used by Corzine, Creech, and Corzine (1983, p. 778). This variable has three categories: the deep South (Alabama, Arkansas, Georgia, Louisiana, Mississippi, South Carolina, and Texas), border Southern States (Florida, North Carolina, Tennessee, and Virginia), and non-Southern states.

2. The other categories of black people who made up the second cluster were black people who rioted in the streets, blacks who made it by getting around the law, and black people who gave their children African names; insofar as we are interested in how "mainstream" racial identification affects voting behavior, a decision was made not to explore how this second factor of identification might affect turnout. Though this factor may influence voter turnout, it may be more germane for protest types of behavior among blacks who had been socialized in a severe racial climate. Overall, this factor accounted for 17% of the total variance.

3. A very important issue to consider is whether or not older citizens who were socialized in the deep South moved to more racially tolerate climates. This might help explain the relationships we expected to find. Our analysis of the covariation pattern between region of socialization and current region produced a tau-b of .33 and a gamma of .49. This would indicate that most residents were likely to remain in region of origin. But movement away from the deep South among the elderly increased significantly the voting level of only elderly blacks who currently reside in the West. Without further analysis, its not altogether clear why older blacks in the West are more likely to report voting. This issue will be explored in future analyses and papers.

References

Aberbach, J. D. (1977). Power consciousness: A comparative analysis. *American Political Science Review, 71,* 1544-1560.

Aberbach, J. D., & Walker, J. L. (1970). The meaning of black power: A comparison of white and black interpretations of a political slogan. *American Political Science Review, 64*, 367-388.

Apfelbaum, E. (1979). Relations of domination and movements for liberation: An analysis of power between groups. In W. G. Austin & S. Worchel (Eds.), *The social psychology of intergroup relations* (pp. 188-204). Monterey, CA: Brooks/Cole.

Brown, R., Jackson, J. S., & Bowman, P. J. (1982). *Racial consciousness and political mobilization of black Americans.* Paper presented at the American Political Science Association meeting, Chicago.

Campbell, A., Converse, P. E., Miller, W. E., & Stokes, D. E. (1960). *The American voter.* New York: John Wiley.

Caplan, N. (1970). The new ghetto man: A review of recent empirical studies. *Social Issues, 26*(1), 59-73.

Cohen, J. E., Cotter, P. R., & Coulter, P. (1983). The changing structure of southern political participation: Matthews and Prothro 20 years later. *Social Science Quarterly, 3,* 536-549.

Corzine, J., Creech, J., & Corzine, L. (1983). Black concentration and lynchings in the South: Testing Blalock's power-threat hypothesis. *Social Forces, 61,* 774-796.

Danigelis, N. L. (1977). A theory of black political participation in the United States. *Social Forces, 56,* 31-47.

Danigelis, N. L. (1982). Race, class and political involvement in the U.S. *Social Forces, 61,* 532-550.

Dawson, R. E., Prewitt, K., & Dawson, K. S. (1977). *Political socialization: An analytic study* (2nd ed.). Boston: Little, Brown.

Goldstein, L. M. (1982). *The voting rights act: A reassessment.* Paper presented at the American Political Science Association meeting, Denver, CO.

Gurin, P., Miller, A. H., & Gurin, G. (1980). Stratum identification and consciousness. *Social Psychology Quarterly, 43*(1), 30-47.

Hamilton, C. V. (1979). The patron-recipient relationship and minority politics in New York City. *Political Science Quarterly, 94,* 211-227.

Jackson, J. J. (1980). *Minorities and aging.* Belmont, CA: Wadsworth.

Jackson, J. S., Brown, R. E., Hatchett, S. J., & Shepard, L. J. (1985). *Correlates of registration and voting patterns in the 1984 National Black Election Study.* Paper presented at the League of Women Voters Education Fund's Conference on Electoral Participation, Washington, DC.

Jackson, J. S., Gurin, G., McCullough, W. R., & Tucker, M. B. (1981). *Black identification, consciousness and mental health.* Unpublished manuscript, University of Michigan.

Jackson, J. S., McCullough, W., & Gurin, G. (1981). Group identity development within black families. In H. McAdoo (Ed.), *Black families* (pp. 252-263). Beverly Hills, CA: Sage.

Jennings, M. K., & Niemi, R. E. (1981). *Generations and politics: A panel study of youth and their parents.* Princeton, NJ: Princeton University Press.

Keller, E. (1978). The impact of black mayors on urban policy. In J. Howard & R. C. Smith (Eds.), *The Annals, 439,* 50-53.

Key, V. O. (1949). *Southern politics in state and nation.* New York: Knopf.

Knoke, D., & Burke, P. J. (1980). *Log-linear models.* Beverly Hills, CA: Sage.

Lewin, G. K. (1939). Field theory and experiment in social psychology: Concepts and methods. *American Journal of Sociology, 44,* 868-896.

Lewin, G. K. (1948). Self-hatred among Jews. In G. K. Lewin (Ed.), *Resolving social conflicts: Selected papers on group dynamics* (pp. 186-200). New York: Harper.

Mannheim, K. (1972). The problem of generations. In P. G. Altbach & R. S. Laufer (Eds.), *The new pilgrims: Youth protest in transition* (pp. 101-138). New York: McKay.

Matthews, D. R., & Prothro, J. W. (1966). *Negroes and the new southern politics.* New York: Harcourt, Brace & World.

McAdam, D. (1982). *Political process and the development of black insurgency.* Chicago: University of Chicago Press.

Miller, A. H., Gurin, P., Gurin, G., & Malanchuk, O. (1981). Group consciousness and political participation. *American Journal of Political Science, 25,* 494-511.

Miller, D. S., & Sears, D. O. (1986). Stability and change in social tolerance: A test of the persistence hypothesis. *American Journal of Political Science, 30,* 214-236.

Morris, A. D. (1981). Black southern student sit-in movement: An analysis of internal organization. *American Sociological Review, 46,* 746-767.

Morris, A. D. (1984). *The origins of the Civil Rights Movement: Black communities organizing for change.* New York: Free Press.

Morris, A. D., Hatchett, S. J., & Brown, R. E. (1989). The Civil Rights Movement and black political socialization. In R. Sigel (Ed.), *Political learning in adulthood: A sourcebook* (pp. 272-305). Chicago: University of Chicago Press.

Morris, M. D. (1975). *The politics of black America.* New York: Harper & Row.

Morris, M. D. (1984). Black electoral participation and the distribution of public benefits. In C. Davidson (Ed.), *Minority vote dilution* (pp. 271-285). Washington, DC: Howard University Press.

Preston, M. B. (1983). The election of Harold Washington. *P.S., 16,* 486-488.

Prohansky, H., & Newton, P. (1968). The nature and meaning of negro self-identity. In M. Deutsch, C. Katz, & A. R. Jensen (Eds.), *Social class, race, and psychological development* (pp. 178-218). New York: Holt, Rinehart & Winston.

Sears, D. O. (1983). The persistence of early political predispositions: The roles of attitude object and life stage. In L. Wheeler & P. Shaver (Eds.), *Review of Personality and Social Psychology, 4,* 79-116.

Sears, D. O., & McConahay, J. B. (1973). *The politics of violence.* Boston: Houghton Mifflin.

Shingles, R. D. (1981). Black consciousness and political participation: The missing link. *American Political Science Review, 75,* 76-91.

Simpson, G. E., & Yinger, J. H. (1972). *Racial and cultural minorities* (4th ed.). New York: Harper & Row.

Tajfel, H., & Turner, J. (1979). An integrative theory of intergroup conflict. In W. G. Austin & S. Worchel (Eds.), *The social psychology of intergroup relations* (pp. 33-47). Monterey, CA: Brooks/Cole.

Thibaut, J. W. (1950). An experimental study of the cohesiveness of underprivileged groups. *Human Relations, 3,* 251-278.

Thibaut, J. W., & Kelley, H. H. (1959). *The social psychology of groups.* New York: John Wiley.

Verba, S., & Nie, N. H. (1972). *Participation in America: Political democracy and social equality.* New York: Harper & Row.

Verba, S., Nie, N., & Kim, J. (1978). *Participation and political equality: A seven-nation comparison.* New York: Cambridge University Press.

Walton, H. (1972). *Black politics: A theoretical and structural analysis.* Philadelphia: Lippincott.

Walton, H., Jr. (1985). *Invisible politics: Black political behavior.* New York: SUNY Press.

Wolfinger, R. E., & Rosenstone, S. T. (1980). *Who votes?* New Haven, CT: Yale University Press.

DEMOGRAPHIC AND RELIGIOUS CORRELATES OF VOTING BEHAVIOR

Robert Joseph Taylor
Michael C. Thornton

Recent events bear witness to an accelerating involvement of religious organizations in the political landscape of U.S. life. Although the actual impact of religious organizations is not clear, the interests of religious groups have been expressed in relation to a number of social issues, including abortion, family policy and legislation, and both domestic and foreign policy. This growing religious influence coincides with a period of declining participation in electoral politics among the general population. The emergence of religion as a conduit of political and social change contradicts the traditional belief that religious institutions are apolitical. Political activism within segments of the religious community has generated a renewed interest in how religious beliefs and practices are related to political actions (Beatty & Walters, 1984). Further, there is interest in determining whether this trend toward religious activism is evident broadly in the population or is isolated in particular and identifiable subgroups.

Aging and Religious Participation Among Black Americans

An emerging body of literature indicates that elderly blacks display a very high level of religious participation (see Chapter 7). Older black adults attend religious services on a frequent basis, have a high likelihood of being an official member of a church or other place of worship, pray on a daily basis, and describe themselves as being religious (Taylor, 1986). Findings based on the full age range of National Survey of Black Americans (NSBA) data (18-101 years) reveal that elderly blacks display a consistently higher degree of religious involvement than their younger counterparts (Chatters & Taylor, 1989; Taylor, 1988a, 1988b; Taylor, Thornton, & Chatters, 1987). Age was a significant and positive predictor of the probability of being a religious affiliate, the likelihood of attending religious services as an adult, and whether one attended church and was an official member of a church. Further, older age was positively associated with several informal religious behaviors, such as reading religious materials, listening to and viewing religious broadcasts, private prayer, and requests for prayer from others. Within the area of religious attitudes, older black adults were more likely than younger persons to express greater subjective religious involvement and to evaluate the historical role of black churches in a positive manner. The extensive religious involvement of elderly black adults suggests that they are an optimal group in which to examine the influence of religion on political participation.

Age and Voting Behavior

The literature has been equivocal in its view of the effect of age on political behavior. Early research suggested that similar to the proposed effects of religion, age had a negative impact on political participation. In this vein, the elderly have been described as the most alienated and uninvolved age group (Hudson & Strate, 1985). Emerging work, however, challenges the assumptions of low interest and perceptions of limited political efficacy among this age group (e.g., Glenn & Grimes, 1968; Lupfer & Rosenberg, 1983). Although some researchers describe a linear and positive relationship between age and political interest (Glenn & Grimes, 1968), others have noted that level of political participation increases through late middle age, gradually dropping off in old age (Nie, Verba, & Kim, 1974). It is speculated that the decrease in overall participation reflects the lower socioeconomic status among the elderly (Glenn & Grimes, 1968). In voter turnout studies that control for education and income, the observed reduction in voting associated with age is diminished (Glenn & Grimes, 1968; Nie et al., 1974). The principal conclusion of this body of research on age and political participation is that older persons are more notable for their similarities to other age groups than for their differences. Older adults, similar to the middle aged, are more politically active than young adults (Hudson & Strate, 1985).

Recent research based on studies conducted by the Program for Research on Black Americans at the University of Michigan reveals that older black adults exhibit a high degree of political participation. Using data from the NSBA, Brown and Barnes-Nacoste (Chapter 13) found that 7 out of 10 elderly and middle-aged blacks indicated that they voted as compared to only 1 out of 2 younger black adults. Similarly, data from the 1984 National Black Election Study indicated that both middle-aged and older blacks had a higher probability of voting than did their younger counterparts (Tate, Brown, Hatchett, & Jackson, 1988).

Models of Religion and Political Participation Among Black Americans

Two competing models describe the relationship between religion and political participation among black Americans. The first of these models, religion as opiate, suggests that black religious involvement is directly antagonist to secular concerns. This is particularly evident among Protestant denominations, which are described as being conservative in theology and practice (Hunt & Hunt, 1977a, 1977b). This conservatism is believed to be especially pronounced among black Protestants, who are viewed as escapist, emotional, and otherworldly. Various researchers have suggested that among these groups, secular concerns such as politics are inimical to an afterlife (Hunt & Hunt, 1977a, 1977b).

The contention that religion acts to dampen political activities among blacks is predicated on a number of assumptions. First, it is suggested that economic deprivation and limited opportunities for political effectiveness result in a preoccupation with religion as a means to relieve earthly sufferings: Relying on His will rather than one's own. Religious beliefs alleviate suffering by altering perceived deprivation (Wimberly, 1984) through "compensators" or "theodices" (explanations of the meaning of suffering) (Stark & Bainbridge, 1980).

In one of the few studies to examine the notion of religion as opiate among black Americans, Marx (1967, 1969) found that membership in black denominations discouraged racial consciousness and collective behavior. Participation in religious institutions resulted in an overemphasis on otherworldly matters and only limited concern with issues of social and political change. Involvement in nonsecular types of churches also has a negative affect on activism (Nelsen & Nelsen, 1975). Ultimately, adherents of the religion as opiate model view religious participation as an impediment to obtaining racial equality or political progress.

A competing perspective on religion and political participation is called the ethnic community model. This model emphasizes the role of churches in enhancing individual self-worth and building a functional community based on a sense of group identity and collective interest. Consistent with this model are the notions that religion is a dynamic agent of social change and that black churches serve as institutional bases during struggles against racial injustice. Research utilizing this model alludes to anecdotal and historical evidence that indicates that black churches and their leadership have been indispensable to the struggle for political and social equality for black Americans.

Reflecting their organizational strengths, churches and their officials are key reference points for many blacks (Vedlitz, Alston, & Pinkele, 1980; Washington, 1964) and serve as a resource base for the mobilization of black communities in areas of social protest and electoral politics (Morris, 1984). Black clergy have acted as political middle-persons between the black electorate and interested white politicians (Vedlitz et al., 1980). In addition, Matthews and Prothro (1966) found that black political participation was highest where churches were an integral part of the political process.

Morris's (1984) critical analysis of the civil rights movement highlighted the critically important role of black churches as an effective mechanism within black communities for mobilizing resources and achieving social change. In particular, the resources of black churches include their organized mass base, an independent financial foundation through which protest is funded, the economic and political autonomy of clergy, and a meeting place where tactics and strategies can be planned. Black churches are complex organizations with a well-defined division of labor (Morris, 1984). Their numerous committees and groups make it possible for many churches to hold a scheduled activity every night of the week. Church meetings may stimulate political interest and mobilization through announcements or preachments against discrimination. The organizational structure of black churches may facilitate raising money and mass meetings and other activities that are necessary for collective action. Yet, although black churches have a complex organizational structure, they are not typical bureaucracies. Their organizational structure has been characterized as being relatively informal, with the minister playing a central role in coordinating church activities. Morris (1984) argued against the notion that the fluid organizational structure of black churches reflects disorder and a collectivity motivated by emotionalism, however. Although black churches do serve as important outlets for the reduction of stress, they are also strong mass-based organizations through which diverse goals are achieved.

Focus of Present Analysis

As this literature review indicates, there is little information on political participation among elderly black adults, and even less is known about the impact of religion on political participation among this group. In the present chapter we investigate demographic and religious correlates of the voting behavior of older black adults. We used two measures of voting behavior: presidential voting and state and local voting. A full set of demographic (i.e., age, gender, marital status, education, income, urbanicity, and region) and religiosity (i.e., church attendance, church membership, religious affiliation, and subjective religiosity) variables formed independent variables in this analysis.

Methods

Dependent Variables

The two dependent variables examined in this analysis were measured by the following questions: "Did you vote in the last presidential election (1976)?" and "Did you vote in any state or local election during the last year?"

Religious Involvement Variables

Four measures of religious involvement were utilized in this analysis: religious affiliation, frequency of church attendance, church membership, and the degree of subjective religiosity. Religious affiliation was grouped into five categories: Baptist, Methodist, Catholic, Other, and No Affiliation. Frequency of church attendance was assessed by the question: "How often do you attend religious services? Would you say nearly every day, at least once a week, a few times a month, a few times a year, or less than once a year?" Church membership was determined by asking respondents: "Are you an official member of a church or other place of worship?" In addition, subjective religiosity was measured by the question: "How religious would you say you are—very religious, fairly religious, not too religious, or not religious at all?"

Results

Religious Involvement

The majority of the elderly blacks in this sample were Baptist (58.8%), followed by Methodist (17.1%), Catholic (5.7%), and persons expressing no religious affiliation (4.2%). A total of 14% of respondents indicated that they were affiliated with a religion or denomination other than these major groups. Generally, the respondents attended church frequently; 5% stated that they attended religious services nearly every day, 46.9% at least once a week, 30.2% a few times a month, 9.4% a few times a year, and 7.9% less than once a year. Three out of four (77.6%) respondents said they were official members of a church or other place of worship. Overall, respondents characterized themselves as being religious, with 59.4% stating they were very religious, 35.2% fairly religious, and 5.4% stating that they were either not too religious or not religious at all.

Bivariate Analysis

The majority of the black elderly adults in this sample said they voted in the 1976 presidential election and in state and local elections. Seven out of 10 respondents (69.7%) indicated they voted in the presidential election and 54.5% in state and local elections. Tables 14.1 and 14.2 present the bivariate analysis of the demographic variables on the probability of presidential voting (Table 14.1) and state and local voting (Table 14.2). The pattern of the relationships between the demographic variables and the two measures of voting behavior was consistent with each of the demographic variables except gender achieving statistical significance. Age demonstrated a negative relationship with both measures of voting behavior, with respondents 75 and older being the least likely age group to vote. Among the marital status groups, a higher percentage of married respondents reported voting in presidential and

Table 14.1 Bivariate Analysis of Presidential Voting and Selected Demographic Variables

| Demographic Variables | Presidential Voting | | | | | |
	Yes (%)	No (%)	(N)	χ^2	V	Gamma
Age in Years				8.81*	.12	−.20**
55-64	74.2	25.8	236			
65-74	70.5	29.5	224			
75+	58.6	41.4	111			
Gender				.08	.01	.03
Male	70.4	29.6	213			
Female	69.3	30.7	358			
Marital Status				10.28*	.13	
Married	76.0	24.0	221			
Divorced	71.1	28.9	45			
Separated	71.7	28.3	53			
Widowed	62.5	37.5	232			
Never married	75.0	25.0	20			
Education				40.11***	.27	.47***
0 to 6 years	54.4	45.6	195			
7 to 11 years	73.0	27.0	226			
H.S. graduate	85.5	14.5	145			
Income				44.74***	.31	.52***
Under $5,000	57.7	42.3	222			
$5,000-$6,999	65.3	34.7	72			
$7,000-$11,999	82.5	17.5	80			
$12,000+	91.2	8.8	102			
Urbanicity				4.86*	.09	.21*
Urban	72.4	27.6	409			
Rural	63.0	37.0	162			
Region				18.14***	.18	
Northeast	76.0	24.0	96			
North Central	79.8	20.2	109			
South	63.1	36.9	336			
West	86.7	13.3	30			

*$p<.05$; **$p<.01$; ***$p<.001$.

state and local elections. Both education and income had strong positive associations with presidential and state and local voting. Regional differences were exhibited, with a lower percentage of respondents who resided in the South reporting that they voted than respondents in any other region. Urbanicity was the only variable that displayed a distinctive relationship with the two measures of voting behavior. Urbanicity

Table 14.2 Bivariate Analysis of Demographic Variables on State and Local Voting

Demographic Variables	State and Local Voting					
	Yes (%)	No (%)	(N)	χ^2	V	Gamma
Age						
55-64	56.4	43.6	236	7.77*	.12	-.12
65-74	58.3	41.7	223			
75+	42.7	57.3	110			
Gender						
Male	55.2	44.8	212	.07	.01	.02
Female	54.1	45.9	357			
Marital Status						
Married	62.3	37.7	220	9.55*	.13	
Divorced	55.6	44.4	45			
Separated	49.1	50.9	53			
Widowed	48.5	51.5	231			
Never married	50.0	50.0	20			
Education						
0 to 6 years	41.2	58.8	194	25.37***	.21	.34***
7 to 11 years	56.9	43.1	225			
H.S. graduate	68.3	31.7	145			
Income						
Under $5,000	43.6	56.4	220	35.69***	.27	.40***
$5,000-$6,999	45.8	54.2	72			
$7,000-$11,999	68.7	31.3	80			
$12,000+	74.5	25.5	102			
Urbanicity						
Urban	56.3	43.7	410	2.04	.06	.13
Rural	49.7	50.3	159			
Region						
Northeast	55.2	44.8	96	11.94**	.14	
North Central	64.2	35.8	109			
South	49.4	50.6	334			
West	73.3	26.7	30			

*$p<.05$; **$p<.01$; ***$p<.001$.

was significantly associated with presidential voting but not state and local voting; urban respondents were more likely to vote in presidential elections than their rural counterparts.

In the bivariate relationship between religious involvement and voting, only church attendance and church membership were significantly related to voting behavior (Tables 14.3 and 14.4). Frequent attendance

Table 14.3 Bivariate Analysis of the Religious Involvement Variables on Presidential Voting

Religious Involvement	Presidential Voting Yes (%)	No (%)	(N)	χ^2	Gamma
Church Attendance				18.35**	.29***
Nearly every day	73.3	26.7	30		
Once a week	78.4	21.6	255		
A few times a month	64.9	35.1	168		
A few times a year	61.5	38.5	52		
Less than once a year	53.5	46.5	43		
Church Membership				6.30*	.26*
Yes	73.0	27.0	429		
No	61.2	38.8	121		
Religious Affiliation				10.81*	
No affiliation	45.8	54.2	24		
Catholic	75.8	24.2	33		
Methodist	74.5	25.5	98		
Baptist	71.1	28.9	332		
Other	61.7	38.3	81		
Subjective Religiosity				3.74	.06
Very religious	68.1	31.9	335		
Fairly religious	73.6	26.4	201		
Not too religious	63.6	36.4	22		
Not religious at all	50.0	50.0	8		

*p<.05; **p<.01; ***p<.001.

at religious services was associated with a greater likelihood of voting in both presidential and state and local elections. Similarly, older persons who were church members were more likely to vote than were nonmembers. Additionally, persons who expressed no religious affiliation were significantly less likely to vote in the presidential election than respondents indicating a denominational preference.

Multivariate Analysis

Table 14.5 presents the results of the logit analysis of the religious involvement and demographic variables on the voting behavior of elderly black adults; all tested models achieved statistical significance. Education and income were positively associated with both presidential and state and local voting. Respondents with higher levels of education

Table 14.4 Bivariate Analysis of the Religious Involvement Variables on State and Local Voting

Religious Involvement	State and Local Voting			χ^2	Gamma
	Yes (%)	No (%)	(N)		
Church Attendance					
Nearly every day	66.7	33.3	30	6.55	.16*
Once a week	58.7	41.3	254		
A few times a month	48.8	51.2	166		
A few times a year	51.0	49.0	51		
Less than once a year	48.8	51.2	43		
Church Membership					
Yes	58.8	41.2	427	10.54**	.32**
No	42.1	57.9	121		
Religious Affiliation					
No affiliation	37.5	62.5	24	5.36	
Catholic	45.5	54.5	33		
Methodist	60.2	39.8	98		
Baptist	53.9	46.1	330		
Other	56.8	43.2	81		
Subjective Religiosity					
Very religious	55.0	45.0	333	1.80	-.03
Fairly religious	55.7	44.3	201		
Not too religious	45.5	54.5	22		
Not religious at all	37.5	62.5	8		

*$p<.01$; **$p<.001$.

and income were more likely to vote than were their counterparts (Models 1-4). Respondents residing in the West were more likely than Southerners to vote in presidential elections (Models 1 and 2). In addition, respondents who were never married were less likely to vote in state and local elections than were their married counterparts (Model 4).

Among the religiosity variables, frequency of church attendance and religious affiliation both were associated with presidential voting (Model 2). Those who attended church on a frequent basis were more likely to vote than those who attended less frequently. Similarly, Baptists were more likely to vote than were respondents in the religious affiliation category designated Other. In addition, church attendance bordered significance with the likelihood of voting in state and local elections (Model 4).

Table 14.5 Logistic Regression Analysis of Religious Involvement and Demographic Variables on Presidential and State and Local Voting

Predictors	Presidential Voting		State and Local Voting	
	Model 1	Model 2	Model 3	Model 4
Intercept	15.1***	15.82***	8.3*	8.64*
Church Attendance	—	.43**	—	.23[a]
Church Membership	—	.18	—	.32
Religious Affiliation				
None	—	−.55	—	.40
Catholic	—	.14	—	−.62
Methodist	—	−.27	—	.19
Other	—	−1.01**	—	−.26
Subjective Religiosity	—	−.20	—	.11
Income	.13***	.10**	.08***	.69*
Education	.14***	.15***	.07***	.73*
Age	−.01	−.01	−.01	−.01
Marital Status				
Divorced	−.17	−.15	−.50	−.43
Separated	.02	.18	−.46	−.48
Widowed	−.38	−.27	−.38	−.31
Never married	−.30	.79	−.29	−1.40*
Sex				
Male	−.34	−.03	−.32	−.07
Urbanicity				
Urban	−.36	−.25	.01	−.09
Region				
Northeast	.01	.15	−.29	−.08
North Central	.34	.34	.14	.11
West	1.56*	1.61*	.81	.66
χ^2	75.94***	88.1***	48.72***	53.12***

NOTE: Several of the predictors in this analysis are represented by dummy variables. Baptists, married, female, rural, and South are the excluded categories.
*$p<.05$; **$p<.01$; ***$p<.001$; $.05<a<.10$.

Discussion

Demographic Factors

Consistent with prior research, the set of bivariate results indicated that age, marital status, education, and income all had a significant impact on voting behavior. Wolfinger and Rosenstone (1980) found that married persons were more likely to vote than their widowed, divorced, separated, and never-married counterparts. Similarly, older persons who were 78 years of age and older were less likely to vote than were younger persons (Wolfinger & Rosenstone, 1980, Table 3.2). Across a variety of studies, education and income have demonstrated strong positive relationships with voting behavior (Milbrath & Goel, 1977; Verba, Nie, & Kim, 1978; Verba & Nye, 1972; Wolfinger & Rosenstone, 1980). But for several of these bivariate findings, the introduction of multivariate controls diminished or eliminated these relationships. In particular, it would appear that the effects of education and income are confounded with other factors that have more limited influences on voting behavior.

A recent analysis examining the correlates of education, income, and poverty (Taylor & Chatters, 1988) may inform our efforts to understand the nature of socioeconomic differences in voting behavior. This prior analysis indicated that measures of socioeconomic status (i.e., education, income, and poverty status) were intimately related to age and marital status among this sample of older black adults. In essence, married persons had higher incomes and a lower incidence of poverty than did their nonmarried counterparts, whereas older persons had fewer years of education, lower incomes, and higher rates of poverty than did younger respondents. These findings, in conjunction with the present research, indicate that the bivariate findings for the relationships between voting behavior and age and marital status were spurious and essentially reflected their common association with education and income statuses. The findings of the present research are consistent with other work that suggests that education and income are primary predictors of voting behavior (Verba & Nye, 1972; Wolfinger & Rosenstone, 1980). As distinct from other efforts demonstrating differential effects for socioeconomic factors (Wolfinger & Rosenstone, 1980), among this group of older black adults, education and income were equally strong predictors of the probability of voting.

There were several instances in which other demographic factors sustained their influence even in the presence of controls for income and education. Region was a significant predictor of voting in presidential elections and marital status was a significant predictor of voting in state and local elections. Regional differences indicated that Southerners were less likely than respondents who resided in the West to vote in presidential elections. Rates of voting in the South are lower than those for other regions of the country, and this disparity is evident among both blacks and whites (Wolfinger & Rosenstone, 1980).

Marital status differences indicated that older persons who were married were more likely to vote in state and local elections than were older persons who had never married. The literature on social networks and social support suggests that the statuses of marriage and parenthood function to integrate individuals within families, neighborhoods, and the larger community. It could be argued that never-married elderly (who also would be less likely to have children) would tend to exhibit lower levels of community integration than would older persons who were married. The depressed levels of voting in state and local elections found among never-married respondents could reflect their generally lower levels of community involvement and integration. Further, never-married elderly might exhibit lower levels of voting specifically because state and local ballot issues tend to reflect concerns that directly affect families and children (i.e., elections to the school board, school bond initiatives) to a greater degree than do presidential or national elections. Older persons who are never married might have limited interest or investment in these types of ballot issues.

Taken as a whole, this collection of demographic findings does not bode well for increasing the rates of participation of older black adults in electoral politics. First, it has been documented that Southern residency is associated with diminished levels of political participation. Presently, 60% of the older black population and half of the general adult black population reside in the South. Similarly, low socioeconomic status has been associated with low voter participation. Recent estimates indicate that 39% of older black adults are officially poor (Taylor & Chatters, 1988). Furthermore, research on the black underclass suggests that a sizable and growing segment of the black population is comprised of men who are only marginally attached to the labor force and women and children who reside in female-headed households (Wilson & Aponte, 1985). Given the growing proportion of blacks who can be characterized as members of the underclass, the prospects that future cohorts of older black adults will be economically secure are modest. In sum, residency status (i.e., living in the South) and socioeconomic conditions suggest that participation in electoral politics among older black adults is uncertain. Religious involvement, however, may have a mitigating influence on these impediments to political participation.

Religious Involvement

The present research showed that religiosity had a positive effect on the political behavior of older black adults. Church attendance was associated with a greater likelihood of voting both in presidential and state and local elections. Church attendance remained an important predictor of voting behavior in the presence of controls for education and income. Church membership had a significant positive bivariate relationship with both indicators of voting behavior, but this relationship was eliminated in the presence of multivariate controls. In addition, the findings indicated that individual perceptions of religiosity (i.e., subjective religiosity) were not significant in explaining voting behavior; religiously oriented older black adults were no different from their nonreligious counterparts in their proclivity to vote in national and local elections.

As demonstrated by these findings, religious involvement is a multidimensional construct and different aspects of overall religiosity have varying influences on political participation. Church attendance and church membership assess the organizational component of religious involvement, whereas subjective religiosity measures an attitudinal component of religious involvement. The present findings indicate that organizational religious involvement has a stronger and more pronounced influence on voting behavior than does subjective religiosity. In this investigation, organizational aspects of religiosity were more important than religious attitudes in predicting political participation (i.e., voting behavior). Further work is needed to determine the relative influence of various aspects of religiosity on other forms of political participation.

The relationship described here between church attendance and voting behavior confirms that attendance does not hinder political participation and suggests that churches may be a critical element in political mobilization for social protest and voting behavior within black communities (Morris, 1984; Washington, 1964). The present findings suggest that religion does not directly stimulate voting behavior, but instead the organizational context of churches may increase political participation.

Black churches frequently have been portrayed as having either a salutary or detrimental influence on individuals and collectivities. The tendency to view the influences of black churches as a dichotomy ignores the unique status of religious institutions within black communities. Because of this unique status, black churches can be seen as Christian in a way different from what is normally understood by the term.

Historically, black churches have had two simultaneous principal aims, described by some as the race and Christian focuses (Paris, 1985), whereas others have characterized churches as highlighting the dual purpose of survival and liberation (Wilmore, 1983). Although black religions are depicted as ascetic and otherworldly, they have also produced very secular religious traditions, probably best epitomized by the civil rights movement. Instead of acting to discourage and mollify concerns with social change, black churches have incorporated both a spiritual focus and a secular concern that highlights the liberation of their membership from an oppressive environment; both strategies are basic to African-American life and culture (Wilmore, 1983, pp. 227-230).

Generalizations as to the mission and primary emphasis of black religious institutions on the basis of one dimension of the church severely distort the totality of black religious experience and expression. During a particular historical era, churches may choose to highlight one or another goal, but the underlying themes of secular and religious enlightenment have remained the foundation of their mission. This argument concerning the dual nature of black religious traditions has been made primarily in theological treatises and highlighted in case studies and observed in the historical annals of U.S. life. There is need for empirical research that documents this relationship between the two traditions and their effects on political activism within black communities.

The results of this research are consistent with other work that indicates a positive relationship between black churches and activism within black communities. Given the contemporary state of black America, with few institutional and shrinking governmental resources available, churches often become primary sources of hope, both secular and otherworldly. As this research indicates, the relationship between the church and the black community is complex and the agenda of research issues yet to be addressed is extensive. Future research should explore more closely the role that the church plays in the process of voting and other political behaviors among black adults. It would be particularly significant to identify how the dual focus on secular and religious concerns within many black churches is related to political activism. With state and national governments placing growing emphasis on community initiatives for self-help, churches will become an increasingly important source of resources and direction for black communities. For these and other reasons, black churches and black religious experiences deserve greater attention from the social and behavioral science communities.

References

Beatty, K., & Walters. O. (1984). Religious preference and practice: Re-evaluating their impact on political tolerance. *Public Opinion Quarterly, 48*, 318-329.

Chatters, L. M., & Taylor, R. J. (1989). Age differences in religious participation among black adults. *Journal of Gerontology: Social Sciences, 44*, S183- S189.

Glenn, N., & Grimes, M. (1968). Aging, voting and political interest. *American Sociological Review, 33*, 563-575.

Hudson, R., & Strate, J. (1985). Aging and political systems. In R. Binstock & E. Shanas (Eds.), *Handbook of aging and the social sciences* (pp. 554-585). New York: Van Nostrand Reinhold.

Hunt, L., & Hunt, J. (1977a). Religious affiliation and militancy among urban blacks: Some Catholic/Protestant comparisons. *Social Science Quarterly, 57*, 821-833.

Hunt, L., & Hunt, J. (1977b). Black religion as both opiate and inspiration of civil rights militancy: Putting Marx's data to the test. *Social Forces, 56*, 1-14.

Lupfer, M., & Rosenberg, J. (1983). Differences in adults' political orientations as a function of age. *Journal of Social Psychology, 119*, 125-133.

Marx, G. (1967). Religion: Opiate or inspiration of civil rights militancy among negroes? *American Sociological Review, 32*, 64-72.

Marx, G. (1969). *Protest and prejudice* (rev. ed.). New York: Harper & Row.

Matthews, D., & Prothro, J. W. (1966). *Negroes and the new southern politics.* New York: Harcourt, Brace, & World.

Milbrath, L., & Goel, M. (1977). *Political participation.* Chicago: Rand McNally.

Morris, A. D. (1984). *The origins of the civil rights movement: Black communities organizing for change.* New York: Free Press.

Nelsen, H. M., & Nelsen, A. K. (1975). *Black church in the sixties.* Lexington: University of Kentucky Press.

Nie, N., Verba, S., & Kim, J. (1974). Political participation and the life cycle. *Comparative Politics, 6*, 319-340.

Paris, P. (1985). *The social teaching of the black churches.* Philadelphia: Fortress.

Stark, R., & Bainbridge, W. (1980). Towards a theory of religion: Religious commitment. *Journal of the Scientific Study of Religion, 19*, 114-128.

Tate, K., Brown, R. E., Hatchett, S. J., & Jackson, J. S. (1988). *The 1984 national black election study: A sourcebook.* Ann Arbor: University of Michigan, Institute for Social Research.

Taylor, R. J. (1986). Religious participation among elderly blacks. *The Gerontologist, 26*, 630-636.

Taylor, R. J. (1988a). Correlates of religious non-involvement among black Americans. *Review of Religious Research, 30*, 126-139.

Taylor, R. J. (1988b). Structural determinants of religious participation among black Americans. *Review of Religious Research, 30*, 114-125.

Taylor, R. J., & Chatters, L. M. (1988). Correlates of education, income, and poverty among aged blacks. *The Gerontologist, 28*, 435-441.

Taylor, R. J., Thornton, M. C., & Chatters, L. M. (1987). Black Americans' perceptions of the sociohistorical role of the church. *Journal of Black Studies, 18*, 123-138.

Vedlitz, A., Alston, J., & Pinkele, C. (1980). Politics and the black church in a southern community. *Journal of Black Studies, 10*, 367-375.

Verba, S., & Nie, N. (1972). *Participation in America: Political democracy and social equality.* New York: Harper & Row.

Verba, S., Nie, N. H., & Kim, J. (1978). *Participation and political equality: A seven-nation comparison.* Cambridge, England: Cambridge University Press.

Washington, J., Jr. (1964). *Black religion.* Boston: Beacon.

Wilmore, G. (1983). *Black religion and black radicalism* (2nd ed.). Maryknoll, NY: Orbis.

Wilson, W. J., & Aponte, R. (1985). Urban poverty. *Annual Review of Sociology, 11,* 231-258.

Wimberly, D. (1984). Socioeconomic deprivation and religious salience: A cognitive behavioral approach. *Sociological Quarterly, 25,* 223-238.

Wolfinger, R. E., & Rosenstone, S. J. (1980). *Who votes?* New Haven, CT: Yale University Press.

SECTION V

Retirement and Work

15

THE BLACK AMERICANS
WHO KEEP WORKING

Lerita M. Coleman

Implicit in recent media portrayals of black life is the message that blacks do not work, do not like to work, or avoid working. Given the historical circumstances surrounding the presence of blacks in the United States, it would seem that the emphasis on blacks as nonworkers may be misleading. There are substantial numbers of black men and women who secure employment and maintain high rates of labor force participation throughout their life cycle; many remain in the labor force past retirement age (see Chapter 16).

For black Americans working is a cultural norm. This norm stems from their African heritage, historical origins in the United States as laboring slaves, and other societal influences such as the Protestant ethic. A strong work ethic among blacks is evidenced by the fact that 84% of black women, in comparison to 55% of white women, have worked regardless of their socioeconomic, marital, or family status (Kent & Hirsch, 1972). Many black men have high labor force participation rates (63%), although their employment histories are often disrupted by extended periods of unemployment (U.S. Bureau of Labor Statistics, 1989).

It is important to understand the role of employment in the lives of black Americans aged 55 years and older.[1] This cohort is of particular interest because of possible work norms established earlier in life and the fact that they often leave the labor force despite inadequate incomes.

It is unclear to what extent blacks differ from whites in their motivations to retire, in retiring early or late, and in ability to maintain full-time or part-time employment in the later years. It is not certain whether employment is intrinsically important to older black Americans or if it is an economic requisite (see Chapter 16 this volume).

Why Do the Elderly Continue to Work?

Less is known about why elderly black Americans continue to work than about their white counterparts. In previous studies, the reasons white elderly workers cited for continuing to work are health, education, and occupational status (Palmore, George, & Fillenbaum, 1982; Veroff, Douvan, & Kulka, 1981). White elderly workers also indicated financial need or positive intrinsic rewards as important reasons for working. Working older white women, in particular, expressed positive views about their health and felt work provides a source of dignity, a boost to self-esteem, and a way to maintain a youthful self-image (Jaslow, 1976).

A clear understanding of the patterns of labor force participation among the black elderly may be difficult. Many blacks have more varied work histories than whites. In some cases, the *desire* or ability to retire occurs less frequently among blacks than whites (Kent & Hirsch, 1972). Many black elderly are likely to extend their labor force participation indefinitely and yield it only to health problems. Other researchers argue that the restricted range of occupational opportunities afforded blacks makes work less meaningful to them, and hence, retirement is less disruptive (Palmore, Fillenbaum, & George, 1984). Such arguments do not tell us if older blacks work, why they work, or how much they work, however.

More often than not, the different work histories of elderly black in comparison to elderly white Americans can be attributed to education, occupational status, and racial discrimination. At all income levels, elderly blacks are more disadvantaged educationally than their white counterparts. Although only 25% of whites failed to complete grade school, some two thirds (66%) of elderly blacks completed less than 8 years of school. Further, whereas 20% of whites over age 60 had some high school education, only 8% of blacks attended high school. The statistics on college attendance are equally disparate among whites and blacks (15% and 4% respectively).

Another factor influencing blacks' employment life cycle lies with their overrepresentation in the secondary labor market (Abbott, 1977; Gibson, 1987; Jackson & Gibson, 1985). Secondary labor market occupations are characterized by low wages, lack of health and retirement benefits, and the need for sheer physical strength and endurance. Unfortunately, blacks aged 50-64 years old are twice as likely as whites to suffer a major physical disability, preventing them from working (Abbott, 1980).

Historically, racial discrimination has led to major disparities in income between black and white workers classified in the same occupational groups (Corcoran & Duncan, 1978; Gibson, 1987). Moreover, older blacks have reaped few benefits from the recent gains made by younger black workers as a result of affirmative action and the civil rights struggles (Abbott, 1980). Hence, many elderly blacks may reach the end of a vicious employment cycle in financial destitution and ill health. The black elderly may work because of economic necessity or for survival rather than for fulfillment, recognition, or status (Dancy, 1977; Jackson, 1988; Jackson & Gibson, 1985).

Financial solvency plays a unique role in the employment and retirement patterns of older blacks. Having gainful employment—but with unstable jobs and inadequate income—is not unusual for this cohort. Therefore, the transition from work to retirement is argued to be less traumatic for blacks than whites because of the new income stability (e.g., social security, supplemental security insurance, pension) that accompanies retirement (Jackson & Gibson, 1985).

Social security was originally designed to provide pensioners with supplemental income during retirement. Social security policies, though, encourage near total retirement for those with previous adequate salaries by making deductions from earned income. Many elderly workers, however, prefer to supplement inadequate income (e.g., small social security or retirement pensions) with part-time or full-time employment (Soumerai & Avorn, 1983). The availability of supplemental income in the form of social security and retirement benefits is particularly tenuous for blacks and women who have unstable work histories and low-paying jobs yielding minuscule social security payments and little, if any, pension. This position is substantiated by the work of Abbott (1977), who found that the income of the black elderly is either earned or from public assistance rather than derived from government (e.g., regular social security) or private pensions or assets. Abbott (1977) found that the most financially disadvantaged elderly are black unmarried women. Due to their high concentration in domestic and service occupations, occupations in which many women do not deduct social security, 67% of unmarried black women 60 years of age and older earn annual incomes of less than $3,000, and 17% of these older unmarried black women have incomes of less than $1,000. These elderly black women represent the largest group of all nonbeneficiaries.

In summary, inadequate education, lack of occupational skills and occupational opportunities, and low-wage labor characterize the work histories of many older blacks. It is not surprising, therefore, that older blacks cite economic necessity, economic opportunity, value preference, health, transportation, and personal circumstances as reasons for continued employment (Almquist, 1980). Given that many of these sociodemographic characteristics of the black elderly are based primarily on labor statistics, it is important to verify whether these same factors contribute to the continued presence in the labor force of a sample of older blacks.

Therefore, I pose three questions in the present investigation: (a) Which factors best predict the employment status of blacks aged 55 years and older? (b) Which factors best predict the number of hours blacks aged 55 years or older work each week? and (c) Do the same factors predict employment status after retirement age? The factors under consideration include: age, gender, marital status, household composition, number of household members contributing income, family income, education, occupation, health interference, regional background, urban or rural residence, worries about money, and the presence or absence of an intrinsic desire to work.

Predicted Factors Influencing Work Status Among the Elderly

Why these factors? Age, for example, is important because it helps to establish the parameters for major life cycle transitions like retirement or older age. More specifically, blacks may work full-time until retirement age, but begin to work part-time after age 65. Moreover, people may use age to make decisions about employment status. Age also may be highly correlated with health. This correlation raises questions about whether age or health may be a better predictor of employment status among older blacks.

Although black women constitute a large segment of the total number of respondents and also have very high labor force participation rates earlier in the life cycle, we do not know whether more older females than males work. Based on labor force participation rates, I expect gender to be a significant predictor of employment status; that is, more older women work than do older men. Similarly, older black women may work more hours per week than older black men.

Likewise, marital status may be linked to employment status. Are widowed and divorced older people more likely to be in the labor force than married older people? I would expect that older nonmarried blacks are more likely to be working and working more hours per week than older married blacks. This prediction stems from the assumption that the nonmarried *must* work to support themselves whereas married older people have two potential sources of income.

Family income, number of household members contributing to the income, and household composition are all possible determinants of employment status among the elderly. Many older blacks live in poverty, and as Abbott (1980) suggested, many blacks may work because they need the money. Further, it is unclear whether or not other members of the household (e.g., spouse, children, grandchildren) contribute income or are supported by older blacks. Thus, one reason for working may be to supplement family income or support other household members.

Level of education frequently correlates with subsequent labor force experiences and may be a good predictor of the employment experiences of the black elderly. Previous literature indicates that people with higher educational levels often work in some capacity (perhaps on a part-time basis) on their jobs past retirement age. Older blacks with less education may be more compelled to work than more educated older blacks. Thus, although I expect education to be a significant predictor of employment status, I cannot specify whether it will be positively or negatively related.

Likewise, occupation may determine whether or not older blacks remain in the labor force. Most elderly blacks are employed in menial and low-paying occupations (e.g., service and manual labor). Blue-collar positions or secondary labor force occupations may be linked to the health problems that cause blacks to retire early from the labor force. Therefore, I hypothesize that occupational status will predict employment status and may be related to the number of hours an older person works.

Perhaps the primary factor determining employment among the black elderly is health. Although several studies report the high number of chronic health problems cited by older black Americans (Jackson & Gibson, 1985), they also suggest that many older blacks continue to work despite the presence of health problems. Thus, "health interference," or the extent to which health interferes with one's ability to work, is very important. I expect, then, that health interference will be a major predictor of employment status and the number of hours older blacks work.

Other factors such as regional background and geographic location of residence may also figure into whether older blacks work. Unemployment rates suggest that some regions (Northeast, North Central) may provide more occupational opportunities for blacks than other regions (South) (U.S. Bureau of Labor Statistics, 1989). Based on these figures, I hypothesize that older blacks residing in the Northeast would be more likely to be employed. In addition, one could logically extrapolate from previous research (Jackson, Tucker, & Gurin, 1979) that although blacks have greater numbers of job opportunities in urban areas, employment for workers in smaller rural communities (e.g., farmers, service occupations) may extend into the later years. Occupations in rural communities, however, often involve hard physical labor. Therefore, I predict that older blacks living in urban areas are more likely to be working than blacks living in rural areas.

Finally, older blacks may be worried about money or have some intrinsic desire to work. Thus, these psychological factors were included in the analysis. I expect older blacks who worry more about money to report working more hours per week than older blacks who are not worried about money. Further, I expect that some blacks like to work; that is, they would work even if they did not need the money. Hence, I hypothesize that intrinsically motivated blacks also work and work more hours than blacks who are less intrinsically motivated to be in the labor force.

Knowing whether or not older blacks work and how many hours they work may give us greater insight into how labor force experiences in older age affect blacks. Moreover, the factors predicting employment status for blacks after retirement age (65 years and older) may vary from the significant predictors of employment status for the total older sample (55 years and older). Overall, the analyses may tell us about how employment acts as a role and resource for the black elderly.

Method

Measures

The survey used in the face-to-face interviews addressed many important issues of concern to black Americans, including perceptions of neighborhoods, importance of religion, physical and mental health problems and service utilization, family relationships and social support, labor market participation, and group and personal identity. The section on labor market participation was one of the most substantial sections of the survey. Utilizing pretest information, questions were designed not only to gather information regarding groups of working and not-working individuals, but also on the discouraged, or hidden, unemployed, who often do not appear in the not-working (unemployed) statistics. Questions in the labor market section were often asked of both working and not-working respondents.

Two major dependent measures were included: employment status and number of hours working. Employment status (working/not working) was a dichotomous variable. Working was defined as any amount of paid employment (including part-time work). Included in the non-working sample were retirees and people who were disabled or unemployed. In the 55 years and older group, 33% were working and 67% were not working. For the postretirement age group (65 years and older), 18% were working and 82% were not working. Number of hours working was a continuous variable designating the number of hours per week working. Mean number of hours of work per week of the 55 years and older group was 33, and mean of the 65 years and older group was 27.[2]

Age was coded as a continuous variable designated as number of years with a range of 55-101 years of age. The mean age of the 55 years and older sample was 67 years and the mean age of the 65 years and older sample was 73 years. Gender was coded as 0 = male, 1 = female. Sixty-three percent of the 55 years and older sample were female and 37% were male. The same percentages exist in the 65 years and older sample. Marital status was coded into three categories: married, widowed, and not married (which included separated, divorced, and never married).[3] Among those 55 years and older, 39% were married; 20% were divorced, separated, or never married; and 41% were widowed. In the 65 years and older sample, 37% were married; 13% were divorced, separated, or never married; and 50% were widowed.

Household composition was coded as a three-level variable designating whether or not other people (e.g., spouse, child, relative, or nonrelative) resided with the head of household. For example, head only was coded "1," head and other relative/nonrelative was coded "2," and male head and spouse (no children) was coded "3." Among the 55 years and older sample, 43% of the heads of households resided alone, 34% contained head and relative/nonrelative, and 23% were headed by male with spouse but no children. In the households of respondents 65 years and older, 47% consisted of the head only, 24% contained a head and spouse, and 29% contained a head and relative/nonrelative.

Number of household members contributing to the family income was a four-level variable (1 = one person, 4 = four or more people). Among the 55 years and older group, 63% of the households had one person contributing income, 31% had two people, 5% had three people, and 1% had four or more people. Similarly, for the 65 years and older group, 62% had only one person contributing income, 33% had two, 4% had three, and 1% had four or more household members contributing income.

Other sociodemographic measures included family income, education, and occupational status. Family income was a 17-level variable ranging from less than $1,000 to $30,000 and over; the mean was $8,000 for the 55 years and older group and $7,000 for the 65 years and older group. Education was defined as years of school completed, ranging from 0 to 17 or more. For the 55 years and older group, mean level of education was 8.2 years, and for the 65 years and older group, mean level of education was 7.5 years. The occupational status measure (present occupation or last occupation) was divided into three levels: 1 = white collar, 2 = blue collar, 3 = service. Among the 55 years and older group, 13% were classified as white collar, 38% as blue collar, and 49% as service workers. The percentages were exactly the same for older respondents.

A summary score was used for health interference and assessed the degree to which each of 13 doctor-diagnosed health problems (e.g., high blood pressure, diabetes, or respondent-named health problems) prevented the respondent from working or carrying out daily activities. Individual levels of disability resulting from health conditions were assigned a value from 1 to 3 (higher values reflecting greater disability) and were summed across health problems. Resulting disability scores ranged from 1 to 22 (Chatters, 1983). In the 55 years and older sample, the mean health interference score was 5.43, and among the older group (65 years and older) the mean score was 5.55. Of the 575 respondents in the sample of older blacks who answered this question, 65 indicated that they had not been told by a doctor that they had any of the listed health problems, nor did they indicate any self-generated health problems. This group of black elderly with no health problems was coded at the first level of the health interference measure.

Other measures included region, resides in urban versus rural area, worried about money, and the intrinsic desire to work. Region was divided into Northeast, North Central, South, and West. Of the 55 years and older group, 17% of the population lived in the Northeastern part of the United States, 19% in the North Central portion, 59% in the South, and 5% in the West. Similarly, 14% of the 65 years and older sample lived in the Northeast, 16% in the North Central portion, 65% in the South, and 5% in the West. Residing in urban versus rural area was coded as 1 = urban, 2 = rural. The majority of blacks 55 years and older (72%) live in urban areas whereas 28% live in rural areas. The same proportions of the 65 years and older sample live in urban and rural areas, respectively. Worry about money was a 4-level variable with responses ranging from 1 = a great deal to 4 = not at all. Among the 55 years and older age group, 12% worried about money a great deal, 7% a lot, 25% a little, and 56% not at all. Among the 65 years and older age group, 9% worried a great deal, 6% a lot, 22% a little, and 63% not at all. Intrinsic desire to work (work commitment) was examined by an item assessing whether respondents would continue to work if they did not have to in order to make a living. This two-level variable was coded 1 = no, 2 = yes. A majority (61%) of the 55 years and older group said they would continue working, and 39% said they would not continue to work. Likewise, 71% of the 65 years and older said they would continue working, but 29% said they would not continue to work.

Characteristics of the Black Elderly

The measures chosen as independent and dependent variables provide important information about the employment life of the black elderly and help to answer my questions about the best predictors of employment status and number of hours working. Since part-time work is common among retirees and those approaching retirement age, initial descriptive information differentiates the sample into three rather than two (work/nonwork) categories: no work (retired, disabled, or unemployed), part-time work (less than 20 hours of work per week), and full-time work (20 hours or more of work per week).

Overall, in this sample of 577 respondents 55 years of age and over, 6.2% ($N = 36$) work less than 20 hours, 26.9% ($N = 155$) work 20 or more hours, and two thirds (66.9%) ($N = 386$) are not working (0 hours) for pay outside the home. Basically, there are very small numbers of part-time older workers ($N = 36$) and a large number of nonworking older people ($N = 366$). The nonworking people include 63% retirees, 25% disabled people, and 12% unemployed people.

With respect to age, most of the part-time workers are of preretirement or retirement age. Similar to the general population, the vast majority of full-time workers are in the preretirement group, with a substantially smaller number (26%) of retirement age or older. As one might expect, the greater percentages of the nonworking elderly are concentrated in the 65-75 years (47%) and 75 years and older (26%) age categories. This age by work status breakdown highlights some intriguing and paradoxical patterns. It appears that many blacks work full-time until retirement age, although many begin to work part-time before retirement age. Age appears to play an important role in determining employment patterns among elderly blacks (Table 15.1).

Females compose a large segment of the total number of elderly respondents (63%), and this proportional distribution is not reflected in work status categories. The majority of part-time workers (67%) and nonworking older blacks (67%) are females. In contrast, nearly equal numbers of males (48%) and females (52%) are working full-time.

I hypothesized earlier that widowed older blacks would remain in the labor force. The descriptive data indicate, however, that although the majority of part-time workers are widowed, over one third of them are married. A similar pattern exists for the nonworking blacks: The majority are widowed, but a large number of them are married. In contrast, most full-time workers are married. One explanation for the discrepancy may be that married blacks work full-time in order to support a nonworking or ill spouse. Widows may also need to work to support themselves, but only part-time.

The number of household members contributing income may be another important component in understanding who is working among the black elderly. In most households, only one (63%) or two people (31%) contribute to the overall income. Moreover, at least one third of older blacks, regardless of employment status, are supporting two or more people. Thus, many black elderly support other household members as well as reside in households with members who do not contribute income. It will be interesting to see how these household patterns affect work and nonwork.

Table 15.1 Selected Characteristics of 55 Years Old and Older Working and Nonworking Blacks ($N = 581$) (in percentages)

Category	Working 1-20 Hours ($N = 36$)	Working 20+ Hours ($N = 155$)	Not Working ($N = 386$)
Age in Years			
55-64	47.3	73.6	27.2
65-74	44.4	21.9	46.6
75+	8.3	4.5	26.2
Gender			
Male	33.3	47.7	32.6
Female	66.7	52.3	67.4
Marital Status			
Married	36.1	43.8	37.0
Never married, divorced, separated	22.2	26.5	17.4
Widowed	41.7	29.7	45.6
Household Composition			
Head only	47.2	36.1	45.3
Head, other relative or nonrelative	33.4	38.1	32.1
Male head, spouse (no children)	19.4	25.8	22.6
Number of Household Members Contributing Income			
1	61.8	58.9	65.0
2	35.3	35.8	28.9
3	2.9	5.3	4.5
4 or more	0.0	0.0	1.6
Family Income			
$0-$4,999	56.7	15.9	58.5
$5,000-$9,999	20.0	31.1	23.6
$10,000-$19,999	13.3	31.1	13.1
$20,000+	10.0	22.0	4.8
Education			
0-11 years	80.6	59.9	79.8
High school graduate	11.1	26.0	12.2
Some college	5.6	6.5	4.3
College graduate	2.8	7.8	3.7
Occupation			
White collar	16.7	18.8	10.4
Blue collar	8.3	35.1	41.6
Service	75.0	46.1	48.0

continued

Table 15.1 Continued

Category	Working 1-20 Hours	Working 20+ Hours	Not Working
Region			
Northeast	13.9	22.6	14.5
North Central	8.3	21.9	18.7
South	66.7	47.1	63.4
West	11.1	8.4	3.4
Urbanicity			
Urban	80.6	76.1	69.4
Rural	19.4	23.9	30.6
Worried About Money			
A great deal	2.9	11.5	12.5
A lot	5.7	4.7	7.7
A little	34.3	27.7	23.3
Not at all	57.1	56.1	56.5
Intrinsic Desire to Work*			
Yes	66.7	60.1	
No	33.3	39.9	

* Questions asked only of those respondents currently employed.

Despite the fact that they have worked hard throughout their lives, most black elderly live in poverty. The large percentage (57%) of part-time workers earn less than $5,000 per year. Nonworking blacks closely parallel this pattern: The majority (58%) have an income less than $5,000 a year, 24% have an income between $5,000 and $10,000, 13% have incomes between $10,000 and $20,000, and 5% earn $20,000 or more. In contrast, one third of the full-time workers earn $5,000-$10,000 annually. These descriptive data confirm the reports of the impoverished conditions of the black elderly—especially for those who are not *earning* income.

It is not clear how education affects the work patterns of the elderly black. Regardless of employment status, the vast majority (90%) of older blacks have attained 12 years or less of education. These older blacks reared during the first quarter of the 20th century reflect the historical undereducation of blacks in the United States. One quarter of the full-time workers, however, graduated from high school.

Occupation is linked to employment in a number of intriguing ways. Most of the part-time workers (75%), for example, are in service occupations. Fewer numbers of part-time workers have white-collar (17%) or blue-collar (8%) jobs. In contrast, 46% of the full-time workers are in service occupations, whereas over one third (35%) have blue-collar jobs. As expected, only a small number of full-time workers hold white-collar positions (19%). Overall, occupational trends among the black elderly reflect those for the larger black population; there are fewer blacks in white-collar positions and a larger proportion in blue-collar positions. The vast majority of black workers, however, are concentrated in service occupations.

The health interference variable, having 20 levels, was too difficult to display in these categories. Yet 50% of the black elderly report some form of health problem. Many working older blacks score low on the health disability index (1 or 2). In contrast many nonworking blacks have fairly high disability scores (8 or 9). This descriptive analysis suggest that health interference should be a significant predictor of work/nonwork in the logit analysis.

The majority of older blacks reside in the South. Therefore, it is not surprising that the vast majority of part-time (67%) and full-time (47%) workers also reside in the South. Other full-time and part-time workers live in the Northeast, although some 22% of the full-time workers also live in the North Central portions of the United States.

Residing in a large urban area appears to have no effect on elderly workers. Many (81%) part-time older workers reside in urban areas whereas fewer part-time workers (19%) reside in rural areas. The vast majority of full-time workers also reside in large urban areas (76%). Likewise among those not working, 70% reside in urban areas compared to 30% in rural areas.

I hypothesized that financial concerns might influence the employment status of the black elderly. However, regardless of the employment status, most black elderly report that they do not worry about money. Thirty-four percent of part-time workers report that they worry a little about money, which may account for why they work. The logit analysis will be able to specify more precisely the role finances play in determining employment status.

Finally, many black elderly may possess some intrinsic motivation about work. Sixty-seven percent of part-time workers reported that they would continue to work even if they did not need the money, as compared to 60% of the full-time workers (see Table 15.1).

Predicting Employment Status

Two kinds of analyses were selected to illustrate how the factors described above affect employment status and the number of hours employed per week. First, the measures were included as predictor variables in a logit regression designed to predict employment status (work/nonwork) among the black elderly for the total sample. An additional logit analysis was computed for black elderly 65 years and older.[4] Logit analysis is a statistical technique similar to multiple regression but created specifically for analyses involving dichotomous dependent measures, which traditional multiple regression analysis cannot accommodate. In the present investigation, the logit (logarithm of the odds of working or not working) was regressed on the measures described above. Hence, logit allows an estimate of the probability of work or nonwork for any older black from factors such as age, marital status, health interference, and so forth. The Dichotomous Regression Analysis (DREG) package of the Organized Set of Integrated Routines for Investigation of Social Science Data (OSIRIS IV) program was used to compute the logit analysis. Multiple regression analyses were incorporated to assess the relative importance of these factors in predicting the number of hours the black elderly work. Multiple regression was used in this case because number of hours of working is a continuous dependent variable.

Logit Analysis—Black Elderly Aged 55 and Over

Logit analysis often includes an assessment of the bivariate relationships between individual predictor variables and the dependent variable. The logit is then computed to determine if the individual predictors remain significant when all other predictor variables are entered into the analysis. I had hypothesized earlier that age, gender, marital status, household composition, number of household members contributing income, family income, education, occupation, health interference, region of the country, residing in urban versus rural area, worry about money, and an intrinsic desire to work would have a significant relationship with and predict work status. The present analysis reveals several significant bivariate relationships.

Table 15.2 presents the logit model of working versus nonworking. This model accounts for 6% of the predictive error of the log odds of working. This amount is statistically significant. Age and health inter-

Table 15.2 Logit Model of Employment Status for Selected Social and Demographic Variables for Respondents 55 Years and Older ($N = 571$)

Parameter	b
Intercept	4.47
Age	−5.80***
Health Interference	−5.22***
Region	5.09***
Northeast	.44
North Central	−1.09
South	−.40
West	2.01*
Marital Status	5.08***
Married	−2.16*
Widowed	2.17*
Not married	.75
Occupation	4.25**
White collar	.50
Blue collar	−2.06*
Service	1.59
Family Income	2.43*
Gender	2.94
Male	1.72
Female	−1.72
Household Members Contributing Income	1.45
Education	.42
Urban vs. Rural	.22
Worried About Money	.05
Household Composition	.29

*$p<.05$; **$p<.01$; ***$p<.001$.

ference were the strongest predictors, both having significant multivariate relationships with the dependent variable. In terms of age, the older the respondent, the less likely he or she is employed. Not surprisingly, older blacks with interfering health problems are less likely to be working.

The next significant predictor of working status were marital status and region. Married respondents were less likely to be working, although widowed respondents were more likely to be in the labor force. Surprisingly, black elderly residing in the West are more likely to be in the labor force than those residing in the Northeast, North Central, or

South. Two other significant predictors, occupation and total family income, complete the logit analysis. As predicted, black elderly respondents who are or were engaged in blue-collar occupations are less likely to be employed. Elderly respondents with higher incomes were more likely to be working.

To summarize, age, health interference, marital status, region, occupation, and family income were significant predictors of work status among respondents 55 years of age and older. Although my hypothesis is supported in part, two variables (gender, education) that had significant bivariate relationships, were not significant predictors in the multivariate analysis. Moreover, household composition, number of household members contributing income, residing in urban versus rural setting, worry about money, and an intrinsic desire to work were not significantly related to work status (see Table 15.2).

Logit Analysis—Black Elderly Aged 65 and Over

A similar logit analysis was conducted for a smaller proportion of the sample: those 65 and older. This analysis was conducted to examine whether or not similar predictor variables might account for labor force participation after retirement age. Twenty percent (20%) of the black elderly were classified as working, 80% as not working. In this analysis the same predictor variables were included. The bivariate analysis reveals three significant relationships: employment status with age, occupation, and the amount of health interference (see Table 15.3).

The model is significant in predicting 4% of the predicted error of the log odds of working. In this multivariate analysis, controlling for all other factors, the two significant predictors were age and health interference. Similar to the analysis on the larger older sample (55 years and older), older respondents and respondents with greater amounts of health disability were less likely to be working. Hence, several factors that figure importantly in work status prior to retirement age appear to drop out (see Table 15.3). It is not clear, however, if similar factors will predict the number of hours working.

Predicting Number of Hours Working—
Respondents 55 Years and Older

The final set of analyses focused on the segment of the black elderly population who are employed. A multiple regression analysis was com-

Table 15.3 Logit Model of Employment Status for Selected Social and Demographic Variables for Respondents 65 Years and Older ($N = 201$)

Parameter	b
Intercept	2.33
Age	−2.95*
Health Interference	−2.33*
Region	5.61
Northeast	−.75
North Central	−.62
South	.21
West	2.22
Marital Status	3.46
Married	.84
Widowed	−1.80
Not married	1.27
Occupation	−1.22
White collar	−1.22
Blue collar	1.17
Service	.47
Family Income	1.34
Gender	1.32
Male	1.15
Female	−1.15
Household Members Contributing Income	1.30
Education	−.14
Urban vs. Rural	.02
Worried About Money	.15
Household Composition	.56

*$p < .01$.

puted to examine which among the measures were the best predictors of the number of hours worked per week. Each employed respondent was asked to provide the number of hours he or she worked each week.

A smaller number of predictor variables were entered into these regression equations than in the previous logit analyses because of the small number of respondents working: 55 years and older ($N = 161$) and 65 years and older ($N = 52$). The predictor variables included marital status, age, gender, occupation, health interference, intrinsic desire to work, and total family income. In order to avoid multicolinearity problems stemming from highly correlated independent measures, age,

Table 15.4 Regression Analysis of Number of Hours Worked for Respondents Aged 55 Years and Older and 65 Years and Older

Variable	55 Years and Older (N = 161)			65 Years and Older (N = 52)		
	Partial R	β	t	Partial R	β	t
Constant						
Sex (Male)	.22	.22	2.64*	.09	.08	.54
Health Interference	−.24	−.22	2.81**	−.39	−.41	2.53*
Marital Status (Widowed)	.11	.12	1.3	0.20	.23	1.24
Not Married	.11	.12	1.35	.07	.07	.42
Income	.26	.29	3.14*	.24	2.90	1.50
Desires to Work	.04	.04	.55	.22	.19	.38

NOTE: For 55+ sample, $R = 4.8$, $R^2 = .23$, $SE = 13.24$; for 65+ sample, $R = .57$, $R^2 = .32$, $SE = 14.34$.
*$p<.05$; **$p<.01$.

health interference, income, and occupation, variables that were highly correlated, were used interchangeably in the equations. Equations with the highest amount of variance accounted are reported here.

The results for the larger sample (55 years and older) revealed a significant regression equation ($F(182) = 6.90$, $p<.001$), with gender (male), health interference, and family income as significant predictors of number of hours working per week. This equation accounted for 23% of the variance. Males and older blacks with greater family incomes worked more hours. Older blacks with health problems worked fewer hours (see Table 15.4).

Predicted Number Hours Working— Respondents 65 Years and Older

The patterns were somewhat different for the elderly population who work past retirement age. The regression equations, including age (with income or occupation) instead of health interference, were not significant. But in the regression equation that included marital status, gender, health interference, and total family income, health interference was the only predictor of number of hours worked. This equation accounted for 32% of the variance. Basically, health disability determines the number of hours worked by elderly blacks who remain in the labor force past retirement age (see Table 15.4).

Discussion

The present analysis illustrates how work operates in a number of important ways in the life of older blacks. We can also learn why older blacks participate and remain in the labor force. Further, the analyses help to identify which factors influence the number of hours blacks work during the later years.

There are several significant predictors of employment status for the total sample of black elderly respondents 55 years of age and older. The most significant predictor is amount of health interference: Those who have health problems and are restricted by them are less likely to be in the labor force before or after retirement age. Health problems plague most elderly adults, and this finding substantiates earlier claims that blacks, in particular, may reduce work activities prior to retirement age due to health problems (Jackson & Gibson, 1985). The overwhelming significance of this measure in all of the logit and multiple regression analyses suggests that health alone may prevent employment from being a major role and resource for the black elderly. Health limitations may affect physical mobility and therefore the ability to earn income. Specifically, many black elderly cannot continue to work in the occupations (e.g., blue collar, service) that require physical strength and good health. At the same time, working in secondary labor occupations may contribute to health problems in later life. Further exploration of this causal relationship between health and occupation would greatly elucidate our knowledge about work and the black elderly.

Similarly, age, which is obviously linked to health interference, also predicts work status. It seems likely that as blacks age, interference from health problems increases, thereby ensuring permanent absence from the labor force. In addition, being eligible to retire or reduce work activities may also be related to age.

Another important predictor of employment status is family income. Older blacks with higher incomes are working, and working more hours. This result substantiates earlier work by Abbott (1977, 1980), noting that most income of elderly blacks is *earned* income. Income appears to be a less significant factor in work/nonwork among the postretirement group. But it is also likely that blacks in higher income occupations may remain in the work force. A more in-depth analysis of this causal relationship is needed.

As predicted, marital status was a significant predictor. Specifically, those who are widowed are more likely to be working whereas those who are married are not. It appears that the two potential sources of income of a married couple may allow one of the individuals to leave the labor force. Widows, who have no other sources of income and may live alone, may be required to continue to work. Lack of companionship in the home may also account for large numbers of widows engaged in part-time work.

I also predicted that occupational status would play a significant role in the work status of the black elderly. People who presently or formerly occupied blue-collar positions are not working. This finding confirms other studies (Gibson, 1987; Jackson & Gibson, 1985) that discuss the impact of secondary labor force participation on older blacks. There is no mandatory retirement for many blue-collar positions and most blue-collar workers are full-time workers. Due to the need for heavy physical labor and lack of substantial health benefits, though, many blacks involved in blue-collar jobs may physically wear down and retire early from the labor force. Further, part-time work may not be available for blue-collar workers.

Finally, region of the country appears to have some effect on working in older age. I expected region to be a significant predictor but the West (versus South or North Central) was not expected. In this study black elderly living in the Western part of the United States constitute the smallest percentage (3%) of nonworking blacks. This effect may be due to the small number of people in this category. There may be greater employment opportunities, though, for older workers in the Western states. Geographical differences in the availability of work for older adults is an issue that is in need of further study.

Respondents 65 Years and Older

Very different results were found when the same analysis was conducted for the black elderly of postretirement age. The only significant predictors of employment status are age and health interference. Health interference accounts for 8% of the variance in the model. Again, these results point to the saliency of health as a major determinant of work among elderly blacks. The smaller number of respondents in this sample may also contribute to the lack of other significant predictors.

Number of Hours Worked Per Week

This set of analyses provided some description of the black elderly who work by focusing on the number of hours worked per week. Among the most significant predictors in the regression analyses for the total population of respondents 55 years and older were gender, age, health interference, and family income.

The interchangeability of age and health interference, as well as income and occupation, indicate the high correlation of the variables. As mentioned earlier, as older black adults age, they continue to acquire more debilitating health problems. Likewise, blue-collar or service occupations produce limited incomes and account for the strong relationship between occupation and income.

It is noteworthy, however, that older black males are likely to be working more hours than older black females. These findings contradict my prediction that more black women than black men work in older age. Although throughout the life cycle black females have higher labor force participation rates than black males, it appears that with age, the labor force participation rate does not differ significantly (as evidenced by the logit analysis where gender was not a significant predictor), but black males appear to work more hours. Black males may be participating in more flexible, part-time work. In contrast, most black women in this age cohort, many of whom may have been restricted to domestic work, may not have the physical strength to continue working in this occupation. Also note that health disability is the sole predictor of number of hours working per week in the postretirement group. Again, this illustrates the important relationship between health and work in older age.

A comparison of the total older sample (55 years and older) and the subsample (65 years and older), therefore, indicates that older blacks, who are working before retirement age, may work until aged 65 or until they qualify for social security or SSI.[5] After retirement age, many cease working. More stable income (e.g., SSI, pensions) may allow the black elderly to redirect their energies into other uncompensated activities, like church work or extended family responsibilities, which may not require as much physical exertion as service or blue-collar jobs.

It is important to comment on a series of factors that were predicted to be significantly related to work status, but were not. Education, living in an urban versus rural setting, household composition and number of members contributing to income, worry about money, and intrinsic desire to work were not significant in either of the logit analyses. Little variation in years of education among elderly blacks may account for its lack of significance as a predictor of work status. Most older blacks have little or no education, and historically, given racial discriminatory practices, level of education may exert little influence on the occupational status or work status of this cohort.

Living in an urban versus rural setting did not influence work status. Although urban settings may offer more employment opportunities than rural areas, elderly blacks may be limited to similar jobs (i.e., blue-collar or secondary labor occupations) in both settings. As the results demonstrate, older blacks who occupied blue-collar jobs are not in the labor force.

In terms of household membership and household members contributing income, it appears that the majority of black elderly workers and nonworkers live alone or with a spouse. Therefore, the households of older blacks may not vary much in composition nor in number of persons contributing income. Although older blacks may have a great deal of contact with relatives and nonrelatives, these relationships may not be income related. Thus, the household composition may not affect labor force participation in older age.

Finally, the psychological measures regarding worry about money and an intrinsic desire to work were not significant employment status predictors. The amount older blacks vary on these two measures can provide clues to their lack of significant relationships to employment status. Most older working and nonworking blacks reported they do not worry about money. Clearly, having a stable income from social security or pension may contribute to the lack of worry about money. Religiosity may also be an important explanation for the reason older blacks are not concerned about money and why worry about money does not motivate them to remain in the labor force.

A large number of older blacks said they would continue to work even if they were financially secure. Perhaps older blacks have internalized the work norm and have an intrinsic desire to work. Yet, health and age may supersede the *desire* to work. Historical evidence also suggests this pattern. Many blacks worked on plantations until they could not physically work (Genovese, 1974). This work norm appears to be represented in this cohort of blacks. Health interference and age may be the large deterrents to a desire to work among the black elderly.

In summary, work serves as a financial resource for the black elderly prior to retirement age and is a major source of income especially for widowed black elderly. Due to the kinds of occupations available to this cohort of blacks (e.g., service, blue collar), work may provide a functional role for them, a means through which they economically sustain themselves and their extended families.

An enormous untapped potential resides in our elderly population. There are a growing number of occupations that require little if any physical mobility. Part-time work may be a way to keep black elderly active and alert. There may be ways in which older blacks can become involved in the mentoring of younger cohorts of black men and women. Private industry, government, society, and the black elderly may all benefit from harnessing this great human resource through new forms of work and work-related activities.

Notes

1. Some people may question the inclusion of blacks 55 years and older in an "elderly" cohort when the more popular designation of elderly is 65 years or older. Given the lower life expectancy for blacks and the availability of many senior citizen services for people aged 55 and older, elderly appears to be an appropriate designation for this group.

2. The number of respondents aged 65 years and older reporting the number of hours worked per week is 59.

3. The categories of separated, divorced, and never married were combined because of the relatively small number of respondents in these status groups. This is particularly the case among respondents 65 years and older.

4. Respondents who reported working part-time, working full-time, or laid off but expecting to return to work in the next 6 months were categorized as working. The nonworking category consisted of elderly who reported not working for any reason (e.g., retired, disabled) and those who classified themselves as laid off and not expecting to return to work within the next 6 months.

5. It should be noted that any direct comparisons of the 55 years and older and 65 years and older groups would be misleading. These two groups cannot be compared because the 65 years and older is a subsample of the larger 55 years and older sample. Thus, it is not surprising that many of the predictors of employment status in the 55 years and older sample are the same for the 65 years and older sample.

References

Abbott, J. (1977). Socioeconomic characteristics of black elderly: Some black-white differences. *Social Security Bulletin, 40,* 16-42.

Abbott, J. (1980). Work experience and earnings of middle-aged black and white men, 1965-1971. *Social Security Bulletin, 43,* 16-34.

Almquist, E. M., et al. (1980). Ethnic differences in the labor force participation of older women. *Journal of Minority Aging, 5,* 174-181.

Chatters, L. M. (1983). A causal analysis of subjective well-being among elderly blacks. Unpublished doctoral dissertation, University of Michigan, Ann Arbor.

Corcoran, M., & Duncan, G. J. (1978). A summary of part 1 findings. In G. J. Duncan & J. N. Morgan (Eds.), *Five thousand American families* (Vol. 6). Ann Arbor: University of Michigan, Institute for Social Research.

Dancy, J. (1977). *The black elderly: A guide for practitioners.* Ann Arbor: University of Michigan, Institute of Gerontology.

Genovese, E. D. (1974). *Roll, Jordan, roll.* New York: Pantheon.

Gibson, R. C. (1987). Reconceptualizing retirement for black Americans. *The Gerontologist, 27*(6), 691-698.

Jackson, J. S. (1988). *The black American elderly: Research on physical and psychological health.* New York: Springer.

Jackson, J. S., & Gibson, R. C. (1985). Work and retirement among the black elderly. In Z. Blau (Ed.), *Current perspectives on aging and the life cycle* (pp. 193-222). Greenwich, CT: JAI.

Jackson, J. S., Tucker, M. B., & Gurin, G. (1979). *The National Survey of Black Americans.* Ann Arbor: Inter-University Consortium for Political and Social Research, Institute for Social Research, University of Michigan.

Jaslow, P. (1976). Employment, retirement, and morale among older women. *Journal of Gerontology, 31,* 212-218.

Kent, D. P., & Hirsch, C. (1972). *Needs and use of services among negro and white aged.* University Park: Pennsylvania State University.

Palmore, E. B., Fillenbaum, G. G., & George, L. K. (1984). Consequences of retirement. *Journal of Gerontology, 39,* 109-116.

Palmore, E. B., George, L. K., & Fillenbaum, G. G. (1982). Predictors of retirement. *Journal of Gerontology, 37*(6), 733-742.

Soumerai, S. B., & Avorn, J. (1983). Perceived health, life satisfaction, and activity in urban elderly: A controlled study of the impact of part-time work. *Journal of Gerontology, 38,* 356-362.

U. S. Bureau of Labor Statistics. (1989). *Employment and earnings, 1970-1986.* (Monthly).

Veroff, J., Douvan, E., & Kulka, R. (1981). *The inner American: A self-portrait from 1957 to 1976.* New York: Basic Books.

16

THE BLACK AMERICAN
RETIREMENT EXPERIENCE

Rose C. Gibson

This chapter presents descriptive analyses of the National Survey of Black Americans (NSBA) data (1979-1980) exploring older black Americans' retirement roles and resources and describing the differences by gender and socioeconomic status (SES). Specifically, I analyze differences in late-life roles: differences in the timing of and plans and reasons for retirement, and differences in activities after retirement.

A theoretical framework for understanding black Americans' late-life roles is presented. A literature review follows of blacks' retirement roles and experiences. Then, after presenting the NSBA findings, the chapter concludes with recommendations for approaches to future black American retirement research.

Conceptual Framework for Studying Late-Life Roles

The "Unretired-Retired" Concept

Three fairly new social trends are creating a new type of black retiree, referred to as the *unretired-retired* (Gibson, 1986a). The trends for middle-aged and older blacks are: declining labor force participation, increasing physical disability, and increasing disability pay availability. The unretired-retired are individuals aged 55 and over who do not consider themselves retired despite their nonworking status (Gibson, 1986b).

This unretired-retired group appears to be the most deprived of the black elderly (Gibson, 1987a, 1988; J. S. Jackson & Gibson, 1985). The unretired-retired do not meet traditional retirement criteria, and therefore, they are screened by definition from major national retirement research. This excludes them from planning and policy stemming from the research. Whether older blacks view themselves as retired is influenced by their lifetime disadvantaged work patterns, current work income, and psychological or economic need for the disabled worker role. Each of these issues is discussed in turn.

Relationships Between Lifetime Work and Retirement Experiences

Black Americans' disadvantaged work experiences across the life course have been reported in the more than 20 years of published work and retirement literature. These unchanging disadvantaged work patterns, over time, create an unclear line between work and retirement experiences. This ambiguity, in turn, influences late-life role choices.

The current generation of older black Americans is more likely to have worked in low-status jobs characterized by sporadic work patterns and small earnings (Abbott, 1980; Anderson & Cottingham, 1981; Cain, 1976; Corcoran & Duncan, 1978; U.S. Department of Commerce, 1980; Gibson, 1982, 1983; Gordon, Hamilton, & Tipps, 1982; Hill, 1981; Montagna, 1978; Munnell, 1978). These work patterns threaten black Americans' economic well-being as they reach old age (Abbott, 1980). Work in old age in the same low-status jobs becomes a necessity for many (Abbott, 1977). The result is a continuity of disadvantaged work patterns from youth through old age.

Income from paid work rather than from traditional retirement sources also could cause uncertainty as to whether one is working or retired. This complicates blacks' adoption of the retirement role. Blacks' lifetime work experiences have influenced income levels and sources in old age (Abbott, 1980). Restriction to unstable jobs with low earnings and few benefits relates directly to low levels of retirement pensions and social security benefits. Thus, compared to other groups, older blacks' income packages contain a greater proportion of money from work and nonretirement sources (Abbott, 1977; J. S. Jackson & Gibson, 1985; Parnes & Nestel, 1981).

The Retirement Versus the Disability Role

The attractiveness, availability, and appropriateness of roles alternate to retirement may interfere with blacks' adoption of the retirement role. Role theory literature lends additional insights into the reasons blacks might prefer the disability role to the retirement role (see Biddle & Thomas, 1966; Sarbin & Allen, 1968, for analyses of role theory). In general, these theories suggest individuals select new roles under these conditions: when forced out of the old role, when the new role is different from the old role, or when the new role offers greater benefits than the old role. Blacks' inclination to take on the retirement role is interpreted within this general framework.

To begin, William James's (1910/1950) identity theory posits that individuals change their self-identity when changes in the opportunities or demands of current social situations occur. At this point, individuals formulate different sets of expectations of what are appropriate or desirable self-meanings. Changes in demands or opportunities in the work sphere could encourage a search for more appropriate self-meanings, such as the retiree role. Blacks experience few changes in their work spheres in old age and thus may be less likely to search for or take on a new retiree identity.

Stryker (1968), expanding James's identity theory, offered another framework in which to interpret blacks' reluctance to adopt the retirement role. He suggested that individuals have a hierarchy of available roles, with the most salient in priority positions. Individuals change identities by selecting roles from this hierarchy that have the highest probabilities of being invoked across situations and of congruence between the expectations of the individual and the expectations of society in regard to appropriate role behaviors.

Extrapolated to work and retirement, this might mean that when the work role is no longer available, individuals choose the retirement role if (a) the retirement role is the most salient in their hierarchy of roles, (b) the retirement role is applicable across a variety of life situations, and (c) the individual and others agree to the behaviors of the retiree role. For older blacks whose work is still contributing to their income and for whom the line between work and retirement is unclear, the retiree role would not meet these three conditions.

The theory that individuals give up and take on new roles according to the margin of benefits over costs offers yet another framework in which to examine blacks' adoption of the retirement role. Thus blacks would adopt the retirement role if its benefits outweighed the benefits of other available roles. The disability role possibly pays larger benefits to blacks than the retirement role.

The special profits of the disability role for blacks might be explained by new versions of sick-role theory. First, intolerable social and psychological conditions encourage individuals to adopt the sick role as an escape from a less desirable current role (Phillips, 1965; Thurlow, 1971). Second, the secondary *economic* gains of illness encourage adoption and maintenance of sick-role behavior (Lamb & Rogawski, 1978; Ludwig, 1981; Prince, 1978). Chirikos and Nestel (1983) demonstrated that reports of disability are related to economic need. Individuals who expected lower future wages were more likely to say they were work disabled. Interestingly, this influence of expected income on self-reported disability was stronger for blacks than whites.

Ellison (1968) suggested that among blue-collar workers, the sick role is a substitution for the retirement role. Intolerable social and psychological experiences create a "lack of fit" in the retirement role for this group. Considering both the Chirikos and Nestel and Ellison findings, the sick role may have a better fit and greater economic benefits for disadvantaged black workers than the retirement role. Disability pay may be greater than retirement pay in this group. The availability of disability pay cannot be ignored in blacks' failure to adopt the retirement role.

Thus far, it has been suggested that taking on the retirement role among black Americans is a function of lifetime and current labor force experiences; source of income; and the availability, attractiveness, and appropriateness of the disability role. The disability role appears to have larger social, psychological, and economic payoffs than the retirement role.

Empirical Work on Late-Life Roles

The general unretired-retired conceptual framework and reasons for adopting a disabled-worker instead of a retirement role shaped the existing research on black American late-life roles. Work in this area has progressed from descriptive, to multivariate, to analyses of the very meaning and measurement of the late-life role constructs.

Three studies focused exclusively on black American retirement-role adoption. The first study (J. S. Jackson & Gibson, 1985) examined the possibility that self-definitions of retirement among elderly blacks were complicated by an indistinct line between work patterns earlier in life and work patterns in old age and a large part of income stemming from work. They found those who did not call themselves retired were more likely than those who did to never have had a full-time job in life, to have been lifetime part-time workers, and to be working currently from time to time. These black elderly who did not view themselves as retired also had a large portion of their income coming from their own work. These unretired-retired individuals were more disadvantaged economically and socially than the retired individuals. These findings suggest that two factors are related to ways in which older blacks define retirement for themselves: unchanging disadvantaged work patterns and source of income. This study, however, was descriptive and did not determine the relative or collective effects of factors on adopting a retirement role.

The second study (Gibson, 1987b) extended the earlier J. S. Jackson and Gibson study by exploring the complexity of older blacks' adoption of the retirement role. These multivariate findings, based on logit regression (Hanuschek & J. E. Jackson, 1977), confirmed the descriptive J. S. Jackson-Gibson findings, indicating that four factors decreased the odds of calling oneself retired: (a) having worked discontinuous types of patterns over the lifetime, (b) viewing oneself as disabled, (c) receiving income from one's own work, and (d) receiving income from sources other than retirement pensions, annuities, or assets.

The issues raised by J. S. Jackson and Gibson (1985) and by Gibson (1987b) set the theoretical framework for a third study. Gibson (1991a), using latent variable analyses, explored the meaning and measurement of the retirement and disabled-worker constructs. Gibson identified a role negotiation process:

1. Perceptions of a discontinuous work life, by creating an ambiguity of work and retirement, discouraged adoption of the retirement role.
2. Those in economic need, feeling more compelled to work intermittently, were less inclined to view themselves as retired.
3. The greater economic and psychological rewards of the role encouraged the disabled-worker role.
4. Taking on a disabled-worker role decreased the inclination to take on the retirement role.

Three other findings raise two additional issues. First, the failure to adopt the retirement role may be more a matter of socioeconomic status than race. For example, in the Gibson (1987b) study those black elderly who did not call themselves retired were more economically deprived than those who did. There also were fewer compulsions to work among those receiving retirement pensions. The second issue is that the older-worker roles of black Americans may be more necessity than choice. For example, J. S. Jackson and Gibson (1985) found lower morale among black elderly who were *in* the labor force than among those who were *out* and receiving retirement pensions. The lower worker morale and other characteristics suggest work was a necessity and not a choice.

Both theory and empiricism, then, suggest that late-life roles in the black population are influenced by having to work in old age, perceptions of how little lifetime work patterns have changed, and by the forces of economic and psychological need.

Empirical Work on Retirement Experiences

For more than 50 years, considerable research has been devoted to the retirement decisionmaking process (see, e.g., Fillenbaum, George, & Palmore, 1985; Morgan, 1980; Streib & Schneider, 1971). Several factors were found to predict retirement: poor health, socioeconomic status, financial readiness, the interaction of poor health and financial readiness, job dissatisfaction, extended periods of unemployment, and work and retirement attitudes (cf. Gibson, 1991c).

Virtually no studies focus on black American retirement experiences. The findings of a few race comparisons do suggest, however, that blacks compared with whites are more likely to: retire at earlier ages, retire because of poor health, have been forced to retire, have been unemployed in the 12-month period prior to retirement, and have reported job dissatisfaction and job search discouragement prior to retirement (cf. Gibson, 1991c). In short, there are race differences in the factors that determine the retirement process and decision. Poor health and disadvantaged labor force experiences are more influential for blacks, whereas financial readiness is more influential for whites.

Life after retirement also has been frequently studied. Researchers have examined such factors as morale, physical and mental health, and leisure and productive activities (Gibson, 1991c). Although this research has increased steadily over the past two decades, little work focuses specifically on black Americans. Earlier descriptive analyses of the NSBA data (Gibson, 1991c) reveal some common responses to a question asking how retired blacks spend their time. In order of frequency these were: housekeeping; leisure activities, such as sports and hobbies; gardening; nothing; sitting; and resting. Only a small percentage of the responses were church or church related, reading, listening to the radio, watching television, visiting, or talking. Even smaller percentages of responses were in the categories of caring for others, clubs, organizations, volunteer work, or travel.

These recent studies of the late-life roles and retirement experiences of black Americans are informative and valuable. They do not, however, explore the possibility that the retirement experience differs within the black population—notably in socioeconomic status (SES) and gender subgroups. We turn now to new descriptive analyses of the NSBA data that begin to identify differences in late-life roles and retirement experiences between men and women and between individuals in income, education, and occupation groups.

Late-Life Roles: Gender and SES Differences

About one third of black Americans ages 55 years and over who are not working refer to themselves as retired (Table 16.1). About one fourth, in spite of not working, view themselves as disabled workers instead of as retired. Another fourth are still working. These findings are consistent with past research (Gibson, 1987a, 1987b, 1991a; J. S. Jackson & Gibson, 1985) and illustrate the heterogeneity of black Americans' late-life roles.

Men were slightly more likely than women to call themselves retired and still to be working. Women, however, were more likely than men to call themselves disabled. Individuals with incomes less than $6,000 were more likely than those with incomes $6,000 and over to call themselves disabled. They also were less likely to be working. The two income groups were about equally likely to call themselves retired.

Those with low levels of education (0-8 years) were more likely than those with higher levels to call themselves disabled workers. Individuals with some college were the least likely of all to call themselves disabled workers. Individuals with low (0-8 years) and high (some college) levels of education were more likely than individuals with mid levels of education (9-12 years) to call themselves retired. Those with less than 9 years of education were the least likely still to be working.

Individuals in blue-collar and service occupations were more likely than those in white-collar occupations to call themselves disabled

text continued on page 286

Table 16.1 Late-Life Roles of Black Americans Aged 55-101 by Gender, Income, Education, and Occupation (N = 581)

	Gender			Income		
	Men	Women	Total	<$6,000	≥$6,000	Total
Role						
Retired	86	111	197	96	101	197
	(41.0)	(30.9)	(34.6)	(36.4)	(33.1)	(34.6)
Disabled worker	38	101	139	90	49	139
	(18.1)	(28.1)	(24.4)	(34.0)	(16.1)	(24.4)
Working[a]	76	81	157	34	123	157
	(36.1)	(22.6)	(27.6)	(12.9)	(40.3)	(27.6)
Homemaker	2	16	18	11	7	18
	(1.0)	(4.5)	(3.2)	(4.2)	(2.3)	(3.2)
Other[b]	8	50	58	33	25	58
	(3.8)	(13.9)	(10.2)	(12.5)	(8.2)	(10.2)
Total	210	359	569	264	305	569
	(100.0)	(100.0)	(100.0)	(100.0)	(100.0)	(100.0)

Table 16.1 Continued

Role	Years of Education					Occupation			
	0-8	9-11	12	Some College	Total	Service	Blue Collar	White Collar	Total
Retired	120	25	24	25	194	81	78	27	186
	(38.8)	(24.3)	(26.1)	(45.5)	(34.8)	(32.4)	(40.3)	(40.3)	(36.4)
Disabled worker	93	20	18	5	136	62	46	9	117
	(30.1)	(19.4)	(19.6)	(9.1)	(24.3)	(24.8)	(23.7)	(13.4)	(22.9)
Working[a]	51	42	41	22	156	71	54	29	154
	(16.5)	(40.8)	(44.5)	(40.0)	(27.9)	(28.4)	(27.8)	(43.3)	(30.1)
Homemaker	9	6	2	0	17	6	1	1	8
	(2.9)	(5.8)	(2.2)	(0.0)	(3.0)	(2.4)	(0.5)	(1.5)	(1.6)
Other[b]	36	10	7	3	56	30	15	1	46
	(11.7)	(9.7)	(7.6)	(5.5)	(10.0)	(12.0)	(7.7)	(1.5)	(9.0)
Total	309	103	92	55	559	250	194	67	511

NOTES: Column percentages are in parentheses below each number. Columns fail to add to 581 due to missing data. Blue-collar occupations are craftspersons, operatives, laborers, farmer, and farm workers. Service occupations include all service workers. White-collar occupations are professional, managerial, sales, and clerical.

a. Working 20 or more hours per week.
b. Includes student and welfare recipient.

285

workers. The three occupation groups were about equally likely to call themselves retired. The most likely to be working were those in white-collar occupations.

In sum, gender seems slightly associated with the work, retirement, and disabled-worker roles in late life; whereas SES is not associated with the retirement role, but rather with the worker and disabled-worker roles.

The Retirement Experience: Gender and SES Differences

Age at Retirement

Black Americans are least likely to retire "on time" (age 65 years) and most likely to retire at earlier ages (55-64 years) (see Table 16.2). There were no notable gender or SES differences in age at retirement. It is interesting to note, however, that about 15% of the sample retired at or after age 70. This was especially true of those with incomes less than $6,000. This supports prior research and theory and also reinforces the idea that the black American older worker role is one of economic necessity. This black elderly group that works well into old age may be the group to which Jacqueline Jackson refers as "dying from, rather than retiring from, the work force."

Retirement Planning

About half the black American elderly retired unexpectedly whereas half planned to retire. Similarly, about half retired willingly and half retired unwillingly. Differences in these two aspects of retirement were clearer by SES than by gender. Occupational level, unlike income and education, however, seemed unrelated to retirement planning and willingness to retire.

Retired men were more likely than retired women to have planned their retirement, whereas men and women were equally likely to be willing to retire. The lowest income and education groups (less than $6,000 and 0-11 years) were more likely than the higher groups ($6,000 or more and 12 or more years of education) to have retired unexpectedly and unwillingly. It is interesting to note that those with mid-level education (9-11 years) were more disadvantaged in regard to unexpected and unwilling retirement than were those with less education (0-8 years).

text continued on page 290

Table 16.2 Age at and Plans and Reasons for Retirement of Black Americans Aged 55-101 Years by Gender, Income, Education, and Occupation ($N = 259$, the retired only)

	Gender			Income		
	Men	Women	Total	<$6,000	≥$6,000	Total
Age in Years at Retirement						
Less than 55	13	20	33	19	14	33
	(12.9)	(14.4)	(13.8)	(14.7)	(12.7)	(13.8)
55-64	45	62	107	55	52	107
	(44.5)	(44.9)	(44.8)	(42.7)	(47.3)	(44.8)
65	14	13	27	13	14	27
	(13.9)	(9.4)	(11.3)	(10.1)	(12.7)	(11.3)
66-69	15	22	37	19	18	37
	(14.8)	(15.9)	(15.5)	(14.7)	(16.4)	(15.5)
70+	14	21	35	23	12	35
	(13.9)	(15.2)	(14.6)	(17.8)	(10.9)	(14.6)
Plans for Retirement[a]						
Planned to retire	54	63	117	48	69	117
	(54.0)	(44.7)	(48.5)	(36.6)	(62.7)	(48.5)
Retired unexpectedly	46	78	124	83	41	124
	(46.0)	(55.3)	(51.5)	(63.4)	(37.3)	(51.5)
Retired willingly	59	84	143	55	88	143
	(56.7)	(57.9)	(57.4)	(41.4)	(75.9)	(57.4)
Retired unwillingly	45	61	106	78	28	106
	(43.3)	(42.1)	(42.6)	(58.6)	(24.1)	(42.6)
Reasons for Retirement[b]						
Job related	7	17	24	16	8	24
	(14.3)	(21.0)	(18.5)	(19.3)	(17.0)	(18.5)
Age	3	4	7	7	0	7
	(6.1)	(4.9)	(5.4)	(8.4)	(0.0)	(5.4)
Poor health	28	40	68	42	26	68
	(57.2)	(49.4)	(52.3)	(50.7)	(55.4)	(52.3)
Other (personal, new interests)	1	1	2	1	1	2
	(2.0)	(1.2)	(1.5)	(1.2)	(2.1)	(1.5)
Family responsibilities	4	11	15	9	6	15
	(8.2)	(13.6)	(11.5)	(10.8)	(12.8)	(11.5)
Financial readiness	0	3	3	2	1	3
	(0.0)	(3.7)	(2.3)	(2.4)	(2.1)	(2.3)
Mandatory	6	5	11	6	5	11
	(12.2)	(6.2)	(8.5)	(7.2)	(10.6)	(8.5)

continued

Table 16.2 Continued

	Years of Education				
	0-8	*9-11*	*12*	*Some College*	*Total*
Age in Years at Retirement					
Less than 55	16	4	6	5	31
	(11.2)	(11.8)	(18.8)	(19.2)	(13.2)
55-64	66	15	13	13	107
	(46.1)	(44.1)	(40.6)	(50.1)	(45.5)
65	18	5	1	3	27
	(12.6)	(14.7)	(3.1)	(11.5)	(11.5)
66-69	23	5	4	4	36
	(16.1)	(14.7)	(12.5)	(15.4)	(15.3)
70+	20	5	8	1	34
	(14.0)	(14.7)	(25.0)	(3.8)	(14.5)
Plans for Retirement[a]					
Planned to retire	70	11	17	18	116
	(47.9)	(34.4)	(51.5)	(69.2)	(48.9)
Retired unexpectedly	76	21	16	8	121
	(52.1)	(65.6)	(48.5)	(30.8)	(51.1)
Retired willingly	81	17	20	22	140
	(54.4)	(50.0)	(58.8)	(81.5)	(57.4)
Retired unwillingly	68	17	14	5	104
	(45.6)	(50.0)	(41.2)	(18.5)	(42.6)
Reasons for Retirement[b]					
Job related	13	3	5	2	23
	(16.9)	(13.0)	(29.4)	(22.2)	(18.4)
Age	6	1	0	0	6
	(7.8)	(4.3)	(0.0)	(0.0)	(4.8)
Poor health	41	11	8	6	66
	(53.2)	(47.9)	(47.0)	(66.7)	(52.8)
Other (personal, new interests)	1	1	0	0	2
	(1.3)	(4.3)	(0.0)	(0.0)	(1.6)
Family responsibilities	9	3	2	0	14
	(11.7)	(13.0)	(11.8)	(0.0)	(11.2)
Financial readiness	3	0	0	0	3
	(3.9)	(0.0)	(0.0)	(0.0)	(2.4)
Mandatory	4	4	2	1	11
	(5.2)	(17.5)	(11.8)	(11.1)	(8.8)

continued

Table 16.2 Continued

	Occupation			Total
	Service	Blue Collar	White Collar	
Age in Years at Retirement				
Less than 55	13 (12.9)	14 (15.4)	5 (15.1)	32 (14.2)
55-64	44 (43.5)	45 (49.4)	12 (36.4)	101 (44.9)
65	11 (10.9)	9 (9.9)	4 (12.1)	24 (10.7)
66-69	15 (14.9)	14 (15.4)	6 (18.2)	35 (15.5)
70+	18 (17.8)	9 (9.9)	6 (18.2)	33 (14.7)
Plans for Retirement[a]				
Planned to retire	47 (46.5)	50 (53.2)	17 (54.8)	114 (50.4)
Retired unexpectedly	54 (53.5)	44 (46.8)	14 (45.2)	112 (49.6)
Retired willingly	61 (59.2)	56 (57.7)	21 (63.6)	138 (59.2)
Retired unwillingly	42 (40.8)	41 (42.3)	12 (36.4)	95 (40.8)
Reasons for Retirement[b]				
Job related	10 (18.2)	8 (17.4)	4 (25.0)	22 (18.8)
Age	4 (7.3)	3 (6.5)	0 (0.0)	7 (6.0)
Poor health	25 (45.5)	26 (56.7)	8 (50.0)	59 (50.4)
Other (personal, new interests)	1 (1.8)	1 (2.1)	0 (0.0)	2 (1.7)
Family responsibilities	9 (16.4)	2 (4.3)	2 (12.5)	13 (11.1)
Financial readiness	1 (1.8)	2 (4.3)	0 (0.0)	3 (2.6)
Mandatory	5 (9.1)	4 (8.7)	2 (12.5)	11 (9.4)

NOTES: Percentages are in parentheses below each number. Columns fail to add to 259 due to missing data. Blue-collar occupations are craftspersons, operatives, laborers, farmer, and farm workers. Service occupations include all service workers. White-collar occupations are professional, managerial, sales, and clerical.
a. Categories are not mutually exclusive.
b. Multiple mentions are possible; asked only of those who retired unexpectedly and are currently working less than 20 hours per week.

Reasons for Retirement

Black Americans retired mainly due to poor health. Job-related reasons ranked next, with financial readiness and new interests at the bottom of the list. Age and mandatory retirement were named by a few. Reasons for retirement did not appear to vary that much by gender or SES. There were, however, a few exceptions:

1. Women were slightly more likely than men to retire because of job-related and family responsibilities, and men more likely to retire mandatorily.
2. Those with incomes less than $6,000 were more likely than those with higher incomes to retire for reasons of age.
3. Surprisingly, the more highly educated (some college) were the likeliest to give poor health as the reason for retiring; and those with 12 or more years of education were more likely than those with less than 12 years to give job-related reasons.
4. White-collar workers were slightly more likely than blue-collar or service workers to retire for job-related and mandatory reasons.

Activities After Retirement

The activity most frequently engaged in by the black retired was housekeeping (Table 16.3). Nothing, sitting, or resting were second in rank. About 15% engaged in sports, hobbies, and other leisure activities, and another 10% in gardening. Church, reading, radio, television, visiting, and talking ranked next. Very few were engaged in helping others, clubs, organizations, travel, or volunteer work.

There were practically no gender or SES differences in most retirement activities. There were some exceptions, however, that should be interpreted with caution because percentage bases and percentage differences were small.

1. Women were more likely to be engaged in housekeeping and men in gardening.
2. Those with incomes less than $6,000 were slightly more likely than those with higher incomes to be doing nothing, sitting, or resting.
3. Those with the lowest levels of education (0-8 years) were slightly more likely than those with higher levels (9 or more years) to name keeping house, gardening, nothing, sitting, and resting; but less likely to name sports, hobbies, and other leisure activities.

Table 16.3 Activities of Black Americans Aged 55-101 After Retirement by Gender, Income, Education, and Occupation (N = 245, the retired only)

	Gender			Income		
	Men	Women	Total	<$6,000	≥$6,000	Total
Housekeeping	14 (13.5)	41 (29.1)	55 (22.4)	29 (22.1)	26 (22.9)	55 (22.4)
Gardening	18 (17.3)	6 (4.3)	24 (9.8)	13 (9.9)	11 (9.6)	24 (9.8)
Helping Others	1 (1.0)	6 (4.3)	7 (2.9)	4 (3.0)	3 (2.6)	7 (2.9)
Church Related	10 (9.6)	10 (7.1)	20 (8.2)	10 (7.6)	10 (8.8)	20 (8.2)
Clubs/Organizations	3 (2.9)	4 (2.8)	7 (2.9)	4 (3.1)	3 (2.6)	7 (2.9)
Sports, Hobbies, Other Leisure	12 (11.5)	25 (17.7)	37 (15.1)	19 (14.5)	18 (15.8)	37 (15.1)
Travel	3 (2.9)	2 (1.4)	5 (2.0)	1 (0.8)	4 (3.5)	5 (2.0)
Reading, Radio, Television	6 (5.8)	10 (7.1)	16 (6.5)	9 (6.9)	7 (6.1)	16 (6.5)
Visiting, Talking	5 (4.8)	10 (7.1)	15 (6.1)	7 (5.3)	8 (7.0)	15 (6.1)
Volunteer Work	1 (1.0)	2 (1.4)	3 (1.2)	1 (0.8)	2 (1.8)	3 (1.2)
Nothing, Sitting, Resting	24 (23.0)	24 (17.0)	48 (19.6)	30 (22.9)	18 (15.8)	48 (19.6)
Other	7 (6.7)	1 (0.7)	8 (3.3)	4 (3.1)	4 (3.5)	8 (3.3)

continued

Table 16.3 Continued

	Years of Education					Occupation			
	0-8	9-11	12	Some College	Total	Service	Blue Collar	White Collar	Total
Housekeeping	37 (25.0)	6 (18.2)	5 (15.2)	5 (18.5)	53 (22.0)	26 (26.0)	18 (18.8)	6 (18.8)	50 (21.9)
Gardening	20 (13.4)	2 (6.1)	2 (6.1)	0 (0.0)	24 (10.0)	3 (3.0)	19 (19.8)	2 (6.3)	24 (10.5)
Helping Others	4 (2.7)	1 (3.0)	1 (3.0)	1 (3.7)	7 (2.9)	5 (5.0)	1 (1.0)	1 (3.1)	7 (3.1)
Church Related	5 (3.4)	8 (24.2)	4 (12.1)	3 (11.1)	20 (8.3)	9 (9.0)	6 (6.3)	3 (9.3)	18 (7.9)
Clubs/Organizations	4 (2.7)	0 (0.0)	1 (3.0)	1 (3.7)	6 (2.5)	2 (2.0)	2 (2.1)	1 (3.1)	5 (2.2)
Sports, Hobbies, Other Leisure	18 (12.2)	7 (21.2)	7 (21.2)	5 (18.5)	37 (15.4)	19 (19.0)	12 (12.5)	3 (9.3)	34 (14.9)
Travel	4 (2.7)	0 (0.0)	0 (0.0)	1 (3.7)	5 (2.1)	2 (2.0)	2 (2.1)	1 (3.1)	5 (2.2)
Reading, Radio, Television	9 (6.1)	2 (6.1)	3 (9.1)	2 (7.4)	16 (6.6)	8 (8.0)	5 (5.2)	2 (6.3)	15 (6.6)
Visiting, Talking	5 (3.4)	4 (12.1)	1 (3.0)	4 (14.9)	14 (5.8)	5 (5.0)	5 (5.2)	3 (9.3)	13 (5.7)
Volunteer Work	1 (0.7)	0 (0.0)	1 (3.0)	1 (3.7)	3 (1.2)	0 (0.0)	1 (1.0)	2 (6.3)	3 (1.3)
Nothing, Sitting, Resting	37 (25.0)	2 (6.1)	6 (18.2)	3 (11.1)	48 (19.9)	17 (17.0)	23 (23.9)	6 (18.8)	46 (20.2)
Other	4 (2.7)	1 (3.0)	2 (6.1)	1 (3.7)	8 (3.3)	4 (4.0)	2 (2.1)	2 (6.3)	8 (3.5)

NOTES: The figure on top is the number of people who responded in that activity category, and the figure on the bottom is the column percent. Blue-collar occupations are craftspersons, operatives, laborers, farmers, and farm workers. Service occupations include all service workers. White-collar occupations are professional, managerial, sales, and clerical. Columns fail to add to 259 due to missing data.

4. White-collar workers were the most likely to name visiting, talking, and volunteer work; blue-collar workers were the most likely to name gardening, nothing, sitting, or resting.

5. Service workers were the most likely to name housekeeping.

In summary, SES may influence retirement roles, planning, and activities. SES, however, may not influence age at and reasons for retirement. Gender may influence the retirement roles and experiences of the black elderly less than SES. This is in spite of the fact that clear gender differences in these aspects of retirement have been found in the general population. Race differences in the importance of gender in the retirement experience are suggested.

The Future of Black Retirement Research

The findings of this descriptive analysis of the NSBA work, retirement, and disability data warrant new multivariate research. In this new research, models of late-life roles and retirement experiences should be developed separately for black and white men and women, and for blacks of lower and higher SES.

Analyzing SES Differences

Because the present findings suggest that late-life roles and retirement experiences vary by income and education, new retirement research should take into account the different circumstances of those in lower and higher socioeconomic status groups. The findings did not differ much by occupation. Is occupation not a valid social class indicator for the present generation of older black Americans? If not, the reason might be that racial discrimination placed a ceiling on their occupational mobility. The increasing validity of occupation as a measure of social class among blacks, then, would be a good barometer of widening occupational opportunities for them.

Analyzing Race Differences in the Effects of Gender

The findings suggest that gender is less important in the late-life roles and retirement experiences of black than white Americans. This may be because black men and women in the present elderly cohort, unlike their white counterparts, had similar work lives. Both black men and women were lifetime workers with discontinuous work patterns. New research should focus on such race and gender differences when examining late-life roles and retirement experiences.

Revising Retirement Definitions

Definitions of retirement need recasting if a most disadvantaged group of the black elderly is to be included in future retirement research, planning, and policy. Findings in this chapter highlight the diversity of black Americans in late-life roles. They are workers, disabled workers, and retirees. Prevailing procedural retirement definitions may be inappropriate for those individuals, although eligible, who do not call themselves retired (the unretired-retired).

This sizable and deprived segment of older blacks by definition could be omitted from retirement research. These are individuals who do not choose to call themselves retired, who have never had a regular job, who do not have pension benefits, and for whom there is no clear cessation of work. Because alternate definitions of retirement change the findings of retirement research (Palmore, Fillenbaum, & George, 1984), expanding current definitions of retirement to include the unretired-retired black elderly could change some of the past findings and paradigms of retirement research.

Toward New Retirement Models

Although discussions in this chapter have focused on relationships among source of income, work history, the disabled worker, and retirement roles, the choice of late-life roles undoubtedly is a more complex social-psychological process. Variables excluded from our discussion are likely to be cognitive-motivational and personality factors such as: ways individuals make sense of their world, values they have (and perceive society has) about retirement, external barriers (real and perceived) to carrying out a full retirement role, and various other psychological costs and benefits of the retirement role. These variables could affect choice of late-life roles and retirement experiences directly, as mediators, or as intervenors, as recent latent variable analyses demonstrate (Gibson, 1991a, 1991b).

The models should be tested across national samples to determine whether blacks and other minorities (Gibson & Burns, 1992) and whites differ in the factors influencing late-life roles and retirement experiences. The models also should be tested in longitudinal data to determine the special effects of social change and civil rights legislation on the late-life roles and retirement experiences of blacks, and to determine the causal ordering of work, disability, and retirement roles. For maximum planning and policy benefit, new research on black American late-life roles and retirement resources should employ similar constructs, personal biographies, and methods of analysis.

References

Abbott, J. (1977). Socioeconomic characteristics of the elderly: Some black/white differences. *Social Security Bulletin, 40,* 16-42.

Abbott, J. (1980). Work experience and earnings of middle-aged black and white men, 1965-1971. *Social Security Bulletin, 43,* 16-34.

Anderson, B. E., & Cottingham, D. H. (1981). The elusive quest for economic equality. *Daedalus, 110,* 257-274.

Biddle, B., & Thomas, E. (Eds.). (1966). *Role theory: Concepts and research.* New York: John Wiley.

Cain, G. G. (1976). The challenge of segmented labor market theories to orthodox theory: A survey. *Journal of Economic Literature, 14,* 1215-1257.

Chirikos, T., & Nestel, G. (1983). *Economic aspects of self-reported work disability.* Columbus: Center for Human Resource Research, The Ohio State University.

Corcoran, M., & Duncan, G. J. (1978). A summary of part 1 findings. In G. J. Duncan & J. N. Morgan (Eds.), *Five thousand American families* (Vol. VI, pp. 3-46). Ann Arbor: University of Michigan, Institute for Social Research.

Current Population Reports. (1980). *The social and economic status of the black population in the United States 1970-1978.* (Special Studies Series P-23, No. 80). Washington, DC: Bureau of the Census, U. S. Department of Commerce.

Ellison, D. L. (1968). Work, retirement, and the sick role. *The Gerontologist, 8,* 189-192.

Fillenbaum, G., George, L., & Palmore, E. (1985). Determinants and consequences of retirement among men of different races and economic levels. *Journal of Gerontology, 40,* 85-94.

Gibson, R. C. (1982). *Race and sex differences in the work and retirement patterns of older heads of household* (pp. 138-184). (Minority Research Monograph). Scripps Foundation.

Gibson, R. C. (1983). Work patterns of older black female heads of household. *Journal of Minority Aging, 8*(2), 1-16.

Gibson, R. C. (1986a). *Blacks in an aging society* (pp. 1-41). New York: Carnegie.

Gibson, R. C. (1986b). Blacks in an aging society. *Daedalus, 115*(1), 349-371.

Gibson, R. C. (1987a). Defining retirement for black Americans. In D. E. Gelfand & C. Barresi (Eds.), *Ethnicity and aging* (pp. 224-238). New York: Springer.

Gibson, R. C. (1987b). Reconceptualizing retirement for black Americans. *The Gerontologist 27*(6), 691-698.

Gibson, R. C. (1988). The work, retirement, and disability of older black Americans. In J. S. Jackson (Ed.), *The black American elderly: Research on physical and psychosocial health* (pp. 304-324). New York: Springer.

Gibson, R. C. (1991a). The subjective retirement of black Americans. *Journal of Gerontology, 46*(2), 204-209.

Gibson, R. C. (1991b). Race and the self-reported health of elderly persons. *Journal of Gerontology, 46*(5), S235-S242.

Gibson, R. C. (1991c). Retirement in black America. In J. S. Jackson (Ed.), *Life in black America* (pp. 179-198). Newbury Park, CA: Sage.

Gibson, R. C., & Burns, C. J. (1992). The work, retirement, and disability of aging minorities. *Generations,* Fall/Winter, 31-35.

Gordon, H. A., Hamilton, C. A., & Tipps, H. C. (1982). *Unemployment and underemployment among Blacks, Hispanics, and women.* (U. S. Commission on Civil Rights Clearinghouse Publication No. 74). Washington, DC: Government Printing Office.

Hanushek, E. A., & Jackson, J. E. (1977). *Statistical methods for social scientists.* New York: Academic Press.

Hill, M. S. (1981, January). *Trends in the economic situation of U. S. families and children: 1970-1980.* Paper presented at the Conference of Families and the Economy, Washington, DC.

Jackson, J. J. (1980). *Minorities and aging.* Belmont, CA: Wadsworth.

Jackson, J. S., & Gibson, R. C. (1985). Work and retirement among the black elderly. In Z. Blau (Ed.), *Current perspectives on aging and the life cycle* (pp. 193-222). Greenwich, CT: JAI.

James, W. (1950). *The principles of psychology.* New York: Dover. (Originally published 1910)

Lamb, H. R., & Rogawski, A. S. (1978). Supplemental security income and the sick role. *American Journal of Psychiatry, 135,* 1221-1224.

Ludwig, A. (1981). The disabled society? *American Journal of Psychotherapy, 35,* 5-15.

Montaga, P. D. (1977). *Occupations and society: Toward a sociology of the labor market.* New York: John Wiley.

Morgan, J. N. (1980). Retirement in prospect and retrospect. In G. J. Duncan & J. N. Morgan (Eds.), *Five thousand American families: Vol. 8. Patterns of economic progress.* Ann Arbor: University of Michigan, Institute for Social Research.

Munnell, A. H. (1978). The economic experience of blacks: 1964-1974. *New England Economic Review,* January/February, 5-18.

Palmore, E. B., Fillenbaum, G. G., & George, L. K. (1984). Consequences of retirement. *Journal of Gerontology, 39,* 109-116.

Parnes, H., & Nestel, G. (1981). The retirement experience. In H. S. Parnes (Ed.), *Work and retirement: A national longitudinal study of men.* Cambridge, MA: MIT Press.

Phillips, D. (1965). Self-reliance and the inclination to adopt the sick role. *Social Forces, 43,* 555-563.

Prince, E. (1978). Welfare status, illness and subjective health definition. *American Journal of Public Health, 68,* 865-871.

Sarbin, T., & Allen, V. (1968). Role theory. In G. Lindzey & E. Aronson (Eds), *The handbook of social psychology* (2nd Ed., pp. 223-258). Reading, MA: Addison-Wesley.

Streib, G., & Schneider, G. (1971). *Retirement in American society: Impact and process.* Ithaca, NY: Cornell University Press.

Stryker, S. (1968). Identity salience and role performance: The relevance of symbolic interaction theory for family research. *Journal of Marriage and the Family, 30*, 558-562.

Thurlow, H. J. (1971). Illness in relation to life situation and sick role tendency. *Journal of Psychosomatic Research, 15*, 73-88.

SECTION VI

Life Course of
African Americans

17

STATUS AND FUNCTIONING
OF FUTURE COHORTS
OF AFRICAN-AMERICAN ELDERLY
Conclusions and Speculations

James S. Jackson
Linda M. Chatters
Robert Joseph Taylor

In this volume we have addressed several substantive issues and the deficit in empirical data that has plagued previous research on the status and functioning of African-American elderly. We have placed these empirical findings within a larger theoretical context that views such statuses and functioning within a model of role changes and adaptations over the individual and group life course. In this concluding chapter we would like to highlight and synthesize the major findings in the book and speculate about what coming decades may portend for future cohorts of African-American elderly.

In this chapter we summarize the major findings in the previous 16 empirical chapters, re-engaging the themes propounded in Chapter 1, examining briefly the general issues of the middle-aged "Negro" of 1967, and speculating on where that and subsequent cohorts of middle-aged and older blacks might be in the 21st century. This perspective highlights the importance of life span continuity in the black experience in the United States, reflected in cumulative individual and social deficits, the strength of birth cohort experiences for an oppressed minority, and the important effects that aging and period events may have in shaping the future of existing cohorts of black American adults (J. S. Jackson, in press).

The findings from the first Nationwide Conference on the Health Status of the "Negro" in 1967 at Howard University are still applicable today and succinctly make the point of this chapter. During the conference, Cornely (1968) reported on the widening health gap between blacks and whites, pointing specifically to fetal death rates, life expectancy, childhood health risks, and disease-specific causes of death, all indicating significant increased risks in the "Negro" population. Since this notable conference and report there has been both improvements in black health status over the early and middle stages of the life course and continued discrepancies from that of the general population. The realization that today's African-American elders were the middle-aged "Negroes" of 1967 when this report was written, starkly highlights the importance of a life span framework in interpreting and understanding the life circumstances of African Americans at every position in the life-cycle, but most importantly in older adulthood.

At many points in this chapter we will refer the reader to Table 17.1. This table provides a brief examination of change and stability among middle-aged and older cohorts over the period 1979-1980 to 1987 in several life domains. These data are based upon the NSBA respondents and a second wave of data collection on the original sample, the Panel Survey of Black Americans (J. S. Jackson & Wolford, 1992). This table provides a summary of gross changes in several life domains as the middle-aged and older black cohorts aged from 1979-1980 to 1987. These data are based upon the 915 respondents for whom we have complete responses from both points in time and are weighted to reflect the distribution of the original NSBA sample. These percentages indicate whether individuals in a given cohort show decreases, stability, or increases on a particular indicator as they age over the 7-8 year period. Thus, Column 1 shows the changes or stability in life satisfaction and indicates the proportions of individuals who showed increases, decreases, or remained the same in reported life satisfaction from 1980 to 1987 as they aged from 35-44 to 43-52, 45-54 to 53-62, and so on, through those who were 75 and over in 1979-1980 and over 83 years of age in 1987. Other domains include the amount and frequency of help gained from church members, amount of health satisfaction, the degree of health disability, whether the amount of informal support changed, whether the respondents were more or less likely to vote in presidential and local elections, the degree of race group identity, and whether different age cohorts were more or less likely to show a change in work status.

Population Composition Trends: The Aging of Black America

This chapter highlights the importance of the demographic changes in the older total and black populations. The transformation of the age structure will have important effects on the work and retirement experiences, health, and functioning of older blacks and the availability of informal and formal supports. Based upon the middle projection series of the U.S. Census Bureau (1.9 ultimate lifetime births per woman, mortality life expectancy of 79.6 years in 2050, and annual net immigration of 450,000), it is projected that sustained growth will occur in the over age 65 group until the year 2010. From 2010 through 2030 the postwar baby boom cohorts will increase the over age 65 group from 39 to 65 million. By the year 2030, every fifth American will be over the age of 65 (Siegel & Taeuber, 1986).

Of those individuals over the age of 65, one of the most rapidly growing demographic groups are persons over the age of 85 (Suzman & Riley, 1985). The baby boom cohorts will continue to have a major impact on the societal age structure and will swell the ranks of the over age 85 group from an expected 9 million in 2030 to 16 million by 2050. These projections also suggest comparable effects on estimates for other age groupings, 75 years and older, for example, in the elderly population. As pointed out by several authors, however, reductions in current mortality rates would lead to even greater increases in these projected numbers (Seigel & Davidson, 1984; Seigel & Taeuber, 1986; Suzman & Riley, 1985).

The projected changes in the age structure of the population has resulted in much speculation regarding the social and policy implications of an aging society (Neugarten & Neugarten, 1986; Palmer & Gould, 1986), the rise in the total dependency ratio (Seigel & Taeuber, 1986), individual health, health service delivery, and rising health costs in a population with a large proportion of longevous members (Davis, 1986; Gibson, 1986; Manton & Soldo, 1985; Soldo, 1980). Morbidity and mortality will continue to increase within the older population as an outcome of the increasing numbers of individuals living to older ages (Davis, 1986; Siegel & Davidson, 1984).

Racial and ethnic minorities are also contributing to the aging of the United States at a slightly higher rate than in the general population (J. S. Jackson, Burns, & Gibson, 1992; Siegel & Davidson, 1984). Demographic trends over the last four decades and projections over the next four indicate a significant upward shift in the mean age of the black population and greater concentrations of blacks in all age ranges over 45, with the largest *percentage* shift to occur in blacks 85 years of age and older. Most projections (Siegel & Davidson, 1984) suggest rather large increases in both blacks and whites over the age of 65, particularly for the oldest old, with commensurate larger proportionate increases among the black elderly. These latter increases undoubtedly reflect the greater environmental advantages of these recent black older cohorts in comparison to previous cohorts. Because blacks show greater morbidity at each point in the life span prior to age 65, the relative meaning of increasing proportions and numbers of older blacks in the population must be examined.

Life Course of African Americans

Although little theory exists regarding life span continuity and discontinuity of racial and ethnic group members (J. J. Jackson, 1985; J. S. Jackson, in press; J. S. Jackson et al., 1992), it is clear that life circumstances during younger ages have significant influences upon the quality of life in the latter stages of the life course. From a social problems perspective, some have marked this as the multiple jeopardy hypothesis (Dowd & Bengtson, 1978; J. J. Jackson, 1980, 1985). This hypothesis holds that negative environmental, social, and economic conditions early in the life course of blacks have deleterious effects on later social, psychological, and biological growth (J. J. Jackson, 1981). These accumulate over the individual life span and when combined with the negative consequences of old age itself, eventuate in higher levels of morbidity and mortality at earlier years in old age than is the case for whites.

At almost every point of the life span blacks have greater disability and morbidity (J. J. Jackson, 1981). In infancy this is marked by higher mortality figures as well as accident and disease rates. Adolescence, young adulthood, and even older ages of blacks are characterized by comparatively higher homicide deaths than whites. Middle age and early old age show increased disability, early retirement, and ultimately higher death rates in the black as compared to the general population. It is only after the age of 75 to 80 that blacks tend to show increased longevity in comparison to whites (J. S. Jackson et al., 1992; Manton, 1982; Manton, Poss, & Wing, 1979; Markides, 1983).

It has been suggested that this racial crossover phenomena in the oldest old black and white populations is an artifact of age misreporting in older cohorts, particularly the tendency of older blacks to inflate their ages. Others have argued strongly that this is a consistent finding with cross-national support in other cultures (J. J. Jackson, 1985; J. S. Jackson, Antonucci, & Gibson, 1990a; Manton, 1982; Omran, 1977). In support of the substance of this observed crossover it has been suggested that genetic and environmental factors act in tandem on an heterogeneous black population to produce hardier older blacks (Gibson & J. S. Jackson, 1987, 1992; Manton et al., 1979). One direct implication of this explanation is the existence of differential aging processes within black and white populations (Manton, 1982). As noted by J. J. Jackson (1985), however, no research findings yet support this latter claim. This issue is still under investigation, prompted by recent research showing positive outcomes in aging and effective functioning in the black oldest old (Gibson & J. S. Jackson, 1987, 1992).

In fact, the two chapters that address work and retirement experiences of older blacks in this volume make the point that many older blacks continue to work in very productive formal employment roles. In Chapter 15 Coleman's analyses support a traditional finding in the literature that good health is positively related to employment in older ages. She then speculates on what this employment may mean, given that blacks have a long history of secondary labor market involvement. Marital roles and need also appear to play a role in accounting for who is working or not. She concludes that work for older blacks, as in the younger populations, serves a variety of functional and need-reduction roles and that there is no inevitable decline with age that necessarily drives older black workers from the labor force. At the same time, in Chapter 16 Gibson shows that traditional definitions of retirement are misapplied in this cohort of older blacks. Though one can find the traditionally retired individual, many older African Americans defy easy description and seem to fall into underemployed worker, disabled workers, and people whose retired status is not clearly ascertained ("unretired-retired"). As shown in Table 17.1, different age cohorts show stability of initial work patterns through the 65-74 years of age

Table 17.1 Change From 1980 to 1987 in the Proportion of People Showing Increases, Stability, or Decreases in Life Satisfaction, Help From the Church, Frequency of Help From Church, Health Satisfaction, Health Disability, Amount of Informal Help, Voting in Last Presidential Election, Voting in Last Local Election, Racial Identification, and Employment Status (in percentages)

Life Domain Age Change in Years 1980-1987	Type of Change 1980-1987	Life Satisfaction	Church Help	Often Church Help	Health Satis-faction	Health Disability	Help Receipt	Vote President	Vote Local	Race Identity	Employment Status
35-44 to 45-52	Increases	31	16	33	17	29	31	16	19	15	13
	Stability	51	54	32	59	54	42	82	74	64	73
	Decreases	18	30	25	24	17	27	2	7	21	14
45-52 to 53-62	Increases	26	15	22	20	35	33	19	14	18	6
	Stability	50	51	38	53	55	37	75	72	66	79
	Decreases	24	34	40	27	10	30	6	4	16	15
55-64 to 63-72	Increases	25	27	32	19	24	14	13	22	17	2
	Stability	53	42	29	58	59	32	85	71	74	76
	Decreases	22	31	39	23	17	54	2	7	9	22
65-74 to 73-82	Increases	22	15	44	17	25	16	11	22	12	2
	Stability	63	50	32	56	57	40	75	64	75	62
	Decreases	15	35	24	27	18	44	14	14	13	36
75+ to 83+	Increases	12	13	24	26	3	0	5	9	20	0
	Stability	53	74	48	35	62	69	92	83	70	13
	Decreases	35	13	28	39	35	31	3	8	10	87

cohort (73%, 79%, 76%, and 62%). It is only as the 75 and older cohort ages over the 7-year period that work shows a decided decrease (87% indicating a decrease in working). Interestingly, each of the five age cohorts examined shows a significant decline in work status and a significant increase in reported health disability. Issues of choice, a lifetime of labor force participation in secondary sector jobs, and structural impediments to mobility all could contribute to the wide diversity of work and retirement roles discussed in Chapters 15 and 16, and supported by the patterns over the 7-year period shown in Table 17.1.

There is a general tendency in the United States to view African Americans in simplistic and undifferentiated ways, assuming a large degree of homogeneity in values, motives, social and psychological statuses, and behaviors (J. S. Jackson, in press; Jaynes & Williams, 1989). Although racially based categorical treatment results in some extent of group uniformity in attitudes and behaviors, it has always been true that there exists a rich heterogeneity among blacks (J. S. Jackson, in press). Research demonstrates that African Americans span the same spectrum of structural circumstances, psychological statuses, and social beliefs as the millions of other Americans of different ethnic and cultural backgrounds (J. S. Jackson, in press; Stanford 1990). But a unique history and the nature of their group and individual developmental and aging experiences, all serve to place vast numbers of Americans of African descent in the United States from cradle to grave at disproportionate risk for physical, social, and psychological harm.

In the face of these harsh realities of life, our research findings show older African Americans to be a diverse and heterogenous population, possessing a wide array of group and personal resources at every point in the age span (J. S. Jackson, 1991; Stanford, 1990). For example, R. J. Smith and Thornton in Chapter 12 point to the continuing importance of group solidarity among older blacks. Their results indicate that this solidarity is related in very complex ways to socioeconomic factors and defies simple characterization. These results point to the importance of group consciousness and group interests as a continuing potential resource in older ages among blacks. Table 17.1 indicates a great deal of stability in race group identity among the different age cohorts as they age. These data also point to the possibility that this race group identity may be linked to age, as both stability and increases over time are more prevalent in the older cohorts. In Chapter 13, Brown and Barnes-Nacoste demonstrate the power and efficacy of this solidarity as it relates to political empowerment and participation. Their findings clearly implicate group solidarity as a mediator of racial socialization in the voting process among this older cohort of blacks. As shown in Table 17.1, remarkable stability and increased political participation (presidential and local voting) is found across all age cohorts with some increments in the original older age cohorts. Like most of the chapters in this volume, the data in Table 17.1 and the results in Chapters 12 and 13 document the continuing potency and significance of group interest and racial solidarity in today's older black cohorts.

Brown and Barnes-Nacoste in Chapter 13 notably develop a conceptual model that attempts to place region of early socialization experiences in a causal chain of group interest and ultimate political behavior. The companion Chapter 14 by Taylor and Thornton further examines the correlates of voting, suggesting that organized religious involvement is important in the voting behavior of older blacks. These findings suggest that both group interests, as expressed in group identity and consciousness, and organizational memberships have important, independent influences on political behavior. It may be that the organizational aspects of attachment, whether to the group or to a social and political structure like the church, provide the underlying mediating factor.

The changing age structure will have important influences on the health and effective functioning of older blacks (Gibson, 1986; Richardson, 1991). Because older black Americans of the year 2047 have already been born, the continuing imbalanced sex ratio, segregated geographic distribution, and proportion in poverty, among other structural factors, will have profound influences upon family structure, health status, and the well-being of older blacks over the next 50-60 years (J. S. Jackson, in press). A life span framework is needed to explore how environmental stressors influence and interact with group and personal resources (e.g., in Chapters 12 and 13) to impede or facilitate the quality of life of successive cohorts of African Americans (Baltes, 1987; Barresi, 1987).

Notable improvements in the life situations of blacks (Farley, 1987), particularly health, have occurred over the last 40 years (J. J. Jackson, 1981; J. S. Jackson et al., 1990a). Recent literature (e.g., Farley, 1987; Gibson, 1986; Jaynes & Williams, 1989), however, points to significant remaining structural barriers, particularly for poor blacks. These problems include the difficulties of single-parent households, high infant mortality and morbidity, childhood diseases, poor diets, lack of preventive health care, deteriorating neighborhoods, poverty, adolescent violence, un- and underemployment, teen pregnancy, drug and alcohol abuse, and broken marriages. Although the causal relationships are not known (Williams, 1990), it is clear that these are predisposing factors for high morbidity and mortality across the life span (Dressler, 1991; Haan & Kaplan, 1985; Hamburg, Elliott, & Parron, 1982).

Concurrent with changes in the age composition of the population, trends in poverty status and family structure among black Americans have important consequences for future cohorts of older persons. In the past 30 years, the structure of U.S. families has undergone substantial changes. During this period, both white and black families have witnessed higher divorce rates, increases in female-headed households, a higher proportion of births to unmarried mothers, larger percentages of children living in female-headed households, and a higher percentage of children living in poverty. Although these demographic changes have been experienced by both blacks and whites, black families have disproportionately suffered their impact (Jaynes & Williams, 1989; Taylor, Chatters, Tucker, & Lewis, 1990).

One of the major causes of these changes in poverty status and family structure among blacks is the declining rate of marriage. Over the past 30 years, larger proportions of black adults have either postponed marriage or have declined to marry at all. Although most black women will marry at some point in their lives, the overall proportion who ever marry could range as low as 70% or 80% (Rodgers & Thornton, 1985). In contrast, 94% of black women born in the 1930s eventually married. Currently, these women make up the cohort of older black women 53-62 years of age. Recent trends suggest that as a result of later marriages; higher rates of separation, divorce, and widowhood; and more time spent in separated, divorced, and widowed statuses, black females as a whole will spend a greater part of their lives unmarried (Taylor et al., 1990).

The decrease in length of time in marriage is an important contributing factor in the substantial increases in nonmarital births, childhood poverty, and female-headed households. Presently, about 6 of 10 black births are to unmarried mothers, half of all black children live in poverty, half of all black children live with their mothers but not their fathers, and over one in four black households is headed by a single female. All of these trends have increased over the past two decades and coincide with the reduced length of time spent in marriage by black Americans (Taylor et al., 1990).

Although the impact of the decrease in the length of time in marriage has definite consequences for the status of black children and young adults, additional effects can be predicted for later portions of the life span. In particular, fewer years in marriage would likely act to intensify rates of being unmarried among older women. We can expect that, distinct from past cohorts, older women who are widowed would make up a smaller proportion of the group of older unmarried women. Further, the trend toward a decline in marriage suggests that the proportion of never-married older women will increase in future cohorts of black elderly. Older black women will spend more time without marital partners, a trend that would seemingly exacerbate the present economic and social problems facing this group.

In particular, the companionship of a spouse, wider informal support relationships within families, living arrangements, and income adequacy will all be affected. These factors have been identified in the literature as having particular and significant impacts on the quality of life among older adults. Spouses are consistently noted as important sources of instrumental and socioemotional assistance and as central figures in informal support networks (Chatters, Taylor, & Jackson, 1985). Further, married status has been associated with enhanced perceptions of well-being among older black adults (Chatters, 1988). Although the specific life course patterns of support will vary across marital status designations, overall family resources to these women may be unavailable or truncated. Family support networks are particularly crucial in the areas of health status, formal health resource use, and self-care activities (e.g., medication use, diet, therapies) of older persons. As shown in Table 17.1, one of the most volatile domains of life is the amount of informal help received over the 7-year period. For the two younger cohorts, increased age is almost equally likely to result in reports of both increased and decreased assistance from family and friends. In the three older cohorts, reports of decreased support are from 30% to 40% greater than indications of increased assistance. The changes in spousal and friend networks discussed here could account for this observed diminishment in informal assistance over time.

With regard to living arrangements for older black women, in 1940, 9.4% lived alone as compared to 31.4% of older black women in 1980. As living alone is an important predictor of nursing home utilization, it is anticipated that the increased tendency to live alone may lead to greater institutionalization for this group (Shapiro & Ross, 1989). But although older black women are less likely to be married than their white counterparts, about equal percentages share households with others (Sweet & Bumpass, 1987). Consequently, the existence of extended family households may, in part, mitigate this situation. Similarly, older never-married, divorced, and widowed black women will have fewer economic resources than their married counterparts. Although older blacks generally experience high rates of poverty, married couples have higher incomes and a lower incidence of poverty than do their non-married counterparts (Taylor & Chatters, 1988).

We have been attempting to develop a coherent life span framework within which the nature of the economic, social, and psychological lives of black Americans can be understood and explained in the context of historical and current structural disadvantage and blocked mobility opportunities (J. S. Jackson, 1991; J. S. Jackson, in press; J. S. Jackson et al., 1990a, 1990b; J. S. Jackson, Taylor, & Chatters, this volume). In general, our data collections have been designed to explore scientifically the nature of African Americans' reactions to their unequal status in the United States. Specifically, the research reported in this volume has addressed the question of how structural disadvantages in the environment are translated at different points in the individual and group life cycle into physical, social, and psychological aspects of group and self.

This work has focused on such things as neighborhood and family integration, self-esteem, personal efficacy, closeness of personal and social relationships, physical and mental health, group solidarity and political participation, and work and retirement. Thus, McAdoo in Chapter 3 notes the deterioration in urban neighborhoods and the resultant victimization, stress, and perceptions of vulnerability among older African Americans. His findings indicate that black older adults may have very effective mechanisms for handling the stress and strains caused by environmental stressors. The findings of Jayakody in Chapter 1 provide one possible mechanism by which this positive adjustment may occur. Her findings suggest the overall importance of the neighborhood and neighbors in providing a psychologically supportive environment as well as a tangible source of resource potential for older blacks. Notably, her findings point to some peculiar cultural and historical legacies, that is, the fact that older African Americans living in the South are more likely to report neighborhood integration, even controlling for urbanicity. Even though as we point out, deteriorating neighborhoods provide an increasingly "dry" source of support for this generation of older blacks, neighbors are a continuing source of psychological, social, and tangible support. At the same time, the data in

Table 17.1 indicate low stability in reported life satisfaction and a decrease over the 7-year period.

In Chapter 4, Taylor, Keith, and Tucker point out the complicated role relationships that exist among older men and women and the potential changes over the individual life course in the assumption of helper roles. In Chapter 5, Chatters and Taylor make a similar point indicating the importance of adult children in providing tangible and intangible support to older blacks. Finally, Engram and Lockery in Chapter 6 remind us of the intimacies and close relationships that exist among older African-American partners and the importance of love, companionship, and support in the well-being and effective functioning of older black adults. These findings stand in marked contrast to the almost total avoidance in the literature of the investigation of close personal relationships among older African Americans. As might be expected, these relationships are important, and when combined with the findings on neighboring, family, and friend relationships paint a picture of older black Americans in more variegated and contexualized manner. This richer perspective counters the sterile and sexless portrait of older blacks that has dominated historical and contemporary mass media and research presentations. Because historical trends and projections continue to herald unbalanced sex ratios in older ages, the root causes of widowhood and single status among older blacks must be examined.

Both Taylor in Chapter 7 and J. M. Smith in Chapter 8 point to complex and important roles of organized religion in the lives of older blacks. Importantly, both these chapters provide debunking information to simplistic notions of religious belief among blacks. Taylor's findings point to the heterogeneity among blacks in religious affiliations and the multidimensional nature of religious involvement that exists. His findings suggest that older blacks perceive the role of the church in this broad sense and seek succor from the church and religion in both a spiritual and tangible sense. J. M. Smith provides some support for the structural analysis of Taylor and attempts to model the potential dynamic interplay of structural position, family processes, and church involvement. Her findings belie previous work that has ascribed a simple relationship between social structural position and religious involvement. Historically, many writers have viewed the church in simplistic terms of salvation, denying its fundamental position in the secular life of African Americans. J. M. Smith's work suggests that in the presence of controls for primary and secondary group integration as well as frequency of service and urbanicity, clear relationships among achieved socioeconomic status and religious involvement are not present. Rather than denying the importance of achieved socioeconomic statuses in religious involvement, these results suggest that a much more complicated set of causal relationships may exist among these statuses, neighborhood, and family and friend integration. Somewhat disturbing are the trends suggested in Table 17.1, indicating that African Americans of all age cohorts were more likely to report decreased support from church sources over the 7-year period of 1980 to 1987. When combined with the previous deterioration in informal family and friend support, this paints a possibly bleak picture for future cohorts in what has been historically an important source of sustenance for black elders.

We have oriented our studies to examine how the age cohort into which blacks are born; the social, political, and economic events that occur to blacks born together; and the individual aging process at different points in a person's life course influence the adaptation and quality of life of individuals, families, and larger groups of African Americans. For example, we recognize that blacks born before the 1940s faced very different environmental constraints and have experienced a very different set of life tasks, events, opportunities, and disappointments than those born in the 1970s (Baker, 1987). In addition to significant changes in the legal structure, health care advances, family changes, urban migration, and macroeconomic influences all differed dramatically for these very different birth cohorts, as they will for future cohorts of blacks (J. S. Jackson, in press; Richardson, 1991).

How these different birth cohorts, historical and current environmental events, and individual differences in aging processes interact with one another forms the overall context of this research. Although one focus is on the scientific aspects of phenomena such as political behavior, mental disorder, or service provision, the overarching framework is one that contextualizes these individual and group experiences by birth cohort, period events, and individual aging processes.

A set of fairly firm conclusions can be drawn from a review of the material on health, mortality, morbidity, and risk factors. It appears that the examination of black status and functioning, at least that of aging adults, has been conducted in a relative vacuum. Although several authors have indicated the necessity of considering life course models (e.g., Barresi, 1987; Manton & Soldo, 1985), and history, cohort, and period effects in the nature of black statuses and functioning, few have actually collected the type of data or conducted the types of analyses that would shed any light on this process. This has been the fault as much of a lack of good conceptual models of older black adults as a lack of quality data over time on sizable numbers of representative samples of black Americans.

Blacks arrive at older ages with significant amounts of previous disease and ill health. The available cohort data for cause specific mortality and morbidity across the life course over the last few decades indicates that there are accumulated deficits that perhaps place black older people at greater risk than comparably aged whites (J. S. Jackson, 1991). Similarly, the fact that blacks actually outlive their white counterparts in the very older ages suggests possible selection factors at work that may result in hardier oldest old blacks (Gibson & J. S. Jackson, 1987, 1992). Cohort experiences of blacks play a major role in the nature of their health experiences over the life course in terms of the quality of health care from birth, exposure to risk factors, and the presence of exogenous noxious environmental factors. Additionally, and with possible differences due to birth cohort and period, prejudice and discrimination as a source of stress and blocked opportunities are pervasive across the life span (Baker, 1987; Cooper, Steinhauer, Schatzkin, & Miller, 1981; Dressler, 1991).

In Chapter 9 Edmonds provides graphic illustration of the self-reported health conditions of African-American elderly. Her findings show that self-reported diseases and health satisfaction do not bear simple linear relationships to age among elderly African Americans (Gibson & J. S. Jackson, 1987). Similarly, in Chapter 10 Chatters notes the complexity of understanding health disability and concomitant stress and perceived strain. Chatters suggests that health disability may serve to debilitate coping resources that themselves play important roles in militating the stress-distress relationship. Edmonds notes that structural position and location (rural and Southern) can have negative influences on health outcomes and perceptions of individual satisfaction. Table 16.1 shows significant percentage decreases in health satisfaction and increased reports of health disability over all age cohorts during the 7-year period.

Somewhat disturbingly, in Chapter 11 Greene, J. S. Jackson, and Neighbors find that for stressful problems, oldest old black Americans may experience the lowest levels of formal and informal assistance, and that this relationship may hold across socioeconomic and gender groups. This finding is made even more worrisome by the previously reported trends in decreased informal support shown in Table 16.1. We believe that these three chapters (9, 10, and 11) provide a clear example of the role of health as both a resource for older blacks as well as a stressor that has influences in other domains of life. In the presence of good physical and mental health, older blacks report active and effective lives. In the absence of such good health and in the presence of significant disability, older blacks report poor functioning and concomitant stress and strains. These data also show that informal and professional help is not always readily available, even though prior chapters (e.g., 1 through 5) show the important role that informal supports among older blacks play in preventing and alleviating deleterious environmental problems.

Conclusions and Implications

We have argued in this volume that previous and contemporary cohorts of blacks have been and are at considerable risk. Blacks have in the past spent and are most likely in the future to spend the majority of their childhood in low-income, single-parent, female-headed households and to be exposed to inadequate educational opportunities. Their job prospects early in life have been poor and will be perhaps even poorer in future cohorts. And a large proportion have suffered and will continue to suffer chronic disease prior to reaching middle adulthood.

None of these structural and health deficits strikes at the psychological and social-psychological phenomena of life among black Americans—lack of perceived control, discouragement, and other effects of discrimination that impede the development of motivating aspirations and expectations of a successful life. When these social and psychological reactions are combined with substantial structural barriers to educational and occupational mobility and high probability of exposure to environmental risk factors, the success of blacks in achieving older ages is remarkable (Jaynes & Williams, 1989).

The results of the reviews and empirical analyses in this volume, however, clearly indicate that older age among blacks is not a time of inevitable decline (J. S. Jackson, in press; J. S. Jackson et al., 1990a; Rowe, 1985). The evidence points to the fact that real changes in life-style, environmental risk reduction, and medical interventions can have positive influences on the quantity and quality of late life among older black adults, even given negative life course experiences. Some data (e.g., Gibson & J. S. Jackson, 1987, 1991) show that many older blacks are free from functional disability (Edmonds, Chapter 9, and Chatters, Chapter 10, this volume) and limitations of activity due to chronic illness and disease. In fact, after the age of 65, blacks and whites, within sex groups, differ very little in years of expected remaining life. Health care has improved significantly for older black adults and consecutive cohorts have been better educated and better able to take advantage of available opportunities.

At the same time, without extensive environmental interventions, it is highly likely that a significant, and we suggest growing, proportion of older black adults of the year 2047—those being born in 1992—are at severe risk for impoverished conditions and poor social, physical, and psychological health in old age. This is particularly true compared to the middle-aged cohort of 1967—the elderly of today with whom we began this chapter. This gloomy prediction is not predicated on biological dimensions of racial differences, but instead is based upon the physical, social, psychological, and environmental risk factors intimately correlated with racial and ethnic group membership in U.S. society and the inevitable poor prognosis of the life experience paths into older ages of so many African Americans (J. S. Jackson, in press).

References

Anderson, N. B., & Shumaker, S. A. (1989). Race, reactivity, and blood pressure regulation. *Health Psychology, 8,* 483-486.

Baker, F. M. (1987). The Afro-American life cycle: Success, failure, and mental health. *Journal of the National Medical Association, 7,* 625-633.

Baltes, P. B. (1987). Theoretical propositions of life-span developmental psychology: On the dynamics between growth and decline. *Developmental Psychology, 23,* 616-626.

Barresi, C. M. (1987). Ethnic aging and the life course. In D. E. Gelfand and C. M. Barresi (Eds.), *Ethnic dimensions of aging* (pp. 18-34). New York: Springer.

Chatters, L. M. (1988). Subjective well-being evaluations among older black Americans. *Psychology and Aging, 3,* 184-190.

Chatters, L. M., Taylor, R. J., & Jackson, J. S. (1985). Size and composition of the informal helper network of elderly blacks. *Journal of Gerontology, 40,* 605-614.

Cornely, P. B. (1968). The health status of the negro today and in the future. *American Journal of Public Health, 58*(4), 647-654.

Davis, K. (1986). Aging and the health-care system: Economic and structural issues. *Daedalus, 115,* 227-246.

Dowd, J. J., & Bengtson, V. L. (1978). Aging in minority populations: An examination of the double jeopardy hypothesis.

Dressler, W. W. (1991). Social class, skin color, and arterial blood pressure in two societies. *Ethnicity and Disease, 1,* 60-77.

Farley, R. (1987). Who are black Americans?: The quality of life for black Americans twenty years after the civil rights revolution. *Milbank Memorial Fund Quarterly, 65*(Supp), 9-34.

Gibson, R. C. (1986). Blacks in an aging society. *Daedalus, 115*(1), 349-371.

Gibson, R. C., & Jackson, J. S. (1987). Health, physical functioning, and informal supports of the black elderly. *Milbank Quarterly, 65*(Suppl. 1), 1-34.

Gibson, R. C., & Jackson, J. S. (1992). The black oldest old: Health, functioning, and informal support. In R. M. Suzman, D. P. Willis, & K. G. Manton (Eds.), *The oldest old* (pp. 506-515). New York: Oxford University Press.

Haan, M. N., & Kaplan, G. A. (1985). The contribution of socioeconomic position to minority health. *Report of the Secretary's Task Force on Black and Minority Health: Vol. 2. Crosscutting issues in minority health.* Washington, DC: U.S. Department of Health and Human Services.

Hamburg, D. A., Elliott, G. R., & Parron, D. L. (1982). *Health and behavior: Frontiers of research in the biobehavioral sciences.* Washington, DC: National Academy Press.

Jackson, J. J. (1980). *Minorities and Aging.* Belmont, CA: Wadsworth.

Jackson, J. J. (1981). Urban black Americans. In A. Harwood (Ed.), *Ethnicity and health care* (pp. 37-129). Cambridge MA: Harvard University Press.

Jackson, J. J. (1985). Race, national origin, ethnicity, and aging. In R. H. Binstock & E. Shanas (Eds.), *Handbook of aging and the social sciences* (pp. 264-303). New York: Van Nostrand Reinhold.

Jackson, J. S. (Ed.). (1991). *Life in black America.* Newbury Park, CA: Sage.

Jackson, J. S. (in press). Racial influences on adult development and aging. In R. Kastenbaum (Ed.), *The encyclopedia of adult development.* Phoenix, AZ: Oryx.

Jackson, J. S., Antonucci, T. C., & Gibson, R. C. (1990a). Cultural, racial, and ethnic minority influences on aging. In J. E. Birren & K. W. Schaie (Eds.), *Handbook of the psychology of aging* (3rd ed., pp. 102-123). New York: Academic Press.

Jackson, J. S., Antonucci, T. C., & Gibson, R. C. (1990b). Social relations, productive activities, and coping with stress in late life. In M. A. P. Stephens, J. H. Crowther, S. E. Hobfoll, & D. L. Tennenbaum (Eds.), *Stress and coping in later life families* (pp. 193-212). Washington, DC: Hemisphere.

Jackson, J. S., Burns, C. J., & Gibson, R. C. (1992). An overview of geriatric care in ethnic and racial minority groups. In E. Calkins, A. B. Ford, & P. R. Katz (Eds.), *Practice of geriatrics* (2nd ed., pp. 57-64). Philadelphia: W. B. Saunders.

Jackson, J. S., & Wolford, M. L. (1992). Changes from 1980 to 1987 in the mental health status of African Americans. *Journal of Geriatric Psychiatry, XXV*(1), 15-67.

Jaynes, G. D., & Williams, R. M., Jr. (Eds.). (1989). *A common destiny: Blacks and American society.* Washington, DC: National Academy Press.

Manton, K. (1982). Differential life expectancy: Possible explanations during the later years. In R. C. Manuel (Ed.), *Minority aging: Sociological and social psychological issues* (pp. 63-70). Westport, CT: Greenwood Press.

Manton, K. G., & Soldo, B. J. (1985). Dynamics of health changes in the oldest old: New perspectives and evidence. *Milbank Memorial Fund Quarterly, 63,* 206-285.

Manton, K., Poss, S. S., & Wing, S. (1979). The black/white mortality crossover: Investigation from the perspective of the components of aging. *The Gerontologist, 19,* 291-300.

Markides, K. S. (1983). Mortality among minority populations: A review of recent patterns and trends. *Public Health Reports.*

Neugarten, B. L., & Neugarten, D. A. (1986). Age in the aging society. *Daedalus, 115,* B1-49.

Omran, A. R. (1977). Epidemiologic transition in the U.S. *The Population Bulletin, 32,* 3-42.

Palmer, J. L., & Gould, S. G. (1986). The economic consequences of an aging society. *Daedalus, 115,* 295-324.

Richardson, J. (1991). *Aging and health: Black elders.* (Stanford Geriatric Education Center Working Paper Series, No. 4: Ethnogeriatric Reviews). Stanford, CA: Stanford University, Geriatric Education Center, Division of Family & Community Medicine.

Rodgers, W. L., & Thornton, A. (1985). Changing patterns of first marriage in the United States. *Demography, 22,* 265-279.

Rowe, J. W. (1985). Health care of the elderly. *New England Journal of Medicine, 312,* 827-835.

Shaprio, E., & Roos, N. (1989). Predictors and patterns of nursing home and home care use. In M. Peterson, & D. White (Eds.), *Health care of the elderly: An information sourcebook.* Newbury Park, CA: Sage.

Siegel, J. S., & Davidson, M. (1984). *Demographic and socioeconomic aspects of aging in the United States.* Current Population Reports, Series P-23, No. 138. Washington, DC: Government Printing Office.

Siegel, J. S., & Taeuber, C. M. (1986). Demographic perspectives on the long-lived society. *Daedalus, 115,* 77-118.

Soldo, B. (1980). America's elderly in the 1980s. *Population Bulletin, 35,* 3-47.

Stanford, E. P. (1990). Diverse black aged. In Z. Harel, E. A. McKinney, & M. Williams (Eds.), *Black aged: Understanding diversity and service needs* (pp. 33-49). Newbury Park, CA: Sage.

Suzman, R., & Riley, M. W. (1985). Introducing the "oldest old." In R. Suzman and M. W. Riley (Eds.), *The oldest old. Milbank Memorial Fund Quarterly, 63,* 177-186.

Sweet, J. A., & Bumpass, L. L. (1987). *American families and households.* New York: Russell Sage Foundation.

Taylor, R. J., & Chatters, L. M. (1988). Church members as a source of informal social support. *Review of Religious Research, 30,* 193-203.

Taylor, R. J., Chatters, L. M., Tucker, M. B., & Lewis, E. (1990). Developments in research on black families: A decade review. *Journal of Marriage and the Family, 52,* 933-1014.

Wilkinson, D. T., & King, G. (1987). Conceptual and methodological issues in the use of race as a variable: Policy implications. *Milbank Memorial Fund Quarterly, 65*(Suppl. 1), 56-71.

Williams, D. R. (1990). Socioeconomic differentials in health: A review and redirection. *Social Psychology Quarterly, 53,* 81-99.

AUTHOR INDEX

Author Index

SUBJECT INDEX

Subject Index

ABOUT THE AUTHORS AND EDITORS

Rupert W. Barnes-Nacoste is an Associate Professor of Psychology at North Carolina State University. He received his Ph.D. in experimental social psychology from the University of North Carolina at Chapel Hill in 1982. He completed postdoctoral work both at the University of Michigan's Institute for Social Research where he worked with the Program for Research on Black Americans and in the Department of Psychology and the Institute for Research in Social Science at the University of North Carolina at Chapel Hill. He continues to pursue his interests in social interdependence and intergroup relations, procedural justice, affirmative action, and outgroup rejection.

Ronald E. Brown is an Associate Professor of Political Science at Wayne State University and an Adjunct Faculty Associate with the Institute for Social Research at the University of Michigan. Upon receiving his doctoral degree in political science from the University of Michigan in 1984, he accepted a Rockefeller Postdoctoral Scholar position for 1984-1985. His current research interests center around the role of religion and the church in the political action of African Americans.

Linda M. Chatters is an Assistant Professor in the Health Behavior and Health Education Department of the School of Public Health and a Faculty Associate with the Institute for Social Research at the University of Michigan. After earning her Ph.D. in psychology at the University of

Michigan, she completed postdoctoral work supported by the Rockefeller Foundation and the National Institute on Aging. As a recipient of a First Independent Research Support and Transition (FIRST) Award from the National Institute on Aging, she is investigating issues related to the use of survey data among diverse groups of black American respondents. Her work has appeared in *Psychology and Aging, Journal of Gerontology: Social Sciences, The Gerontologist, Journal of Marriage and the Family, Social Work, Family Relations,* and *Journal of Black Studies.*

Lerita M. Coleman received her Ph.D. in social psychology from Harvard University. She has taught at the University of Michigan and the University of Tennessee. Currently, she is an Associate Professor in the Department of Psychology at the University of Colorado. She has been the recipient of numerous honors and awards, including fellowships from the Rockefeller Foundation, Spencer Foundation, and Ford Foundation. She has authored and co-authored several articles and chapters on women, work, and aging. Her present interests focus on stigmatization and its impact on African Americans and others across the life span.

Mary McKinney Edmonds is Vice President for Student Affairs at Stanford University and Clinical Professor in the Department of Health Research and Policy at Stanford Medical School. She is the author of many articles and papers in medical sociology and social gerontology. Her particular research interest is in the health status of black aged females with respect to their health and illness behaviors.

Eleanor Engram is an Assistant Pastor at Gospel Baptist Church, Cleveland, Ohio, and a candidate for the doctor of ministry degree at Ashland Theological Seminary. Her doctor of ministry project examines the role of the African-American church in serving the elderly population. She earned her master's and Ph.D. degrees in sociology from Duke University. She has held faculty positions at the University of California at Berkeley, Morgan State University, and San Jose State University. Her book *Science, Myth, Reality: The Black Family in One-Half Century of Research* received the 1983 Book Award of the Association of Social and Behavioral Scientists.

Rose C. Gibson is a Professor in the School of Social Work and a Faculty Associate at the Institute for Social Research at the University of Michigan. A former National Institute on Aging Postdoctoral Fellow in Statistics, Survey Research Design, and Methodology on Minority Populations, she has participated in the first National Survey of Black Americans. She is the author of *Blacks in an Aging Society* and is Editor-in-Chief of *The Gerontologist,* as well as serving on several editorial boards of journals in the field of aging. Her major research interests are in the area of sociocultural factors in aging.

Ruth L. Greene is the Charles Stewart Distinguished Professor and Professor of Psychology at Johnson C. Smith University. She received her doctorate from the University of Massachusetts and completed postdoctoral work supported by the Ford Foundation at the Center for the Study of Aging and Human Development at Duke University Medical Center. She is also a United Negro College Fund Distinguished Scholar. Currently, she is completing a National Institute of Health Award to survey a community sample of older black and white adults. The survey includes information on health, mental health, family relationships, help resources, and stress and coping.

James S. Jackson is a Professor of Social Psychology and Public Health and a Research Scientist at the Institute for Social Research at the University of Michigan. He is the Director of the Program for Research on Black Americans and the African-American Mental Health Research Center. He is a co-author of *Hope and Independence: Blacks' Response to Electoral and Party Politics* and an editor of the books *Life in Black America* and *The Black American Elderly.* He has also directed nine major national sample surveys of the black population and has conducted research and published in the areas of racial and ethnic influences on life course development, attitude change, reciprocity, social support, and coping and health.

Rukmalie Jayakody, M.S.W., is a doctoral student in the Joint Program in Social Work and Sociology at the University of Michigan. Her research interests include minority families, intergenerational relations, and kin networks as well as neighborhood conditions and neighbor interactions.

Verna M. Keith is an Assistant Professor in the Department of Sociology and is affiliated with the Adult Development and Aging Program at Arizona State University. She has recently completed postdoctoral fellowships in the School of Public Health and the Institute of Gerontology at the University of Michigan. She has authored and co-authored articles on older adults that examine the use of health services by majority and minority elderly, gender differences in social support, and the relationship between social support and psychological distress. Her current research focuses on the linkages between gender, race, life stress, and psychological well-being.

Shirley A. Lockery received her M.S.W., M.P.A., and Ph.D. from the University of Southern California. In 1988, she accepted a National Institute on Aging Postdoctoral Research Fellowship at the University of Michigan School of Social Work. Since 1990, she has been an Assistant Professor at the School of Social Work at the University of Michigan. Her research and professional interests are in the area of health and ethnic minority aging. She is a Gerontological Society of America fellow and currently works on the editorial board of *Gerontology and Geriatrics Education* and the *American Journal of Health Promotion*. She has published numerous book chapters and articles in professional journals.

John L. McAdoo is an Associate Professor in the College of Human Ecology at Michigan State University. He received his master's degree in social work and his Ph.D. in educational psychology at the University of Michigan. He has completed postdoctoral work in mental health epidemiology at Johns Hopkins University, educational research at Harvard University, and survey research at the University of Michigan. He has published articles on many topics, including crime, morale and the urban elderly, the roles of the African-American father in the family, parent-child interaction patterns, self-esteem and ethnic identity of African-American children, and African-American male-female relationships. He is currently completing research related to the morale and well-being of urban elderly families.

Harold W. Neighbors is an Associate Professor in the School of Public Health and a Faculty Associate at the Institute for Social Research at the University of Michigan. After receiving his Ph.D. in social psychology from the University of Michigan in 1982, he did postdoctoral work at the Institute for Social Research, receiving grants from the Rockefeller Foundation and the National Institute of Mental Health. His current research interests include psychiatric epidemiology, risk factor identification, methodological approaches to mental health need assessment, ethnic influences on the perception and classification of mental disorders, help seeking, and service utilization.

Jacqueline M. Smith is an Assistant Professor at the School of Social Work at Howard University in Washington, DC. Her research has examined the relationship of structural factors like race, ethnicity, and the family to the utilization of health care services and the physical and psychological well-being of the aged.

Robert J. Smith is an Associate Professor of Psychology and a Research Scientist at the Institute for Urban Research at Morgan State University in Baltimore, Maryland. He received his Ph.D. in social psychology from Ohio State University. He has been a postdoctoral fellow at the Institute for Research on Poverty at the University of Wisconsin and the Institute for Social Research at the University of Michigan. His research interests are in social gerontology, specifically in the areas of death and dying, the social-psychological aspects of the aging process, and issues related to group consciousness and the use of social support networks among the black elderly.

Robert Joseph Taylor is an Associate Professor of Social Work and a Faculty Associate at the Institute for Social Research at the University of Michigan. After earning his doctorate in social work and sociology at the University of Michigan, he completed both postdoctoral work and a FIRST Award sponsored by the National Institute on Aging. His research focuses on family and friend social support networks across the life span, with a particular emphasis on the networks of older adults. His work has appeared in *The Gerontologist, Journal of Gerontology: Social Sciences, Journal of Marriage and the Family, Journal of Black Studies, Review of Religious Research,* and *Social Service Review.*

Michael C. Thornton is an Associate Professor of Afro-American Studies at the University of Wisconsin at Madison. He received his doctoral degree in 1983 from the University of Michigan. His research focuses on intergroup attitudes, ethnic differences in social support, interracial families, and religion. He has published in *The Gerontologist, Child Development, Ethnic and Racial Studies,* and the *Milbank Quarterly.*

M. Belinda Tucker, a social psychologist, is an Associate Professor in the Department of Psychiatry and Biobehavioral Sciences at the University of California at Los Angeles. She was co-principal investigator on the 1979-1980 National Survey of Black Americans. She has authored numerous articles on marriage and personal relationships, including the forthcoming edited volume *The Decline in Marriage Among African Americans.* She has received a Research Scientist Development Award from the National Institute of Mental Health. Her research interests include the African-American family, the psychological and social structural implications of constrained mate availability, the determinants of changing marriage patterns, and social structural influences on close personal relationships.